Robert L. Roseberry
Chancellor College, University of Malawi

Rachel Weinstock
Consultant, *English Language Services*

Reading, Etc.
AN INTEGRATED SKILLS TEXT

Prentice Hall Regents
Englewood Cliffs, New Jersey 07632

Library of Congress Cataloging-in-Publication Data

Roseberry, Robert L.
    Reading, etc. : an integrated skills text / Robert L. Roseberry,
Rachel Weinstock.
        p. cm.
    Includes bibliographical references.
    ISBN 0-13-763467-6
    1. English language—Textbooks for foreign speakers. 2. College
readers. I. Weinstock, Rachel. II. Title.
PE1128.R674 1992
428.6'4—dc20
                                                                91-17936
                                                                     CIP

Acquisitions editor: Anne Riddick
Editorial/production supervision and
    interior design: Mary McDonald
Copy editor: Sherry Babbitt
Cartoon drawings: Leah Taylor
Cover design: Wanda Lubelska Design
Prepress buyer: Ray Keating
Manufacturing buyer: Lori Bulwin

 © 1992 by Prentice-Hall, Inc.
A Simon & Schuster Company
Englewood Cliffs, New Jersey 07632

Printed in the United States of America
10 9 8 7 6 5 4 3 2 1

ISBN 0-13-763467-6

Prentice-Hall International (UK) Limited, *London*
Prentice-Hall of Australia Pty. Limited, *Sydney*
Prentice-Hall Canada Inc., *Toronto*
Prentice-Hall Hispanoamericana, S.A., *Mexico*
Prentice-Hall of India Private Limited, *New Delhi*
Prentice-Hall of Japan, Inc., *Tokyo*
Simon & Schuster Asia Pte. Ltd., *Singapore*
Editora Prentice-Hall do Brasil, Ltda., *Rio de Janeiro*

Contents

UNIT THREE: GENETIC ENGINEERING

UNIT FOUR: MEDIA

10. Television News: "Now . . . This"   190

11. Teaching as an Amusing Activity   221

Preface

Reading, Etc. is intended for students whose native language is other than English and who wish to study or are already studying at an English language high school, university, or college. The assumption is made that these students have already reached an intermediate level of English skills. Consequently, the materials are written at a high-intermediate level. They are intended to resemble in content and approach many of the texts that students might be expected to read in the last year of high school or the first year of university.

This text is designed to help students acquire the skills that academic study requires. Among these are understanding vocabulary in context; coping with complex grammatical structures in reading passages; understanding the content of reading material on science and social science topics; learning how to organize and write essays; and combining information from several sources to write academic essays on topics related to the reading passages.

Reading, Etc. consists of four units, each of which is subdivided into three chapters. Each unit presents several aspects of a general topic, including economics, exploitation of the sea, genetic engineering, and the media. Every chapter of the book contains the following sections:

1. *chapter focus:* preview of the content of the chapter in point form;
2. *arrangement of information:* discussion of ways that the content of a text is organized (by using enumeration, definition, process, classification, comparison and contrast, and argument); and discussion of the ways that the text is put together so that the reader will see it as a logical, continuous whole (parts of a text, thesis statements, topic sentences, paragraph structure, unity and coherence, and bridging);
3. *vocabulary preview:* words from the reading passage presented in contexts, and exercises to reinforce understanding of word meanings;
4. *discovering word meanings:* words presented in sentences from the text for

practice in using prefixes, suffixes, and roots, and practice in using a dictionary to determine the meaning of the word in its context;

5. *signal words and phrases:* words and phrases from the reading passage that provide clues to the reader about the way the text is organized and the ways that sentences and paragraphs are related to each other;

6. *grammar preview:* exercises using sentences from the reading passage of the chapter;

7. *getting ready to read:* questions that stimulate thought and discussion on the general topic of the reading passage, and practice in finding specific information in or clues to the structure and content of the reading passage;

8. *the reading passage:* a challenging, informative text on a current topic;

9. *questions on the reading passage:* questions divided into three sections—"checking your comprehension," "for discussion," and "analyzing the structure";

10. *the writing process:* a discussion in each chapter of one part of the writing process, with the focus on writing essays; and

11. *writing about reading:* a group of exercises that combines the topics of the reading passages with practice of the writing process, and that provides practice in synthesizing ideas and information from several reading passages.

Biographical Information

Robert L. Roseberry received his A.B. from the University of California, his M.A. and Ph.D. in German Language and Literature from the University of Toronto, and his M.Ed. in Language Education from the University of British Columbia. He has taught at the universities of Winnipeg and Alberta, at Vancouver Community College, at the University of Nigeria, and at the York University English Language Institute, among others. He has written and published curriculum for the Japanese exchange program at Vancouver Community College, and has taught at the Toronto Office Skills Training Project for Southeast Asian Refugee Women. He presently teaches at Chancellor College, University of Malawi.

Rachel Weinstock received her B.A. degree in English and Education at Yeshiva University in New York City, her M.A. in English Literature at the University of Toronto, and her Ph.D. in Education (applied linguistics) at the Ontario Institute for Studies in Education, University of Toronto. Before turning to the teaching of English as a Second Language, she taught English to native speakers in New York and Toronto. She has taught ESL at Glendon College of York University, at York University's Department of Continuing Education, and at the York University English Language Institute. Subsequently, she was Project Manager of the Literacy Institute at George Brown College. She now operates her own consulting firm, *English Language Services,* serving the training and editing needs of corporate and individual clients.

To our mothers and in memory of our fathers
Our first and best teachers

The interior of the Great Weaving Room, Fall River, MA. (Source: Library of Congress)

UNIT ONE

Economics

Economics[1] is a popular subject in modern colleges and universities. Economists study industry and trade. They show how products are converted to money, and how people, businesses, and countries use money. They also study profits, banking, investments, and the use of wealth.

Economics is one of the social sciences, which include such subjects as history; politics; sociology, which is the study of human behavior in society; and anthropology, which is the study of cultures and civilizations.

This unit contains three chapters on economics. The first chapter, on the Industrial Revolution in Britain in the eighteenth and nineteenth centuries, gives the history of modern industrial society.

The second chapter is about the importance of knowledge and information in modern business. This chapter suggests that the modern economy of the West is changing. Large industries are no longer as important as they were a few years ago. Instead, computers and information services are beginning to control the economy.

The third chapter of this unit is about people who are losing their jobs because of the changes in the modern economy. It shows how a healthy, growing economy can help many people while harming others.

[1]*Economics* has a plural ending, but it is a singular noun. Some other similar nouns in English are *physics* and *mathematics*.

Chapter 1

The Industrial Revolution

CHAPTER FOCUS

As you study this chapter, you should focus on the following important points:

Arrangement of information: enumeration

Vocabulary: understanding new words

Signal words and phrases: *indeed, rather, thus, however, it is true that, a further, a/the final*

Sentence grammar: coordination within a clause, adjective clauses, past and present perfect tenses

Writing: overview of the writing process

Content: the causes and results of the Industrial Revolution

Arrangement of Information

Organization of the Content: Enumeration

There are two main types of academic writing: *expository writing,* which presents information, and *persuasive writing,* which argues a point of view. Good writing of either kind is organized in a way that is clear and easy to understand. There are several ways to make writing orderly and easy to read. One way is to use enumeration, which means presenting items in a list. The list can be either very simple or quite complex. An example of a simple list might be the groceries you need to buy at the supermarket. A complex list might be the series of ideas contained in the chapters of a book.

There are many different ways to organize such lists. For example, lists can be alphabetical, which means that they are organized according to the letters of the alphabet; or they can be sequential, which means that they are arranged according to moments in time (chronologically) or steps in a process. Some short lists do not need to be organized. This is true especially if all the items in the list are equally important.

Lists can contain many kinds of information, such as the names of objects or people, ideas, conditions, and categories. A list can be a series of words, phrases, clauses, sentences, or even longer pieces of writing.

Together with enumeration, other methods of organization, including definition, classification, and comparison/contrast, can be used, and these will be discussed in later chapters.

Exercises

1. Can you discover how the following lists are organized?
   a. apples, bananas, oranges, pears
   b. At seven o'clock I got up. Then I got dressed and had breakfast. By eight o'clock I was out of the house and running for the bus.
   c. To cook one cup of brown rice, put two cups of water into a pot. Bring the water to a boil. Pour the rice into the water, stirring gently. Cover the pot, and let it simmer for forty-five minutes. Remove the rice.

2. Here are two examples of enumeration from the reading passage in this chapter. Can you tell what kind of information is listed? Are these lists organized?
   a. There were four main trends that reflected the economic and social changes during the Industrial Revolution. One was the expansion of the economy. Another trend was a structural change. Together with this there was an increase in trade and services. Finally, the division between people with land and those without land began to disappear.
   b. Rooke discusses a number of conditions that existed in eighteenth-century Britain. One of these was the availability of capital for investment. Much of this capital came from overseas trade. Another requirement was the existence of people who were ready to invest that capital in manufacturing rather than in buying land. A third factor was an efficient banking system, for banks helped capital to move easily between investors and manufacturing enterprises.

Vocabulary Preview

Words in Context

The following words, arranged in groups, appear in this chapter's reading passage. Study the words in their contexts. Then complete the exercise that follows each group by writing the correct words in the blanks. Be sure to use the appropriate form of each word.

1. assessment, range of factors, rural, terms, trend, urban, variable

	assess (v.)
-ment (n.)	assessment

Our child was having trouble in school. We wanted to find out what he could do, what he couldn't do, and what level of achievement we could expect in the future. For this *assessment*, we took him to a psychologist. For *assessments* of his physical health, we took him to three different doctors.

range of factors (noun phrase)

To decide what courses to take, a student must consider a *range of factors*. These factors include career goals, interest, the level of difficulty of the courses, and course schedules. The student must then decide which of these different things are most important.

rural (adj.)

Agriculture is usually important to the economies of *rural* areas. Many such areas far from the cities have the necessary climate, resources, and space for growing crops.

terms (n., pl.)

She studied the *terms* of the contract carefully. Since she agreed with all the conditions of the contract, she signed her name.

	trend (n.)
-y (adj.)	trendy
-ness (n.)	trendiness

In the world of fashion, certain designers establish the main directions for clothing styles. These *trends* usually last for several years. Then they are replaced by new *trends*.

	urban (adj.)
sub-	suburban
(= *nearly*)	
-ize (v.)	urbanize
-ation (n.)	urbanization

In the early days of North American societies, very few people lived in cities. Today, however, the *urban* areas contain most of the population. Relatively few people live in the countryside.

	vary (v.)
-ety (n.)	variety
-ed (adj.)	varied

-ation (n.)	variation
-able (adj. or n.)	variable
-ility (n.)	variability
-ous (adj.)	various

It is difficult to conduct psychological experiments on human beings because each person is different. Furthermore, each group of people has many differences. These *variables* include such things as intelligence, age, education, personality, and attitude.

Now use these words to fill in the blanks below. You may have to add endings to some words.

A _variety of people_ has caused a _increase_ toward higher property values in _Rural_ areas. One factor is that each new _trend_ of property value causes a rise in taxes. Another _variable_ is the cost of property insurance, which can be very expensive in cities. In addition, mortgage rates have increased in many areas. Therefore, it is not easy for home buyers to get good _terms_ for their loans. Many people find that they can no longer afford to live in the city. As a result, more and more people are moving into _Urban_ areas not far from major cities.

2. accelerate, fundamental, model, reflect, relevant, shift, trigger

	accelerate (v.)
-ion (n.)	acceleration
-or (n.)	accelerator

Before swimming, he counted the number of times his heart beat in one minute. After swimming he again counted his heartbeats, and he found that their speed had *accelerated*. Then he decided that he would *accelerate* his swimming speed so that his heart would beat even faster.

| | fundamental (adj.) |
| -ly (adv.) | fundamentally |

If a house does not have a solid foundation, it will fall down. In the same way a person needs a good basic education before entering a university. This *fundamental* training gives the person a background in knowledge and study techniques.

	model (n. or v.)
re- (= *again*)	remodel

The child made some tiny copies of a railroad engine. These *models* looked just like the original.

The report contains a drawing that shows how windmills work. This *model* was discussed at the recent conference on alternate energy sources.

	reflect (v.)
-or (n.)	reflector
-ive (adj.)	reflective
-ly (adv.)	reflectively
-ion (n.)	reflection

Her smiling face was *reflected* in the mirror. She *reflected* on the reasons for her recent happiness.

His gloomy attitude *reflected* the unhappiness in his home environment.

	relevant (adj.)
-ce (n.)	relevance

The teacher asked Marika to describe some problems of modern transportation in cities. Marika responded by talking about the mating habits of elephants. Of course, this had nothing to do with the question. We all agreed that Marika's talk was interesting but not *relevant* to the topic.

	shift (n. or v.)
-y (adj.)	shifty

When he was young, the opinions of his friends were very important to him. As he grew older, their opinions became less important. Thus there was a *shift* in his attitude toward his friends' opinions.

trigger (n. or v.)

He had set the burglar alarm system to go off when the windows were opened. The thieves who tried to enter the house through a window *triggered* the alarm. The loud siren frightened them away.

Now use these words to fill in the blanks below. You may have to add endings to some words.

The famous scientist's decision to leave nuclear weapons research

showed a _____ _____ in his thinking. This deci-

sion _____ a popular protest against nuclear weapons. The

protest _____ as more and more people joined. At first,
the movement _____ the views of only a small group of
people. But in time it spread through several countries and began to
have an effect on political decisions _____ to nuclear issues.
The movement became so successful that it was used as
a _____ for other movements.

3. automated, domestic, enterprise, extensive, innovation, stimulate

	automate (v.)
-ion (n.)	automation
-ic (adj.)	automatic
-ally (adv.)	automatically

The Japanese are developing a transportation system that does not
need human drivers. It runs entirely on computers and other
equipment. This completely *automated* system should be safer and
more efficient than one that is operated by people.

	domestic (adj.)
-ally (adv.)	domestically
-ate (v.)	domesticate
-ion (n.)	domestication
-ity (n.)	domesticity

I have lots of work to do. However, the work I do around the
house is the most boring. I really do not like these *domestic* chores.

	enterprise (n.)

The North American economy is based largely on private *enterprise*. People may own and operate their own businesses without
too much government control.

	extent (n.)
	extend (v.)
-ive (adj.)	extensive
-ly (adv.)	extensively
-ion (n.)	extension

It is important to read carefully for specific information. But it is
also important to read a lot. Without *extensive* reading, a person's
knowledge would be very limited.

	innovate (v.)
-ive (adj.)	innovative

-ively (adv.)   innovatively
-ion (n.)   innovation

Some new things are very practical. Other *innovations* seem pretty silly. Personally, I think that see-through plastic clothing is a very silly *innovation*.

                 stimulus (n.)
-ant (n.)   stimulant
                 stimulate (v.)
-ion (n.)   stimulation

I love to study foreign languages. They encourage my interest in the way people in other countries live. In other words, the study of foreign languages *stimulates* my curiosity.

Now use these words to fill in the blanks below. You may have to add endings to some words.

Many _____ have come from small businesses that people

run in their own homes. Economic conditions before the Industrial

Revolution _____ the growth of such so-called cottage in-

dustries. However, these _____ _____ became

less popular when _____ equipment became necessary.

The _____ use of technology made many small businesses

less profitable.

4. conceptual, maintain, norm, per capita

                 concept (n.)
-ion (n.)   conception
-ual (adj.)   conceptual
-ly (adv.)   conceptually
-ize (v.)   conceptualize
-ation (n.)   conceptualization

In some schools, students are required to memorize and repeat facts. They are not trained to ask questions or to deal with ideas. Their teachers do not use a *conceptual* approach in the classroom.

                 maintain (v.)
-ance (n.)   maintenance

When you are hiking in the desert, you should drink a lot of water to *maintain* your physical condition. Your body cannot keep going without water, so you must be sure to take enough with you.

	norm (n.)
-al (adj.)	normal
-ly (adv.)	normally
-ize (v.)	normalize
-ation (n.)	normalization

Our whole class took the university entrance examination. Most of the students achieved a mark that was near the *norm*. A few, however, scored high above or far below the *norm*.

per capita (adj. or adv.)

The government has announced a $1 million increase in the grant to education. But this increase must provide for two million people. Therefore, it is a *per capita* increase of only fifty cents, which is not a large amount.

Now use these words to fill in the blanks below. You may have to add endings to some words.

Two main types of teaching are called the *behavioristic* and the *cognitive* approaches. For many years the behavioristic approach was used in most classrooms and was therefore the _____. According to this theory, students learn by memorizing and imitating.

They _____ their knowledge only by using it frequently. The behavioristic approach is related to the saying, ''Practice makes perfect.'' The cognitive approach, on the other hand, is a _____ system that stresses ideas and original thought. The success of the Soviet satellite *Sputnik* in the 1950s initiated a growing interest in this approach to education. In spite of this, however, relatively little money _____ is spent on cognitive education.

Discovering Word Meanings

Use (1) context clues; (2) your knowledge of prefixes, suffixes, and roots; and (3) a dictionary, if necessary, to discover the meanings of the italicized words in the following sentences from this chapter's reading passage.

1. Many periods of upheaval, or drastic change, have marked the history of Western civilization. These periods have caused major social, political, and cultural changes. For example, the Renaissance, the Reformation, and the French Revolution are *discontinuities* of modern history that had important long-term effects on society.

(What are the Renaissance, the Reformation, and the French Revolution examples of? How does the prefix *dis-* affect the meaning of *continue?* What part of speech is *discontinuities?*)

2. Social and economic life, which had changed relatively little before the Industrial Revolution, now began to change rapidly. Indeed, this process of rapid change has continued to the present day. It has become the norm in our own *postindustrial* society.

   (According to this passage, is today's society still considered industrial? What prefix would you use to describe a society that is not yet industrial?)

3. According to this model, a leading sector of the economy grows more rapidly than the others. It then *activates* the rest of the economy.

   (How does the suffix *-ate* change the part of speech of *active?* What effect does a leading sector of the economy have on the rest of the economy?)

4. A further *prerequisite* for the growth of industry was an adequate supply of labor.

   (What is the root of this word, and how does the prefix change its meaning? What does it mean to fulfill a prerequisite for a university course?)

Signal Words and Phrases

Signal words help the reader predict what kind of information will follow. Study the following signal words and phrases that appear in this chapter's reading passage.

1. indeed

This word emphasizes the information that came before it. The information that follows *indeed* emphasizes the information that precedes it by being stronger, more specific, or more detailed. An expression with a similar meaning is *in fact.*

> I was happy to see her. *Indeed,* I was delighted.

> In the Industrial Revolution, social and economic life began to change quickly. *Indeed,* this process of change has continued to the present day.

> When used in response to a yes/no question, *indeed* intensifies the answer, whether it is positive or negative.

> Hasn't he grown a lot? *Indeed* he has. (or: Yes, *indeed.*)

2. rather

This word has many meanings and uses. As a signal word it follows a negative sentence. A positive restatement is then given. A phrase with a similar meaning is *on the contrary.*

Her name is not Margaret. *Rather,* it is Margot.

None of the individual factors can be singled out as the cause of growth. *Rather,* many were necessary for the process that produced this great economic advance.

3. thus

As a signal word, *thus* often shows a result or consequence of what came before it. Words or phrases with similar meanings are *hence, therefore,* and *as a result.*

Britain was the leader in the change from farming to industry. *Thus* Britain was the world's first industrial state.

4. however

The statement made before this word is true. The sentence after *however* shows an opposite point of view. A word with a similar meaning but different usage is *but.*

Food should be tasty. It is more important, *however,* for food to be healthful.

Some parts of the population suffered during the Industrial Revolution. *However,* most people benefited from it.

5. it is true that

The phrase is used to indicate that what follows is true, but that the opposite position is more important. The next sentence often begins with *however.* A phrase with a similar meaning is *I admit that.*

It is true that taxes are necessary. However, the taxes in this district are too high.

It is true that some parts of the population suffered during the Industrial Revolution. However, most people benefited from it.

6. a further

Use these words to add another item to a list. Other words and phrases with similar meanings are *another, still another,* and *yet another.*

One prerequisite for the growth of industry was a supply of capital. *A further* prerequisite was an adequate supply of labor.

7. a/the final

Use these words to add the last item to a list.

The first course was tomato soup. Then we had a green salad. The main course was poached salmon. *The final* course was a delicious homemade apple pie.

As we have seen, many factors stimulated the economy in Britain during the Industrial Revolution. *A final* significant factor was the British government's encouragement of economic development.

Grammar Preview

Study the following excerpts or paraphrases from this chapter's reading passage, and work through the tasks.

1. Combine the sentences in each group below into one sentence, according to the example. Compare the combined sentence with the series of shorter sentences. Which would you expect to find in academic reading material, and why?

   Example

   This great economic change formed the basis of economic progress. This great economic change laid the foundations for the increasing wealth of nations.

   Combined

   This great economic change formed the basis of economic progress and laid the foundations for the increasing wealth of nations.

   a. Inventions such as automated weaving machines stimulated industrial growth.
   Inventions such as the steam engine stimulated industrial growth.
   b. The Industrial Revolution resulted in far-reaching changes in the British way of life.
   The Industrial Revolution resulted in improved living standards.
   c. Overseas trade led to a superior merchant fleet.
   Overseas trade resulted in more capital for investment.
   Overseas trade provided markets for British textiles and hardware.

2. Rewrite each sentence below as two shorter, simpler sentences, according to the example.

   Example

   Social and economic life, which had changed little over the centuries, began to change rapidly.

   Rewritten

   Social and economic life had changed little over the centuries.
   Social and economic life began to change rapidly.

    a. Rostow's theory identifies the textile industry as the ''leading sector'' that started economic growth.

    b. Another requirement was the existence of wealthy people who were ready to invest their capital in business.

    c. This discussion of conditions in Britain refers to a range of factors that led to the Industrial Revolution.

3. Choose the correct verb tense for each of the following, according to the example. Explain the reason for your choice.

Example

The most important change in history (was/has been) the Industrial Revolution of the eighteenth and nineteenth centuries.

The correct choice is *was*. According to the sentence, the Industrial Revolution ended in the past and did not continue to the present. The use of a specific time reference (eighteenth and nineteenth centuries) tells us this.

Many periods of upheaval (marked/have marked) the history of Western civilization.

The correct choice is *have marked*. The history of Western Civilization continues into the present time. No specific time is mentioned.

    a. Between 1750 and 1850 the population of England and Wales (tripled/has tripled).

    b. The process of rapid change (continued/has continued) to the present day.

    c. At least half the population of Britain in the middle of the eighteenth century (worked/has worked) in agriculture.

Getting Ready to Read

The reading passage in this chapter is about the beginning of modern industry and modern economics. It is also about great social and economic change.

1. Think about an important change in your life. What led to the change or helped cause it?

2. Think about the way you spend an average day. Is there anything you do that would not have been possible 150 years ago?

3. Name several countries that you would describe as highly industrialized and several others that you think are not yet highly industrialized. Why do you think that some countries are more industrialized than others? To what extent is your home country industrialized?

4. Find paragraph 6 in the reading passage. Quickly read this paragraph and the first sentence of paragraph 7. Do not stop to read each word

carefully. Read as fast as you can. Look at the important words only. (You will have time to read the paragraph again later.) When you finish the first sentence of paragraph 7, stop reading. How do you expect the passage to continue?

5. How fast can you find information without reading every word? As quickly as possible, identify the subject of paragraph 6. Then pick the correct choice from the statements below.
   a. the growth of the economy during the Industrial Revolution
   b. models of economic growth during the Industrial Revolution
   c. W. W. Rostow's "take-off" theory
   d. dating the beginning of the Industrial Revolution

6. How quickly can you discover the subject of paragraphs 7 through 16? Pick the correct choice from the statements below.
   a. models of economic growth
   b. the effect of population growth on the expansion of markets
   c. the meaning of the Industrial Revolution
   d. conditions or factors that helped make the Industrial Revolution possible

7. According to Eric Pawson, what conditions were important for population growth?

Now read the passage carefully from beginning to end. As you read, note the conditions that helped to make the Industrial Revolution possible.

READING PASSAGE

The Industrial Revolution

1   Many periods of upheaval, or drastic change, have marked the history of Western civilization.[1] These periods have caused major social, political, and cultural changes. For example, the Renaissance,° the Reformation,° and the French Revolution° are discontinuities of modern history that had important long-term effects on society. The most important such change, however, was the Industrial Revo-

The period from the fourteenth through the sixteenth centuries in Europe is called the Renaissance. The term

---

[1]The discussion in the next five paragraphs is based on Eric Pawson (1979). *The Early Industrial Revolution: Britain in the Eighteenth Century.* (London: B. T. Batsford, Ltd.), pp. 13–14.

lution of the eighteenth and nineteenth centuries.[2] Its profound effect on the pattern of social and economic life has shaped the modern world, formed the basis of economic progress, and laid the foundation for the increasing wealth of nations. Social and economic life, which had changed relatively little before the Industrial Revolution, now began to change rapidly. Indeed, this process of rapid change has continued to the present day. It has become the norm in our own postindustrial society.

2   The Industrial Revolution, then, did more than stimulate industrial growth. It also turned a stable social system into one that experienced constant growth and change. This was a shift in the way that people understood the conditions of their lives. Another shift changed the whole social and economic structure. Because the increase in factory production attracted workers to the cities, it caused a transformation from a rural farming society to an urban industrial one. The leader in this transformation was Britain. Thus Britain became the world's first industrial state. The Industrial Revolution spread to other countries of Europe and later to America as well. For many years, however, Britain maintained its position as the world's industrial leader.

3   There were four main trends that reflected the economic and social changes during the Industrial Revolution. One was the expansion of the economy. This resulted in a rise in the per capita income of the population. These incomes continued to grow as wages rose in many sectors° of the economy. Another trend was a change of structure from an agricultural economy with cottage industries° to an industrial economy. Together with this came an increase in trade and services. A social trend that resulted from this economic shift was the transformation from a rural society to an urban one. Finally, the division between people with land and those without land began to disappear. Instead, a division developed between the middle classes and the working classes.

Renaissance comes from the French word for rebirth. This period was a rebirth of learning and culture. It followed the Dark Ages, a time of widespread ignorance. The Renaissance marks the beginning of modern times.

In the sixteenth century there was an attempt to reform, or make changes in, the Catholic Church. Finally, the reformers left the Church and established the Protestant churches.

In 1789 the people of France overthrew the king and queen to establish a republic. This revolt was the French Revolution.

parts

small manufacturing businesses in private homes

[2]In the Western calendar, the counting of centuries, or one hundred-year periods, begins with the birth of the founder of the Christian religion in the year "zero." This was the first year of the first century. The first one hundred years, beginning with the year "0," are the first century. Thus the next one hundred years are part of the second century, even though they are 100, 101, etc. The years 200, 201, 202, etc., are the third century, and so on. The year 1991 means that we have completed ninety-one years of the twentieth century and are in the ninety-second year of this century. The years after the year "0" are called A.D., or *anno Domini*. This is Latin for "in the year of our Lord." Years before the year 0 are B.C. This means "before Christ."

4   Thus the Industrial Revolution resulted in far-reaching changes in the British way of life. It also caused living standards to improve steadily. It is true that some segments of the population suffered because of Britain's economic progress. However, in the long run the tremendous increases in wealth and opportunity produced great benefits for society as a whole.

5   Economic historians disagree in their assessments of when the Industrial Revolution actually began. Some point to the 1780s as the period when economic growth accelerated greatly. Others, however, suggest that the increased growth rate began in the 1740s. Still other writers have taken the view that the Industrial Revolution started in the seventeenth century.

6   In order to date the beginning of the Industrial Revolution, historians attempt to understand its causes. In discussing this issue, R. M. Hartwell (1967, pp. 78–79) identifies two conceptual models of economic growth. One is a sectoral model of unbalanced growth. According to this model, a leading sector of the economy grows more rapidly than the others. It then activates the rest of the economy. Britain's eighteenth-century textile industry, which grew faster than other sectors of the economy, is an example of a leading sector. The other model is an aggregative° model. Here, a change in one strategic variable, such as savings, affects the entire economy. It then stimulates a process of balanced growth. According to Hartwell, however, the Industrial Revolution can be better explained as a combination of the two models. In his view, "long-term and widespread change" produced balanced growth in England before 1780 (Hartwell, 1967, p. 78). The pressure of this change stimulated important technical advances. After 1780 these advances triggered a "take-off"° in certain sectors, resulting in unbalanced growth.

a collection of individual particles, pieces, or things

7   According to both models, certain conditions were necessary for the Industrial Revolution to occur. P. Rooke (1971) discusses a number of conditions that existed in eighteenth-century Britain.[3] One of these was the availability of capital for investment. Much of this capital came from overseas trade. Another requirement was the existence of people who were ready to invest that capital in manufacturing rather than in land. A third factor was an

When a plane leaves the ground and begins to fly, we say that it takes off. Therefore, a theory that explains an economic take-off discusses how the economy _____ .

[3]Most of the following discussion of conditions leading to the Industrial Revolution, except as noted, is based on P. Rooke (1971). *The Industrial Revolution.* (New York: The John Day Company), pp. 14–20.

efficient banking system, for banks helped capital to move easily between investors and manufacturing enterprises.

8   However, these factors related to capital alone do not explain why the Industrial Revolution occurred. Another important factor in eighteenth-century Britain was the growth of both domestic and overseas markets for manufactured products. This growing demand provided incentives for investment in increased production and new methods of manufacturing.

9   The expansion of the domestic market is closely tied to the growth of population. Between 1750 and 1850 the population of England and Wales nearly tripled. This increase was due largely to a fall in the death rate. According to Eric Pawson (1979, pp. 28–31, 40), improved health and sanitation conditions were important for population growth. At the same time, improvements in agriculture made it possible to feed more people. Of course increased population alone does not necessarily stimulate economic growth. Many modern Third World countries, such as India, have rapidly increasing populations but little economic growth. However, in eighteenth-century Britain the rise in population joined with other conditions to provide an incentive to manufacturers. Especially for producers of clothing, food, and drink, a larger population resulted in the expansion of business. Among these, the most spectacular growth was in the textile, or cloth, industry.

10   The expansion of Britain's foreign commerce throughout the eighteenth century depended on its overseas colonies, which had to trade on terms favorable to Britain. This trade led to a superior merchant fleet, resulted in more capital for investment, and provided markets for British textiles and hardware.

11   Between 1750 and 1770 production for the home market rose by 7 percent because of a relatively steady rise in population. During the same period, export industries increased their output by 80 percent. This rapid expansion of overseas demand reflected the fact that war and colonization had provided completely new markets.

12   In addition to markets for their goods, manufacturers needed adequate supplies of raw materials° and natural resources. Here, too, Britain was in a fortunate position, with a rich supply of farmland, minerals, rivers, and harbors (Pawson, 1979, p. 16). Domestic wool and cotton from the colonies were plentifully available for the textile industry. So were iron ore to supply heavy industry and coal to power the factories.

Raw food is food that has not been cooked or prepared. Therefore raw materials are _____ .

13   Another vital condition for economic growth was Britain's system of transportation and communication. Good transportation was necessary for shipping raw materials to factories, and for sending finished goods to home markets or ports. After 1760 the British built an extensive system of canals for shipping coal and iron ore cheaply across the English countryside.

14   British manufacturers were under pressure to keep up with demand. This provided an incentive for innovations and inventions to solve the production problems of industry. Many inventions and innovations greatly stimulated the rate of industrial growth. Among these were automated spinning and weaving machines and the steam engine. The relevant technical knowledge for many of these inventions had been available in many parts of the world for a long time. British inventors, however, had certain advantages over inventors in other countries. They were protected by a system of patents that guaranteed them the legal ownership of their inventions. As a further incentive to innovators and inventors, the British established a number of societies to encourage specialized or scientific work.

15   A further prerequisite for the growth of industry was an adequate supply of labor. At least half the population of Britain in the middle of the eighteenth century worked in agriculture. However, fundamental changes were taking place° in this area of economic activity too. Before the Industrial Revolution, English farmers used a system of open fields. They divided these fields into strips of land for cultivating, or growing, food, and they shared their tools with other farmers. Now, however, a new system called *enclosure,* in which segments of land were fenced off, gradually replaced the system of open fields. Many farmers who were forced off the land by the expenses of enclosure sought work in factories, workshops, or mines. In addition, the increase in population meant that some workers who could no longer find work on farms found it instead in the growing industries.

16   A final significant factor was the British government's encouragement of economic development. Government policy aimed at promoting and protecting commercial enterprise. This was called *Mercantilism.* Mercantilism resulted in the establishment of the colonial system, the navigation laws, and the protection of agriculture and industry. In addition, the mercantile policy found economic advantages in Britain's eighteenth-century wars.

happening, occurring

As we have seen, no single factor was sufficient to cause the rapid economic growth that led to the Industrial Revolution. Rather, a range of related factors combined to produce this great economic advance that formed modern society.

References

Hartwell, R. M. (1967). *The Causes of the Industrial Revolution in England*. London: Methuen & Co., Ltd.
Pawson, Eric. (*tury*. London: B. T. Batsford, Ltd.
Rooke, P. (1971). *The Industrial Revolution*. New York: The John Day Company.

Checking Your Comprehension

1. What is meant by "discontinuities of history"?
2. How was the Industrial Revolution a discontinuity of history?
3. What four changes in British life accompanied the Industrial Revolution?
4. What are two of the conditions that made the Industrial Revolution possible? How did they help make it possible?
5. Look at Figure 1–1. How did such machinery lower the price of textiles?

FIGURE 1–1 Calico printing in a Lancashire mill, 1834. (Source: the Granger Collection)

For Discussion

1. In what way or ways is the Industrial Revolution still affecting modern society?
2. Why do you think economists are interested in the causes of the Industrial Revolution?

Analyzing the Structure

1. Which words tie the second sentence of the reading passage to the first?
2. What is the function of *then* in the first sentence of paragraph 2?
3. In paragraph 3, four trends are discussed. Two methods of enumeration are used to list these trends. One of these methods is the use of the words *one, another,* and *finally.* What is the second method?
4. Find two sentences in paragraph 4 that partially contradict each other. Explain this contradiction. What signal words are used to convey this meaning?

The Writing Process: Overview

Writing of any kind is a process that stretches over a period of time. Any writing project is begun by thinking about the ideas to be presented. At some stage the writer must work with and refine those ideas and put them in a form that will communicate the writer's intentions to the reader. Each of these phases of the writing process consists of several activities, but not all writers perform these activities in the same order. There are many kinds of writing for different purposes and for different audiences. In this book we shall concentrate on the fundamentals of writing academic essays. Students should remember that the method shown in this book is only one of several approaches to academic writing.

Writing for an Audience: Knowing Your Purpose and Your Reader

One of the first factors we must think about when we write is the audience. This includes knowing why we are writing, who the reader is, and what the reader already knows about the topic. Since this course focuses on writing academic essays, these questions can be answered in fairly specific ways. An academic essay is usually written to survey the information on a topic, to explain an idea, or to present an argument. On an examination, an essay is intended to show the instructor what you know or understand about a specific issue. The readers of academic essays are your instructors or fellow classmates. When you are exploring a topic of your own, you must judge how much your readers are likely to know about it. If there are basic ideas that a reader must know to understand what you are writing about, you may have to explain these, or you may have to define certain words or concepts. There is no rule that you can follow to decide what you have to explain. This decision changes depending on your topic and your readers. To make this decision, try to imagine what kinds of questions your readers might have about the statements you make in your essay.

Overview of the Writing Course

The method of this course will be to present and explain the fundamental activities involved in the writing process and to help you practice these activities. Many of these activities may already be familiar to you. By reviewing them and by learning about the activities that are unfamiliar to you, you will be able to improve your writing ability.

Each chapter will focus on a different activity included in the process of writing, but you will have to use all of the activities in everything you write, even before you have a chance to look at them in detail. For this reason, it is important for you to have an overview of the whole process. This overview consists of two parts: (1) studying a model essay, and (2) familiarizing yourself with a list of the fundamental activities involved in the writing process.

Studying a Model Essay

One of the ways the course will help you to understand the process of essay writing is by showing you a short essay as a model. We will look at different parts of this model essay as we proceed through the course. Read the essay below, and study the notes that are attached to it.

Consequences of Damaging the Amazon Rain Forest *Introductory paragraph*

Living things often depend on each other to survive. In some places, such as the oceans and the tropical forests, thousands of species may be living together in this way. These living creatures also interact with the nonliving, or inorganic, things around them. Such areas of close interdependence in nature are known as ecosystems. These ecosystems, however, do more than support the plants and animals that live in them. They also influence the environment of the entire planet. The ecosystems of tropical rain forests, for example, protect the entire planet by returning water to the air as vapor and by providing much of the oxygen that

Background information that is needed for understanding the thesis

we breathe. One of the largest of these is the rain forest of the Amazon River Basin in Brazil. This forest is almost as large as the United States. It protects many unique species, and it plays a major role in controlling the earth's atmosphere and weather. However, it is being destroyed to provide farm land. Little is being done to prevent this destruction. Many people do not seem to understand that the failure to preserve the Amazon rain forest could have serious consequences for all living things.

Thesis statement

Paragraph bridge

Topic sentence

Some of these consequences are physical or biological. It is estimated, for example, that one million species of animal and plant life depend on the rain forests and on each other to survive. Without this ecosystem, these species, which live nowhere else on earth, would quickly become extinct. Destroying the forests would also speed up the so-called greenhouse effect, which may be causing the earth's temperature to rise at an alarming rate. The rain forests absorb a large amount of carbon dioxide. Scientists believe that this gas is partly responsible for the rising temperatures. A third consequence is the increase in diseases such as malaria. As forests are cleared to make room for hydroelectric dams, large stagnant lakes are formed. These provide breeding grounds for malarial mosquitoes. A final physical consequence of the loss of the Amazon forests might be a significant reduction in the amount of oxygen in the atmosphere. Without the earth's large forests, we might soon run out of air to breathe.

First body paragraph

Example of a transition within a paragraph

Bridge to the previous paragraph →

In addition to the physical effects caused by the destruction of the rain forests, there are social and economic effects as well. The Amazon forests contain many of the world's rubber trees, which are a major source of income for people living in the area. These people would have to find other ways to make a living if the forest disappeared. An even more serious consequence is the introduction of previously unknown diseases, such as malaria, into the region. Poor people, who cannot easily get medicines, often have no protection against these diseases. In addition, native peoples whose tribes have lived for centuries in the area are now being forced to move to escape disease and to find new sources of food as the forests disappear. However, many of the native peoples are hunters and gatherers who are unable to change their way of life. They cannot find food in the areas where they must live. The result is that these people are dying from disease and starvation, and their cultures are vanishing.

Topic sentence

Second body paragraph

It is clear, therefore, that the destruction of the Amazon rain forest must stop. The harm that this destruction is causing is far greater than any benefits it might bring. All the nations of the world must become involved in this problem, for the entire planet depends on the Amazon forest and the other great tropical forests. This involvement must not be one-sided. We must not expect Brazil alone to bear the responsibility or pay the cost. Ecology is an issue that has no national boundaries. We shall all have to make sacri-

Restatement of the thesis

Bridge to the body of the essay

Very general related issues

Call for action

fices, including contributions of money, work, and time. Only by making such a commitment to our planet can we guarantee a safe and healthful environment for our children.

Each part of this essay, and each technique that the writer used to organize the writing and make it easier to understand, required thought and planning. As we proceed through the book we shall focus in turn on each of several fundamental activities involved in the writing process: understanding the topic, narrowing the topic, writing a thesis statement, developing a strategy, arranging and organizing information, writing topic sentences, achieving unity and coherence, getting feedback, writing introductions and conclusions, improving connections within a text, and editing.

Writing About Reading

1. In one paragraph, enumerate the main causes of the Industrial Revolution.

2. Expand your paragraph on the causes of the Industrial Revolution into a short essay on the topic. One approach might be to group the various causes. Remember to add enough supporting information to develop each paragraph.

3. Explain why the Industrial Revolution is important to us today. Do you believe that the Industrial Revolution is continuing? Why or why not?

4. Write a short essay on ''The conditions that stimulated the Industrial Revolution in England are (or are not) sufficient to stimulate industrial revolutions in modern Third World countries.'' To prepare for writing this essay, look at the conditions that stimulated the Industrial Revolution in England. Which of these are present and which are absent in a Third World country that you know? What is the effect on that country's industrialization?

Chapter 2

The Knowledge Economy

CHAPTER FOCUS

As you study this chapter, you should focus on the following important points:

Arrangement of information: emphatic order and enumeration signal words

Vocabulary: understanding new words

Signal words and phrases: *in addition; for example; according to; the/a first, second,* etc.

Sentence grammar: adjective clauses, parallelism, modal verbs

Writing: understanding the topic

Content: the change from an industrial economy to an economy based on knowledge

Arrangement of Information

Organization of the Content: Emphatic Order and Enumeration

Remember that enumeration means presenting items in a list. Often these items move from the less important to the more important. This is called *emphatic order:*

> In order to live we must have relative comfort, stability, and the biological necessities of life.

In some kinds of writing, for example scientific and newspaper writing, the most important information is placed first so that the reader can quickly find the main points. This is called *reversed emphatic order*.

Writers often use such words as *first, second, third, one, another, still another,* and *finally* to mark some of the items in a list. The following lists give two sets of enumerative signal words that follow different grammatical patterns. In the first pattern, a noun follows the signal word:

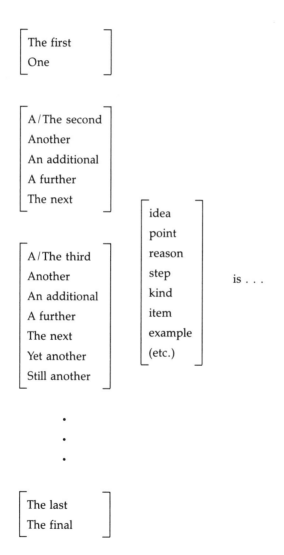

In emphatic order, the importance of the last item can be indicated in ways such as the following:

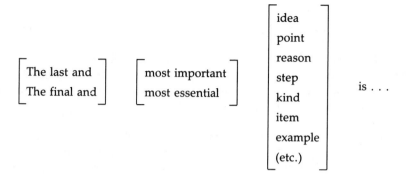

In the second pattern of emphatic order, a complete sentence follows the signal word:

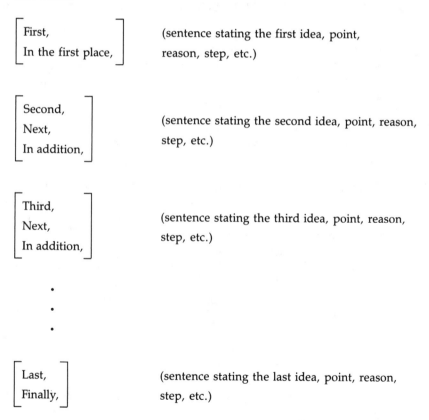

Examples of ways to mark the last item in emphatic order are as follows:

The two patterns may be mixed within one paragraph or essay. Note that it is rarely necessary to use an enumerative signal word for every item in the list.

Items marked by such signal words usually belong to a set or category. The text usually indicates what this set or category is. In the following example this set is "reasons." Each enumerative term—*one, another,* and *third*—refers to one reason in the set.

> There are three reasons he didn't get the job. One is that he had no experience. Another is that his application was late; and the third and most important reason is that the boss's son applied for the same job.

A way of deciding what belongs to the set of three reasons is to insert the word *reason* after each enumerative term. Thus we may rewrite the paragraph as follows:

> There are three reasons he didn't get the job. One reason is that he had no experience. Another reason is that his application was late; and the third and most important reason is that the boss's son applied for the same job.

In the above example, the items listed occur in consecutive sentences. Often, however, such items are separated. Each one can be named and discussed at length before the next item is mentioned:

> There are three reasons he didn't get the job. One is that he had no experience. Until now most of his jobs had been summer jobs or part-time work not related to his chosen profession. Another is that his application was late. This was beyond his control, however. The post office had misdirected his letter, and he had no way of knowing about the mistake. The third and most important reason he didn't get the job is that the boss's son applied for the same position. If he had known this, he would never have bothered to apply for the job in the first place.

Exercises

1. Go back to the reading passage in Chapter 1, "The Industrial Revolution." Paragraphs 7–16 list (enumerate) factors that contributed to the success of the Industrial Revolution. Not all of these paragraphs begin with signal words. How is it possible for the reader to understand clearly that this part of the essay gives an enumeration?

2. To what extent is emphatic order used in paragraph 10 of this chapter's reading passage, "The Knowledge Economy"?

Vocabulary Preview

Words in Context

The following words appear in this chapter's reading passage. Study them in their contexts and carry out the discussion tasks that follow.

	agriculture (n.)
-al (adj.)	agricultural

Twenty years ago I visited the farm where my mother lived as a child. Today the farm is gone; there are houses there instead. *Agricultural* land is disappearing. People are building houses everywhere. How will we eat in the future if there is no land for *agriculture?*

Give an example of agriculture.

	biology (n.)
-ist (n.)	biologist
-ical (adj.)	biological
-ly (adv.)	biologically

Biology was one of my favorite subjects in school. I love to study plants and animals. I want to know as much as I can about the life sciences. I enjoy the *biological* sciences so much that I am planning to become a doctor.

What are some of the fields of study that require a knowledge of biology?

	congest (v.)
-ion (n.)	congestion
-ive (adj.)	congestive

During rush hour, cars and buses *congest* every downtown street. Soon there will be so many cars that nothing will move. The *congestion* is becoming so bad that it takes me two hours to get home from work.

Do you have a suggestion for reducing traffic congestion?

	contemporary (adj. or n.)
-eous (adj.)	contemporaneous

I would like to read a *contemporary* description of the voyage of Christopher Columbus. Did anyone who lived at that time write about it? If any great historians were *contemporaries* of Columbus, did they understand the importance of his voyage to the "New World"?

Have you ever met any of the contemporaries of your grandparents? Are most of your friends contemporaries of yours, or are they older or younger?

	define (v.)
-ite (adj.)	definite
-ly (adv.)	definitely
-ion (n.)	definition
-ive (adj.)	definitive
-ly (adv.)	definitively
re- (= *again*)	redefine

Most words have clear meanings. How can you find a meaning of a word? One way is to look up its *definition* in a dictionary. However, the meanings of words are *definitely* changing. There is no doubt; many words change over time. We must *redefine* these words in new dictionaries so that people can find the new meanings.

How would you define a good student? How would you define a good friend?

	economy (n.)
-ist (n.)	economist
-ic (adj.)	economic
-ics (n.)	economics
-al (adj.)	economical
-ally (adv.)	economically
-ize (v.)	economize

Economics is not an exact science. Some *economists* have studied it all their lives. Still they cannot predict how the *economies* of nations will change. Will the nations get richer or poorer? What *economic* changes will occur? I know that I will get richer if I *economize*. If I am an *economical* housekeeper and save money, I will have money when I need it.

What is the difference in meaning between *economic* and *economical*? In your opinion, how can we improve the economy of our country? How would you advise a family to economize?

	illusion (n.)
-ory (adj.)	illusory
-ive (adj.)	illusive

We went to a magic show and watched a man pretend to cut a woman in half. It looked real, but of course it was just an *illusion*. The woman came out later and bowed to the audience.

Describe an illusion that you have experienced.

	invent (v.)
-or (n.)	inventor
-ion (n.)	invention
-ive (adj.)	inventive
-ly (adv.)	inventively
-ness (n.)	inventiveness

People often talk about *inventing* a better mousetrap. If you could build a better one, you could catch more mice. Such an *invention* might make you rich. Personally, I am waiting for some *inventor* to *invent* a better mouse!

What are some of the most important inventions in daily life? Can you name any of their inventors?

	polute (v.)
-ant (n.)	pollutant
-ion (n.)	pollution

Pollution is becoming a serious problem. Chemical *pollutants* in the air are not safe to breathe. The water is often too dirty to drink. The land is also *polluted* in many places. Trees cannot grow. People and animals cannot live there.

What should the government do about pollution? Name one thing that you personally can do about pollution.

	skill (n.)
-ful (adj.)	skillful
-ly (adv.)	skillfully
-ed (adj.)	skilled
semi-	semiskilled
(= *half*)	

The *semiskilled* workers who put cars together can make more money than workers with no training. Their sons and daughters often go to universities. There they may learn to become *skilled* workers such as engineers and doctors.

Name some jobs for unskilled, semiskilled, and skilled workers.

	talent (n.)
-ed (adj.)	talented

I have met some very *talented* people. One person I know can play music, paint, and write poetry. Another has a *talent* for acting in plays. Do you believe that a person is born with *talent* or that a person can learn to be *talented*?

What talents do you have? Describe the talents of a friend or acquaintance.

	theory (n.)
-ize (v.)	theorize
-etical (adj.)	theoretical
-ly (adv.)	theoretically

Most people want to be practical. That is, they want to make things that work. First, however, one must study *theory.* After one has the general knowledge and understands the ideas, it is much easier to make practical things.

Can you name some practical inventions and the theories that made them possible?

Discovering Word Meanings

Use (1) context clues; (2) your knowledge of prefixes, suffixes, and roots; and (3) a dictionary, if necessary, to discover the meanings of the italicized words in the following sentences from this chapter's reading passage.

1. The *pharmaceutical* industry will use bioengineering to produce a variety of drugs.

   (What is another name for a drug store? What part of speech is *pharmaceutical?*)

2. Semiskilled workers often worked on large *assembly lines.* Many new industries, such as the automobile industry, used *assembly lines* for efficient production.

   (Can you find three clues in this context to help you understand the meaning of this phrase?)

3. In every business field, development guidelines are being *laid out,* long-range retooling of equipment is being hurried along, new personnel are being hired. . . .

   (Use the dictionary to find the appropriate meaning of this term in this context. What other two-word verbs using *out* do you know?)

Signal Words and Phrases

Study the following signal words and phrases that appear in this chapter's reading passage.

1. in addition

These words introduce another item in the enumeration. Words with a similar meaning include *additionally, furthermore,* and *moreover.*

Reading books is a good way to improve your English. *In addition,* it is an enjoyable activity.

The processes that changed rural, agricultural societies into urban, industrial societies have continued to the present day. *In addition,* the growth that began in the Industrial Revolution seems to be continuing even now.

2. for example

This phrase introduces an example. A phrase with a similar meaning is *for instance.*

Some inventors made important contributions to leading industries. *For example,* Alexander Graham Bell invented the telephone.

Animal breeders will be able to design animals to fit economic conditions. *For example,* they could produce animals that eat grass instead of grain.

3. according to

This phrase is followed by the name of a person, theory, law, or the like. After the name comes a paraphrase or a quotation of the words that were used by the person named, or a statement of the theory or law.

According to Drucker, some industries are now becoming economically less important.

According to Rifkin, "In every business field, development guidelines are being laid out. . . ."

4. the/a first, second, etc.

These words show the order of items in an enumeration. In most cases use only *the* with *first.* Use either *the* or *a* with the others.

   a. Use *the* with *first, second, third,* etc., if you know all the items being discussed and if you are listing them in order.
   b. Use *a* with *second, third,* etc., if there are several items, but you don't know how many.

Three children came to the health clinic today. *The first* had a broken arm, *the second* had a high fever, and *the third* was hungry.

A *third* new source of economic growth is the materials industry.

Grammar Preview

Study the following excerpts or paraphrases from this chapter's reading passage, and work through the tasks.

1. Choose a word from the following list to describe the meaning of each of the italicized words in the sentences below: *ability, necessity, permission, possibility, probability, requirement.*

   Example

   You *must* learn English. Answer: *requirement*

   a. Organisms *could* replace miners and machines.
   b. In the future, the energy industry *might* use biological techniques.
   c. The chemical industry *may* learn to use plant and animal materials to produce chemicals.

2. Combine each pair of sentences in more than one way. What changes in meaning can occur when the sentences are combined differently? Is there any advantage to leaving them as shorter, separate sentences?
   a. The main resource of this economy is knowledge. Scientists, technologists, and other professionals use and process this knowledge.
   b. An important part of this revolution is biotechnology. The word *biotechnology* refers to a combination of biology and technology.
   c. In the future the energy industry might use biological techniques to produce special "fuel crops." These crops could provide an endless source of energy.

3. Make changes in the following sentences so that the enumerated items are clearer.
   a. Natural power includes wind power, water power, and we also have to use the muscle power of people and animals.
   b. Services include being transported from place to place, utilities, financial services, and government services.
   c. These changes are already affecting the kinds of work people do, needed training for them, and the products they create.

Getting Ready to Read

The reading passage in this chapter discusses the modern shift from an economy based on machines to an economy based on information. This new economic revolution is changing the world quickly and in many ways.

1. What are some ways that computers affect your daily life? Is your life easier or more difficult because of computers?

2. In your opinion, what kinds of industries will grow in the next ten years? What kinds of industries will become smaller? What reasons can you find for these changes?

3. As quickly as you can, find the following information in the reading passage: (a) Daniel Bell's three stages of civilization, (b) the name of the man

who invented the motion picture, and (c) the name of the man who compared modern industrial processes with "sundials and buggy whips."

4. What are the knowledge-based industries named in the passage?

Now read the passage carefully from beginning to end. As you read, note how information and service industries are becoming more important in our society.

READING PASSAGE

The Knowledge Economy

1 The Industrial Revolution caused great social and economic changes. These changes were the beginning of the industrial age. The nations that made these changes most successfully became the developed nations of the modern world. They owe their prosperity to the Industrial Revolution. The processes that changed rural, agricultural societies into urban, industrial societies have continued to the present day. In addition, the growth that began in the Industrial Revolution seems to be continuing even now. This, however, may be an illusion, at least for the world's developed countries. Economists point to an important shift in the economies of these countries. It is a move away from machinery and toward information exchange. A new economy of knowledge and information is replacing the industrial economy.

2 Human society has developed through several stages. Sociologist Daniel Bell (1983, pp. 500–549) calls these stages "preindustrial," "industrial," and "postindustrial." According to Bell, the economy of the preindustrial society included agriculture, mining, fishing, lumber, oil, and gas. Natural power produced these resources. Such power included wind power, water power, and the muscle power of people and animals. This economy depended on people who worked with their hands. In the next stage, industrial society, people made things by using machines. These machines used new forms of energy such as electricity. The industrial economy employed engineers and semiskilled workers. Semiskilled workers often worked on large assembly lines. Many new industries, such as the automobile industry, used assembly lines for

FIGURE 2–1   The McCormick harvester and twine binder. (Source: International Harvester)

efficient production. The last stage, the postindustrial economy, results from a shift away from the production of goods to the production of services. These services are of several kinds. They include the transportation of people and goods; utilities such as water and power supplies; financial services such as banks, trade, insurance, and real estate; and human services such as health, education, research, government, and recreation. The main resource of this economy is knowledge. Scientists, technologists, and other professionals use and process this knowledge.

3   During the Industrial Revolution, the growing industries needed inventions and new technology. However, according to Bell, these inventions did not come from science and theory. He points out that their inventors were "'talented tinkerers'° who worked independently of or were ignorant of contemporary science" (pp. 501–2). Yet it was they who made important contributions to the leading industries of steel, motors, electricity, telephone, and aviation. Alexander Graham Bell, for example, was a speech teacher. He invented the telephone while he was looking for a way to help the deaf by amplifying sound. Thomas A. Edison invented the light bulb, the motion picture, and

a person who plays around with machines as a hobby

the phonograph, among other things. However, he knew little about theoretical science. And Henry Bessemer created a steelmaking process without knowing about Henry Clifton Sorby's scientific work on metals. Today, such advances are no longer possible without theoretical knowledge.

4   The shift from machine-based industries to knowledge-based industries is a major discontinuity in the economies of developed countries. According to Peter Drucker (1969), a well-known management expert, today's economy still depends on the same major industries that were important in the past. The agriculture, steel, and automobile industries are some of the giants that have led economic expansion. However, Drucker says that these industries are now becoming economically less important. They will probably not continue to grow and expand.

5   Agriculture is a clear example of an important industry that is getting smaller. In 1860 40.6 percent of the U.S. labor force worked in agriculture, but this figure was only 2.1 percent in 1980 (Bell, 1983).

6   Another example is the steel industry. Drucker (1969) notes that this industry is losing its traditional markets. Some products that have been made of steel are now being made of other materials such as glass, plastic, concrete, and paper. Because steelmaking has become too expensive, the industry will not grow again without great changes in the method of production.

7   Drucker also points to the auto industry, which is still growing. Soon, however, it will reach its limits and start to get smaller. The congestion and pollution caused by automobiles will have a serious effect on its decline.

8   What, then, does Drucker suggest are the new knowledge-based industries on which economic growth will depend? He discusses three categories of such industries. The first of these is the information industry. This industry collects, stores, spreads, and applies knowledge. It depends on the computer. In the future, however, the computer itself will probably become less important than communicating and applying knowledge. Drucker foresees a central computer that will make information available to everyone. Another source of new industries is the science of the oceans. New technologies may help to supply food and minerals from the seas. A third new source of economic growth is the materials industry. This industry provides the materials for making objects. One such industry that has already become economically important is the

FIGURE 2–2   Drill presses at Bethlehem Steel Co. (Source: National Archives)

plastics industry. Drucker explains that throughout history our traditional materials have been metals, glass, natural fibers, and paper. Today, with the help of modern science, industries can make many new materials to meet specific needs. Because they will be created to fit a certain product, they will be highly efficient. Consequently, he points out, industries that supply traditional materials such as steel or glass will have trouble competing with those that produce these new materials.

9   Many economists refer to the new knowledge-based industries as a new industrial revolution. An important part of this revolution is biotechnology. The word *biotechnology* refers to a combination of biology and technology. Jeremy Rifkin is one of the leading experts on the biological advances that have made this revolution possible. According to Rifkin (1984, p. 12),

> In every business field, development guidelines are being laid out, long-range retooling° of equipment is being hurried along, new personnel are being hired, all in a mad rush to introduce the life sciences into the economy.

changing machines or tools to do new jobs

10   Leaders in this new field have said that biotechnology will have a great impact on the economy. For example, according to Irving Johnson of the Eli Lilly Company, today's industrial processes will be like "sundials and buggy° whips" compared with the processes of biotechnology (quoted in McAuliffe & McAuliffe, 1981, p. 92). Rifkin (1984, pp. 12–14) lists some specific industries that will be affected. The pharmaceutical industry will use bioengineering to produce a variety of drugs. The mining industry is experimenting with organisms—very small forms of life—that will eat metals or ores. Such organisms could replace miners and machines. The energy industry already uses certain crops to produce alcohol as fuel for cars. In the future it might use biological techniques to produce special "fuel crops." These crops could provide an endless source of energy. The chemical industry may learn to use plant and animal materials to produce chemicals. The agriculture industry is working on methods for destroying pests and diseases without using poisonous chemicals. It is also learning how to improve plant species to help them live under different conditions and thus to increase food production. Animal breeders will be able to design animals to fit economic conditions. For example, they could produce animals that eat grass instead of expensive grain. Finally and most importantly, biotechnology can directly affect human life too. Already it is changing medicine and is beginning to have serious effects on the entire health industry. One day it may even cause us to redefine human biology.

A buggy is a small carriage pulled by a horse.

11   The industrial economy, then, is changing into a knowledge economy in many ways. These changes are already affecting the kinds of work people do, the training they need to do it, and the products they create. Clearly, society and the economy are facing a major discontinuity.

References

Bell, Daniel (1983). The Social Framework of the Information Society. In Tom Forester (Ed.), *The Microelectronics Revolution* (pp. 500–549). Cambridge: The MIT Press.

Drucker, Peter (1969). *The Age of Discontinuity: Guidelines to Our Changing Society*. New York and Evanston: Harper & Row.

McAuliffe, Sharon, & McAuliffe, Kathleen (1981). *Life for Sale*. New York: Coward, McCann & Geoghegan.

Rifkin, Jeremy (1984). *Algeny: A New Word—A New World.* New York: Penguin Books.

Checking Your Comprehension

1. Look at Figure 2–1. What does this picture show about the stages of society? Which paragraph of "The Knowledge Economy" describes these stages? Summarize what this paragraph says about the stages.
2. According to Bell, what is the difference between a "talented tinkerer" and a scientist? How do Bessemer and Sorby illustrate this difference?
3. Explain why industries connected with the oceans and with biology are considered knowledge-based industries.
4. Paragraph 9 begins with the sentence, "Many economists refer to the new knowledge-based industries as a new industrial revolution." Refer to "The Industrial Revolution" in Chapter 1. How is the growth of the new knowledge-based industries similar to the Industrial Revolution in England?

For Discussion

1. Do you think there will be a fourth stage of society after the postindustrial stage? Why or why not? If you think that there will be a fourth stage, what form do you think it will take?
2. How do you expect the change to an information economy to affect you personally?

Analyzing the Structure

1. Paragraph 2 begins with a sentence about "preindustrial," "industrial," and "postindustrial" society. This first sentence is the topic sentence of the paragraph. The rest of the paragraph describes the three types of society that it mentions. Which sentences refer to each of the three types of society?
2. Paragraph 8 is an enumeration. What does it enumerate? How many items are enumerated? Does the paragraph contain any signal words that show enumeration? Find the sentence that begins "This industry . . . ." To what sentence does it refer? Now make an outline showing how all the sentences in this paragraph are related to each other. Indent each sentence under the sentence to which it refers. Number all the sentences. Begin the outline as follows:

Sentences 1 and 2 (topic sentences)
Sentence 3 (first item in the enumeration)
Sentence 4 (refers to sentence 2)
Sentence 5 (refers to sentence 2)
Sentence 6 (refers to sentence 4) etc.

3. The first sentences in paragraphs 8 and 11 use the word *then*. What is its meaning and function?

The Writing Process: Understanding the Topic

In university work, the instructor will often ask you to write about a certain topic. This topic may be very specific, or it may be general enough so that you can choose to concentrate on one issue related to the topic. In either case, the topic will rarely be one that you can write on from your own personal knowledge or experience.

Your first task is to understand what the topic means. Then you are ready to research the topic. Look first at the material in the course to find any information that relates directly to the topic. For most topics, you will then have to continue your research in the library. (For detailed information on how to do library research, see the Appendix at the end of this book.) Your choice of an issue to write about may be influenced by your personal interests. For example, you may be more interested in people than in machines. Therefore, if your assignment is to write about effects of the Industrial Revolution, you may prefer to discuss social consequences rather than technology. More information on how to choose an issue will be presented in Chapter 3.

As an example, consider the model essay in Chapter 1. The writer's assignment was to write an essay on the Amazon rain forest. He went to a library and read several articles on different aspects of rain forests. He noted the following points related to his topic:

description of a rain forest
description of the Amazon rain forest
the importance of rain forests
how rain forests interact with the environment
the destruction of Brazil's rain forest
the effects of destroying a rain forest
politics and the environment
the effects of destroying Brazil's rain forest (the Amazon rain forest).

An essay could be written about any of these issues. Since the writer was primarily concerned about the effects of destruction of the rain forest, he focused his attention on the issues related to this part of the topic.

Exercise

Discuss with a partner the following essay topic: "The Effects of the Knowledge Economy on My Future". Then discuss it further in a small group. Refer to the information provided in the reading passages and write down as many related issues as you and other members of your group can find. Select those issues that interest you the most.

Writing About Reading

1. Write one paragraph enumerating ways in which the knowledge economy affects agriculture. Use emphatic order and the organization and language of enumeration explained in Chapters 1 and 2.

2. Write a short essay of three or more paragraphs on the above topic. One approach is to write a body paragraph on each of the ways in which the knowledge economy affects agriculture. Use the organization and language of enumeration. Arrange your information in emphatic order.

3. Write a short essay of three or more paragraphs listing the advantages and disadvantages of the knowledge economy. Use enumeration and any other methods of organization that are appropriate.

4. Write a short essay of three or more paragraphs about the similarities and differences between the knowledge revolution and the Industrial Revolution in England. Refer to "The Industrial Revolution" in Chapter 1 for information. Use enumeration and any other methods of organization that are appropriate.

Chapter 3

The New Luddites

CHAPTER FOCUS

As you study this chapter, you should focus on the following important points:

Arrangement of information: generalization

Vocabulary: understanding new words

Signal words and phrases: *another, as a result, in turn, on the other hand*

Sentence grammar: future tense, hypothetical *would*, reduction of adjective clauses

Writing: narrowing the topic

Content: the disadvantages of the knowledge economy

Arrangement of Information

Organization of the Text: Generalization

A generalization is a statement about an issue. It consists of one or more complete sentences. Some generalizations are very general; others are less so. Therefore, a generalization might cover everything that is in a text, or it might cover only a part of what is in the text. A generalization that covers everything in a text is called a thesis statement. In other words, if you had to identify the main idea of an entire text in one sentence, that sentence would be the thesis statement of the text. It is usually part of the introduction and most often occurs at the end of the introduction. Some thesis statements can be found elsewhere, and others do not appear at all but are merely implied.

The more limited type of generalization, which covers only a single paragraph, is called a topic sentence. Thus if you had to identify the main idea of a paragraph in one sentence, that sentence would be the topic sentence of the paragraph. The topic sentence is usually the first sentence of a paragraph. Some topic sentences, however, appear elsewhere in the paragraph, while others do not appear at all but are merely implied. (In Chapter 4 you will learn more about generalizations and thesis statements. In Chapter 6 you will learn more about topic sentences.)

Exercises

1. What is the thesis statement of the reading passage in Chapter 2, ''The Knowledge Economy''?

2. What is the topic sentence of the third paragraph of ''The Knowledge Economy''?

3. Does the reading passage in Chapter 1, ''The Industrial Revolution,'' have a clearly written thesis statement? Explain your answer.

Vocabulary Preview

Words in Context

The following words appear in this chapter's reading passage. Study them in their contexts and write the correct forms of the words in the blanks in the exercises that follow. In some cases you may have to include another word, such as a preposition.

	acquire (v.)
-ition (n.)	acquisition
-ive (adj.)	acquisitive

Art dealers often spend very large amounts of money

to _____ famous works of art. Such well-known

_____ may attract buyers from all over the world.

	bridge (n. or v.)
-able (adj.)	bridgeable
un- (= *not*)	unbridgeable

A suspension _____, which hangs from tall towers, makes

it possible for people to cross very wide bodies of water. A famous

example is the Golden Gate _____ in San Francisco. Without

such _____ many wide bodies of deep water would

be _____.

	content (adj.)
-ed (adj.)	contented
-ly (adv.)	contentedly
-ment (n.)	contentment
dis- (= *not*)	discontent, discontented, etc.

When they retired, they wanted their remaining years to be happy

and _____. They bought a smaller house in a warmer cli-

mate and raised a small garden. They got much _____ from

working together in their garden. They have never been bored, un-

happy, or _____ _____ their retirement.

	debate (v. or n.)
-er (n.)	debater
-able (adj.)	debatable
-y (adv.)	debatably

Our school recently held a _____ about taxes.

Each _____ was allowed to speak for ten minutes. The

group that _____ in favor of lowering taxes won. I want to

become a lawyer, so I think I shall take up _____.

	dispute (n. or v.)
-able (adj.)	disputable
-ly (adv.)	disputably
-ant (n.)	disputant
-ation (n.)	disputation

Two cars hit each other in the intersection. This caused

a _____ between the drivers. The two _____

shouted at each other until the police arrived. They were

_____ who had caused the accident.

	disrupt (v.)
-ion (n.)	disruption
-ive (adj.)	disruptive
-ly (adv.)	disruptively

A young couple in the back row kept _____ the politician's

speech. They interrupted the speech by shouting at the politician.

They did not agree with what the politician was saying and would not

allow her to speak. This _____ lasted nearly ten minutes

until the police asked the _____ couple to leave.

onset (n.)

Historians do not agree on the exact year when the Industrial

Revolution began. However, most of them believe that

its _____ was in the early eighteenth century.

	pessimism (n.)
-t (n.)	pessimist
-ic (adj.)	pessimistic
-ally (adv.)	pessimistically

I have a friend who always believes that something bad is going to

happen. She has always been a _____. I wish that she

would give up her _____ thoughts and think more about

good things.

	pole (n.)
-ar (adj.)	polar
-ity (n.)	polarity
-ize (v.)	polarize
-ation (n.)	polarization

The new trade agreement between the two countries has

_____ people into two completely opposite groups. One

group favors the agreement, and the other is completely against it.

There will be no agreement between the two groups as long as

this _____ exists.

	revolt (n. or v.)
-ution (n.)	revolution
-ary (adj.)	revolutionary
-ary (n.)	revolutionary
-ize (v.)	revolutionize

The last decade has seen a _____ _____ biology.

So many different _____ discoveries have come from that

field that almost every kind of business has been affected. Biological

technology is _____ all sectors of the economy.

root (n. or v.)

up- (= *up*)   uproot (v.)

We spent the entire day in the garden pulling up all the weeds. We

were careful to pull up the _____ so that the weeds would

not grow again. After we had _____ all the weeds, we put

them in a pile. Then we put the _____ weeds into garbage

bags.

worthwhile (adj.)

My teeth did not hurt, so I thought that going to the dentist was a

waste of time. However, the dentist found a small cavity in one

tooth. He was able to fix it quickly before it caused any trouble. So the

trip to the dentist was _____ after all.

Discovering Word Meanings

Use (1) context clues; (2) your knowledge of prefixes, suffixes, and roots; and (3) a dictionary, if necessary, to discover the meanings of the italicized words in the following sentences from this chapter's reading passage.

1. Since the onset of the Industrial Revolution, the economies of the *industrialized* nations have continued to expand.

   (How does the suffix change the part of speech and the meaning of this word?)

2. New but different jobs have replaced jobs that machines have *taken over.*

   (Use your dictionary to find the meaning of this two-word verb in this context.)

3. However, Cordell points out that economic changes might be easier to achieve than other changes. Instead of learning how to *make a living,* people will need education in how to live. People will have to change their attitudes about work. They will have to learn not to see value in the idea of work itself. And they will have to learn not to regard paid work as more important than voluntary work.

   (Is *making a living* connected with economic changes or with how to live? How does it relate to the last sentence in this context?)

Signal Words and Phrases

Study the following signal words and phrases that appear in this chapter's reading passage.

1. another

This word introduces an additional item in an enumeration. The expression *a further* has a similar meaning.

> An electronic watch requires the assembly of only five components. *Another* example of a simplified product is the television set.

2. as a result

This phrase introduces the result of what came just before it. Expressions with a similar meaning are *consequently* and *as a consequence*.

> Automated offices can produce more with fewer employees. *As a result*, displaced workers have nowhere to turn for new jobs.

> More and more jobs will require unskilled labor, and *consequently* will offer less pay than skilled jobs.

3. in turn

This phrase introduces an item in a chain of causes and effects: *A* causes *B*. *B*, in turn, causes *C*.

> Increased buying will stimulate more production, and this *in turn* will create more jobs. (*buying = A; production = B; more jobs = C*)

4. on the other hand

This phrase introduces the second item in a choice between two items. The second item contrasts with the first item.

> There will be more jobs for unskilled labor. *On the other hand,* there will be jobs for skilled labor as well.

Grammar Preview

Study the following excerpts or paraphrases from this chapter's reading passage, and work through the tasks.

1. Assume that the following passage comes from a history book written in the year 2100 A.D. It reports events that occurred in the early part of the twenty-first century. You are an economist living in the last decade of the twentieth century. You foresee that these events will happen. Rewrite the passage so that it is a prediction of these events.

   > Increased production brought lower prices, which allowed people to buy additional items. This increased buying then stimulated more production, and this in turn created more jobs.

2. You are an economist writing about the future. You have written the text that appears below. Upon reflection you decide that you are not certain about your predictions. You therefore rewrite them to express your uncertainty.

> People will spend their extra money on services that do not add new jobs, or they will buy goods that are made in automated factories. The scenario of the Industrial Revolution will no longer be valid for these conditions.

3. Suggest how each italicized phrase in the following sentences could be shortened without changing its meaning.
   a. Those *who face unemployment* suffer, but are forgotten in the general prosperity.
   b. In their opinion, increased production will bring lower prices, *which will allow people to buy additional items*.
   c. On the other hand, the new technologies may create employment for people *who design and program machines*, or those *who perform professional services*.
   d. The challenge is to manage this change with a minimum of disruption to the individuals *who need society's protection*.

Getting Ready to Read

The reading passage in this chapter is about some of the disadvantages of the knowledge economy.

1. Consider some ways in which the knowledge economy could affect your future. In what ways might it help you? In what ways might it make your life more difficult?

2. Do you know anyone who lost his or her job because of advances in technology? Describe what happened. What did the person do?

3. The reading passage in this chapter is called "The New Luddites." Quickly find the sentence that explains the term *Luddites*. What does this word mean?

4. Quickly skim through as much of the text as necessary to find examples of how technology can replace workers.

5. Read the first paragraph of the passage. Consider the title. Think about the reading passage in Chapter 2, "The Knowledge Economy." Now predict what this passage will contain.

Now read the passage carefully from beginning to end. As you read, think about the problems that modern computerized technology can cause.

READING PASSAGE

The New Luddites

1 Change on a large scale is often difficult to manage. The economic development of industrial society caused hardship and suffering for some groups and individuals whose jobs were threatened. The storm of rapid change that swept over these people at the beginning of the industrial era uprooted their way of life. The Luddites, for example, were such a group of discontented British workers in the early nineteenth century. The introduction of labor-saving technology in the textile industry had affected their jobs. They protested against the lowered wages and unemployment that resulted by smashing the new machinery. Similarly, in the last quarter of the twentieth century, electronic technology is now revolutionizing all sectors of the working world. As a result, an economic storm is again threatening industrial society.

2   In North America, technological change has been an accepted part of economic development. People invent new machines to replace workers, and therefore jobs are lost. However, so far the new technology has created enough new jobs for almost everyone. Like the Luddites in the nineteenth century, those who face unemployment today suffer, but are forgotten in the general prosperity. Since the onset of the Industrial Revolution, the economies of the industrialized° nations have continued to expand. New but different jobs have replaced those jobs that machines have taken over.

Personalized means that something has been made personal. Therefore industrialized means _____.

3   According to G. G. Schwartz and W. Neikirk (1983), the fear that factory workers would be displaced by machines caused an automation scare in the United States in the 1950s and 1960s. However, those workers who were displaced found jobs in the service sector, for example in offices, banks or government service. In Schwartz and Neikirk's view, the electronics revolution has now reached the service sector as well as the factory. Offices using microcomputers°, word processors, and photocopiers can produce much more with the same number of employees or even with fewer employees. As a result, displaced factory workers can no longer turn to the service sector for new jobs. Both industries and services

Micro means "very small." Therefore microcomputers means _____.

FIGURE 3–1   Robot welders in an auto assembly plant. (Source: Chrysler Corporation)

can now maintain and even increase production without hiring new workers.

4   Many observers dispute this pessimistic conclusion (Schwartz & Neikirk, 1983). In their opinion, increased production will bring lower prices, which will allow people to buy additional items. This increased buying will then stimulate more production, and this in turn will create more jobs. However, Schwartz and Neikirk argue that people today might instead spend their extra money on services that do not add new jobs, or they might buy goods that are made in automated factories. They conclude that the scenario° of the Industrial Revolution may no longer be valid for today's conditions.

a description of the events in a play or movie; in this case, the series of events caused by the Industrial Revolution

5   Let us look more closely at how technological change in industrialized societies can involve both a loss of jobs in some sectors and a change in the kinds of jobs available to workers.

6   We have already discussed the broad reasons for the loss of jobs. It is worthwhile, however, to look at specific examples of the process. A. J. Cordell (1985) points to two kinds of change in manufacturing that affect employment: The product itself is being simplified, and the methods of

production are becoming automated. In either case, fewer people are needed to make a product. As Cordell (1985, p. 26) points out, "the type of production that simplifies the product makes it less expensive to produce and sell. Industries that fail to adopt the new technologies will be greatly affected." His examples are the Swiss° watch industry, where employment fell by 46,000 in the mid-1970s, and the West German watch industry, where jobs decreased by 40 percent at the same time. An electronic watch requires the assembly of five components; a mechanical watch requires one thousand assembly operations. Another example of a simplified product that Cordell cites is the television set. Manufacturers in Japan have cut their staffs by 50 percent. At the same time, production has increased by 25 percent. A second reason for the loss of jobs is the use of microelectronics in all phases of industry. New plants are being built that use robots instead of people. Cordell's example is the Yamazaki factory at Nagoya, Japan, which would have needed 2,500 workers without microelectronics and robots. With this technology, however, it will need only 215 workers.

the adjectival form of Switzerland

7   While some jobs will disappear as a result of these changes, others will change, and still others will be

FIGURE 3–2 "No, B146, you *can't* have a coffee break!"

created. The new jobs, however, will not be of the same types as the old ones. As Cordell suggests, machines are becoming "smarter," so workers will not need to know as much to do their work. This is known as *de-skilling.*° Be- cause of automation, more and more jobs will require un- skilled labor, and jobs for semiskilled workers will disap- pear. On the other hand, the new technologies may create employment for people who design and program ma- chines, or those who perform professional services. These jobs will require a high degree of knowledge and training. Consequently the job market is becoming polarized, for unskilled workers will no longer be able to become semi- skilled workers by acquiring experience. Only training and knowledge will enable a person to perform a skilled job. This will create an unbridgeable gap between the skilled and unskilled members of the work force.

De means "taking away" or "losing." Therefore, de-skilling means _____.

8   Cordell notes that these changes in the conditions of work in industrial societies can lead to important changes in the social structures and attitudes in these societies. He concludes that "the future of work and working in the

FIGURE 3–3 Skilled jobs require graduates like these. (Source: Ken Karp)

evolving information society is subject to much debate.
. . . The new technologies will change the nature of work,
the place of work, and the importance of work to society"
(1985, pp. 42–43). In his view, workers will have to share
jobs and income, for there will not be enough jobs for
everyone. To maintain an economy, members of a society
must have the income to be consumers. However, Cordell
points out that economic changes might be easier to
achieve than other changes. Instead of learning how to
make a living, people will need education in how to live.
People will have to change their attitudes about work.
They will have to learn not to see value in the idea of
work itself. And they will have to learn not to regard paid
work as more important than voluntary work.

9   Industrial nations seem to be in transition from societies based on work to societies in which the meaning of
work has changed. The challenge is to manage this change
with a minimum of disruption to the individuals who need
society's protection.

References

Cordell, A. J. (1985). *The Uneasy Eighties: The Transition to an Infor-
    mation Society.* Background Study 53, Science Council of
    Canada, Minister of Supply and Services. Hull, Quebec:
    Canadian Government Publishing Centre.
Schwartz, G. G., & Neikirk, W. (1983). *The Work Revolution.* To-
    ronto: McClellan & Stewart.

Checking Your Comprehension

1. What are the similarities between certain modern North American workers and Luddites?
2. What analogy does the writer use to describe rapid change? (An analogy
   compares different things or ideas by saying that they are similar in some
   way.)
3. What are the main effects of technological change on the labor market?
   How does Figure 3–1 suggest some of these effects?
4. Explain the two points of view that Schwartz and Neikirk present. Which
   argument do they support, and why?
5. What is *de-skilling,* and how does it affect jobs and salaries?
6. Explain why changes in attitudes toward work will be necessary. What
   are these changes?

For Discussion

1. Why are some countries more likely than others to use robots in their industries? Can you think of any consequences this might have for world trade?
2. Describe a futuristic society in which work no longer has the same value that it has in our society. How is the wealth in such a society distributed? Are wages still connected with work, or do people receive money or goods in some other way? How do people spend their time?

Analyzing the Structure

1. Locate the thesis sentence of the reading passage.
2. Locate the topic sentences of paragraphs 4, 6, and 7. (*Hint:* Sometimes the generalization that states the topic of a paragraph is expressed in more than one sentence.) How did you decide what the topic sentences were?
3. What is the purpose of paragraph 6?
4. Describe how paragraphs 6 and 7 give an enumeration. What do they enumerate? What role does paragraph 5 have in this enumeration?

The Writing Process: Narrowing the Topic

In Chapter 2 we saw that understanding a topic means understanding some of the issues connected with that topic. We also saw that a topic could be general or specific. If the topic is too general, the essay might be longer than necessary. In addition, it may not be clearly focused. One way to narrow the topic, or to make it more specific, is to ask repeatedly, "On which part of the topic do I want to focus?," or more briefly, "What about . . . ?" For example, if the broad or general topic is pollution, the writer may ask, "What about pollution?" One possible reply to this question is "the consequences of pollution." Another useful question is "What kind of . . . ?" If the writer asks, "What kind of pollution do I wish to deal with?," perhaps the reply will be "carbon dioxide pollution in the atmosphere." In this way it is possible to move from a general topic like pollution to a more specific one like the consequences of carbon dioxide pollution in the atmosphere. Using the same technique, the writer could continue to make the topic more and more specific. Sometimes it is useful to do this to get a better overall picture of the possible treatments of a topic. For example, after the writer narrows the general topic of pollution to an issue such as the consequences of pollution, he or she may consider what the consequences of pollution are. The writer then has the option of choosing to write either about all of the consequences or about just one or two of them. This choice will depend on the length and purpose of the essay. The tree diagram on the following page outlines this process.

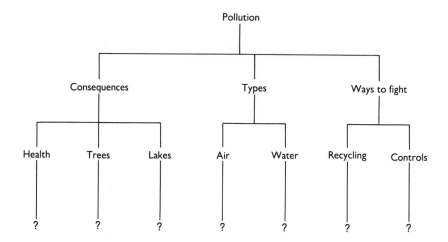

Let us now consider the issues generated by the writer of the model essay on the Amazon rain forests in Chapter 1. As discussed in Chapter 2, some of these issues were the importance of rain forests, how rain forests interact with the environment, and the effects of destroying a rain forest. The writer arrived at his chosen topic by focusing on the effects of destroying a rain forest and asking such questions as, ''What kinds of effects are they?'' and ''Which rain forest will be the subject of the essay?'' He was thus able to move from a rather general issue to the specific topic of the physical and social effects of destroying the Amazon rain forest. This specific topic became the topic of his essay.

Exercise

Consider the essay topic ''Postindustrial Society.'' Narrow this topic so that it is suitable for an essay of about five paragraphs. Explain to the class how you moved from the general to the specific topic.

Writing About Reading

1. The world faces serious economic problems in the near future. In your opinion, what must nations do to survive the next one hundred years? Write one paragraph answering this question. Structure the information in the form of a process.

2. Write a short essay on the above topic. One possible approach is to allow a paragraph for each step in the process.

3. Write a short essay on technological advances. Use enumeration and any other methods of organization that are appropriate.

4. Refer to the sectoral and aggregate models described in ''The Industrial Revolution'' in Chapter 1. Explain how one or both of these theories may account for the new industrial revolution in knowledge and information described in ''The Knowledge Economy'' in Chapter 2 and in ''The New Luddites'' in this chapter. If neither model is sufficient, invent a model of your own.

An ocean scene in Oregon. (Source: Rachel Weinstock)

UNIT TWO

===============

Exploitation of the Seas

To exploit means to use or develop something in order to profit from it. We exploit the land and sea to get the resources that we need for our homes and industries. For example, scientists have found oil deposits in many places along the shores of oceans and seas. Other substances, such as coal and various metals, have been successfully mined from the bottom of the sea. The three chapters of this unit deal with our use and misuse of the seas.

The sea, of course, is a major source of food. Chapter 4 deals with mariculture, a technique that can help increase the amount of food that we can get from the sea. Mariculture is a way of farming in the sea just as we farm on land.

Chapter 5 describes cities of the future that will float on the oceans or cling to the ocean bottoms. These cities will contain all the facilities of land-based cities. They will allow ocean miners and their families to live together near the places where the miners work.

Chapter 6 discusses the kinds of pollution that our modern technological societies are dumping into the seas. It describes the effects of these pollutants and warns of the dangers of misusing the oceans.

Chapter 4

Mariculture

CHAPTER FOCUS

As you study this chapter, you should focus on the following important points:

Arrangement of information: process, parts of a text

Vocabulary: understanding new words

Signal words and phrases: *as an example, next*

Sentence grammar: passive voice, gerunds, future tense, noun + verb combinations, verb + verb combinations, adverb clauses

Writing: the thesis statement

Content: farming and ranching in the sea

Arrangement of Information

Organization of the Content: Process

The term *process* is used to describe a special kind of enumeration. A process is an enumeration of steps that must be followed in a certain order to achieve a desired result. For example, recipes in a cookbook are processes. Suppose that you use the following recipe to prepare a soft-boiled egg:

> Add water to a pot until the water is deep enough to cover the egg, and bring the water to a boil. Place the egg in the water and leave it there for three minutes. Remove the egg and place it in an egg cup for serving.

It is easy to see how important it is to carry out these steps in the correct order. Placing the egg in the water and removing it before bringing the water to a boil would fail to achieve the desired result. In this simple example no signals have been used to suggest the order of the steps. Sometimes, however, the process is more complex. There may be additional descriptions or explanations between one step and the next. In such a case the writer may mark the beginning of each new step by using words such as *first, second, next, then,* and *finally.*

Exercises

1. Look at Figure 4–2 in this chapter's reading passage. How many steps does this process contain? Could any of the steps be carried out in a different order?

2. Write down the steps in a process that is familiar to you.

Organization of the Text: Parts of an Essay

As an advanced student, you will have to read many texts that present complex information. If the writers of those texts have organized them carefully and have shown how the parts are related to each other, they will have provided you with a guide for understanding what they have to say. As a reader, you should learn to recognize the ways of organizing texts.

The first thing to recognize about texts is that there are different levels of structure. The first level deals with the parts of the whole text. On the second level, each paragraph has several parts. A third level has to do with how these parts are combined. In this section we will discuss only the first level, that is, the parts of the whole text.

Most texts have four main parts: the introduction, the thesis statement, the body, and the conclusion.

The Introduction

The introduction of a text introduces the reader to some background information necessary to understand the meaning, relevance, or importance of a topic. In other words, the introduction establishes a context. Then—usually at the end of the introduction—the topic of the text, or the thesis, is stated. Look at "The New Luddites" in Chapter 3. Most of the first paragraph introduces the topic. It establishes a context by discussing who the original Luddites were and when they were active.

The Thesis Statement

The background information supplied in the introduction usually leads up to a thesis statement. This statement is like a contract with the reader, telling the reader what the subject of the text will be. Not all texts have specific sentences that state the thesis. Sometimes the thesis is stated in several sentences, and sometimes it is implied rather than stated. The thesis statement of "The New Luddites" consists of the last two sentences of paragraph 1. It states that another battle between workers and machines is taking place. It informs the reader that this entire essay will be about the struggle between humans and machines in the labor force.

The Body of the Text

The body of the text consists of the number of paragraphs necessary to discuss the thesis. Each paragraph must be related to the thesis in some way. Each of these paragraphs has its own thesis statement, which is called a topic sentence (to be discussed further in Chapter 6). In "The New Luddites," the body paragraphs discuss trends and examples that refer back to the thesis statement and give evidence to support it. Every paragraph in the text should be related, either directly or indirectly, to the thesis statement. Note that, if the body of the text is very long, headings can be used to organize the paragraphs into groups, or sections.

The Conclusion

The conclusion of a text is a mirror image of its introduction. The introduction begins with a wider context and narrows it to the thesis statement, which is a smaller part of the context. The conclusion often echoes or restates the thesis of the essay or even summarizes the main points discussed in the body of the text. It can then reach outward again in a new direction. In "The New Luddites," the last two paragraphs form a conclusion. The first of these paragraphs explains how the economic problem can lead to social changes. The final paragraph points to the future and generalizes the problem to include all technological societies.

Exercises

1. Look at the reading passage "The Knowledge Economy" in Chapter 2. What constitutes the introduction of this essay?
2. What is the thesis statement of "The Knowledge Economy"?
3. What constitutes the conclusion of "The Knowledge Economy"?

Vocabulary Preview

Words in Context

The following words, arranged in groups, appear in this chapter's reading passage. Study them in their contexts and write the correct forms of the words in the blanks in the exercises that follow.

1. conducive, expenditure, overhead

	conduce (v.)
-ive (adj.)	conducive
-ness (n.)	conduciveness

A calm atmosphere is *conducive* to good study habits. In contrast, noise and confusion make studying difficult.

	spend (v.)
ex- (= *out*)	expend
-se (n.)	expense
-ture (n.)	expenditure

If your income is small, you must reduce your *expenditures*. Don't spend too much money, or you will go into debt.

overhead (n. or adj.)

Rent, lighting, and taxes are included in the *overhead* costs of a business. The *overhead* must be kept low if the business is to make a profit.

A young couple wanted to start a new business that produced jewelry.

Part of the business was located in the couple's home, thus reducing

the _____. In this way they were able to minimize

their _____ for electricity and heat. By saving money in

this way, they were able to offer high quality products at low prices.

Such practices are _____ to the financial success of any

business.

2. analogy, feasible, miscellaneous, nutrient, site

	analogy (n.)
-ize (v.)	analogize
-ous (adj.)	analogous

Often it is helpful to explain something complex by comparing it with something similar but easier to understand. For this reason an *analogy* is often drawn between the heart and a pump.

	feasible (adj.)
-ly (adv.)	feasibly
-ility (n.)	feasibility

If enough money is available, and if technical knowledge is sufficiently advanced, a manned flight to Mars may be *feasible* in the near future.

	miscellany (n.)
-ous (adj.)	miscellaneous
-ly (adv.)	miscellaneously

In a business, large expenses are listed separately. The various smaller expenses may be grouped together and listed as *miscellaneous* expenses because they include a number of small, less important items that are difficult to list separately.

	nutrient (adj. or n.)
-tious (adj.)	nutritious
-ly (adv.)	nutritiously
-ness (n.)	nutritiousness

We are more careful about what we eat than our parents and grandparents were. We know that it is important to get the right *nutrients* in our diet if we want to stay well.

	site (n. or v.)
-ate (v.)	situate
-ion (n.)	situation

The architect personally chose the site for the new building. He believed that the location of the building was very important.

Fish farming, known as mariculture, provides an interest-

ing _____ with ranching and farming on land. Similar

costs are involved in both kinds of operations. First, there are the

costs of producing and feeding young fish. Different kinds

of _____ may be necessary. In some cases the food is grown

on _____. Also, the fish must be protected from their natu-

ral enemies, and this will cost money as well. Finally, there are var-

ious _____ costs, such as the costs of shipping and packag-

ing. If the costs cannot be kept lower than the income from the sale of

the fish, the operation will not be economically _____.

3. ecologically, environment, hardy, toxic

	ecology (n.)
-ical (adj.)	ecological
-ly (adv.)	ecologically
-ist (n.)	ecologist

The existence of every form of life on earth is related to the existence of every other form of life. Only when we study this *ecological* system can we understand how complex our world really is.

environs (n.; pl. only)
-ment (n.)	environment
-al (adj.)	environmental
-ly (adv.)	environmentally

The courts often try to remove young criminals from bad *environments*, hoping that placing them in better surroundings will change their behavior.

hardy (adj.)
-ness (n.)	hardiness
-hood (n.)	hardihood

Gardeners in warm climates can grow a large variety of flowering plants that are not *hardy* enough to survive cold northern winters.

toxin (n.)
anti- (= against)	antitoxin
-ic (adj.)	toxic
-ity (n.)	toxicity

Many materials used to clean homes are *toxic* and should be stored in locked cabinets to prevent accidental poisoning of young children.

The thousands of species of plants on earth are an important part of

the planet's _____ system. Many of these plants

are _____. Even _____ chemicals cannot easily kill

them. Other species, however, need a friendly _____ in

order not to die.

4. crucial, impending, spawn

crux (n.)
-ial (adj.)	crucial
-ly (adv.)	crucially

As the plane accelerated down the runway, preparing to take off, the pilot thought that he could hear a strange sound coming from one of the engines. He had to make the important decision whether to take off, and the decision had to be made immediately. He made the *crucial* decision to abort the take-off and to return to the terminal building.

impending (adj.)

Some people live in fear that something dreadful is about to happen. But the *impending* disasters that they imagine rarely occur.

spawn (v. or n.)

When salmon are ready to lay their eggs, they leave the oceans and return to the rivers where they were born. There they *spawn,* and a short time later they die.

A new scientific discovery can result in many related discoveries. Thus one new idea can *spawn* a great many others.

Unlike other fish, salmon remember the waters where their lives began. Returning to these waters is _____ to their reproductive cycle. Oblivious of _____ death, they swim upstream to their home waters to _____.

Discovering Word Meanings

Use (1) context clues; (2) your knowledge of prefixes, suffixes, and roots; and (3) a dictionary, if necessary, to discover the meanings of the italicized words in the following sentences from this chapter's reading passage.

1. Ranchers send herds of animals out to pasture to *graze.* Similarly, fishermen can send young salmon out to sea to grow to maturity without any cost to the producer.

   (What do animals need in order to grow? What part of speech is *graze?* Here, it is used without an object. Use a dictionary to choose the meaning of the word for this context and to find out whether it can be used with an object.)

2. Mussels, which are a species of shellfish, also have the potential for producing large crops. They grow in cold-water regions that are relatively free of shellfish diseases and *predators.*

   (What else, in addition to disease, is a threat to shellfish? What part of speech is *predator?* How do you know this from the context? How could you tell without the context? Use a dictionary to find other parts of speech related to this word.)

3. A kelp plantation could be planted in the North Pacific and drift in the California Current until the kelp matured. Workers on floating platforms would tend the crops, and *tugs* would steer the plantation away from shipping lanes and islands.

   (What is used to push boats through the water? *Tug* is the short form of the answer. Use a dictionary to find the complete word. What part of speech is *tugs* in this context? What is the usual meaning of the word *tug?* What parts of speech can it be?)

4. Most forms of mariculture are at present economically *unprofitable.* However, greater demand for food will produce greater profits.

(What is the meaning of *un-?* What is the meaning of *-able?* What part of speech is *unprofitable?* How can you tell this from the context? How could you tell without the context?)

5. Overhead includes miscellaneous operating expenses, interest, the *amortization* costs of facilities, and the purchase cost of equipment.

   (Find *amortize* in the dictionary. How does *-ation* change the part of speech?)

Signal Words and Phrases

Study the following signal words and phrases that appear in this chapter's reading passage.

1. as an example

These words introduce an example. Expressions with similar meanings are *for example* and *for instance.*

> *As an example,* consider the ways in which mariculture could aid in the commercial salmon industry.

2. next

This word may introduce a second, third, or subsequent idea, point, reason, step, kind, item, example, etc.

> *Next,* control of the biological environment includes the costs of protecting the crop from predators and disease.

Grammar Preview

Study the following excerpts or paraphrases from this chapter's reading passage, and work through the tasks.

1. Why did the writer use the passive voice in the following passages? Try changing the italicized verbs into the active voice to help you understand possible differences in meaning.
   a. Mariculture is the raising of animals and vegetables that live in water, just as crops *are grown* on a farm.
   b. Fish, for example, *are raised* in these pools. Then they *are released* into the ocean to increase existing populations.
   c. In Canada and the United States, mussels *are used* mainly in animal feeds.
   d. Young salmon *could be raised* in fish farms known as hatcheries. They would then stay for several days in floating cages submerged in local

rivers before *being released* to the open ocean. Remarkably, salmon will always remember their home waters. They will cross enormous stretches of ocean to return to those waters to spawn. Traps *can be placed* in rivers during the spawning season to catch some of the returning fish.

2. In the following passages, some of the active voice verbs can be changed to the passive voice, while some cannot. In your opinion, what were the author's reasons for using the active voice in those cases in which the passive voice was possible? Find those that cannot be changed and explain why.

a. In particular, mussels tend to attach themselves to ropes dangling in the water. In this way they can grow in three-dimensional plots. The Lummi Indians of Washington State grow mussels and typically harvest more than 168,000 kilograms of mussel protein per hectare.

b. Most forms of mariculture are at present economically unprofitable. However, greater demand for food will produce greater profits. Mariculture is the feeding, raising, harvesting, processing, and marketing of a marine crop. We can construct a simple bioeconomic model of mariculture.

3. Explain the meaning of the italicized expressions. What question do they answer?

a. In addition, they can control the numbers of salmon *by restricting* the catch or *by releasing* more salmon into the ocean.

b. The mariculturist can reduce these costs *by using* "free" ocean space if possible.

4. A form of the future tense is used in each of the following sentences. Explain the meaning of this tense in each example. Does it refer to future time in each instance? Are there any instances in which it could be replaced by another tense, and if so, which one?

a. Young salmon could be raised in fish farms known as hatcheries. They would then stay for several days in floating cages submerged in local rivers before being released to the open ocean. Remarkably, salmon *will* always *remember* their home waters. They *will cross* enormous stretches of ocean to return to those waters to spawn.

b. Most forms of mariculture are at present economically unprofitable. However, greater demand for food *will produce* greater profits.

c. The cost of these processes must be substantially lowered in a maricultural operation. Otherwise, the operation *will* not *be able* to compete successfully with commercial fishing.

d. The crop, through harvesting, converts to a concentrated state. Processing converts the raw, concentrated crop to a product that people *will buy.*

5. Combine the following sentence pairs according to the example. Is the combined sentence an improvement over the two shorter sentences? Why or why not?

Example

Mussels attach themselves to ropes. Mussels have this tendency.

Combined

Mussels have the tendency to attach themselves to ropes.

Or

Mussels tend to attach themselves to ropes.

   a. Mariculturists reduce costs. They make this endeavor.
   b. Salmon return to their home waters before they die. They make this attempt.

6. Combine the following pairs of sentences by following the instructions in parentheses.

Example

Mussels have not yet achieved wide popularity in North America. They are favored in many parts of the world.

(Begin with a word or phrase that contrasts the two ideas.)

Although mussels have not yet achieved wide popularity in North America, they are favored in many parts of the world.

   a. Such chemicals may be relatively harmless to the mussels themselves. They may affect the consumer.

(Begin with a word that contrasts the two ideas.)

   b. The technique proved economically feasible. A number of kelp farms could be linked together.

(Begin with a word that makes the first part into a condition.)

   c. The fishermen can trap the salmon. They return to spawn.

(Begin the second part with a word that indicates a moment in time.)

Getting Ready to Read

The reading passage in this chapter is about ways to use the oceans to provide food for the earth's growing population.

1. What foods are you accustomed to eating? If these foods were no longer available, what would you eat instead?

2. In many parts of the world, people suffer from lack of food. What are some ways to help solve the problem of food shortage?

3. The essay in this chapter is divided into several main parts. Skim through the essay to identify those parts. Then look again at the first part to discover what its divisions are.

4. Find the part of the text that explains the storage and conversion process (see Figure 4-2).

Now read the passage carefully from beginning to end. As you read, note any information that suggests ways in which mariculture can be used to increase the world's supply of food. Think also about the costs of mariculture and how they might be reduced.

READING PASSAGE

Mariculture

1   An exciting technology that has been recently proposed to combat the impending global food crisis is mariculture, or marine agriculture. Mariculture is the raising of animals and vegetables that live in water, just as crops are grown on a farm. It makes use of either man-made or natural pools. Fish, for example, are raised in these pools. Then they are released into the ocean to increase existing populations (Fishing, Commercial, 1981, pp. 360–61). In the last twenty years mariculture has grown from a small cottage industry to a large high-tech° enterprise. Today governments and large corporations often support mariculture.

using the most modern and advanced technology

2   At present, however, mariculture still lags far behind agriculture. The main problem impeding its expansion is its high cost. To promote the various kinds of mariculture, scientists and farmers must find ways to lower the costs involved. Otherwise, mariculture cannot compete with commercial fishing. Before discussing the economics of mariculture, let us look at some examples of maricultural techniques that are already possible.

Some Techniques of Mariculture

3   J. L. Culliney (1979, pp. 359–68) describes techniques that could be used in three types of mariculture: salmon mariculture, mussel mariculture, and kelp mariculture.

4   **Salmon mariculture.** At present, salmon fishing depends on a large number of vessels, as well as much equipment, and labor. Fleets must pursue the salmon over large areas of the open ocean above the continental shelves. Consequently, salmon fishing is extremely costly. Mariculture could reduce the cost and increase the catch. Young salmon could be raised in fish farms known as hatcheries. They would then stay for several days in floating cages submerged in local rivers before being released to the open ocean. Remarkably, salmon will always remember their home waters. They will cross enormous stretches of ocean to return to those waters to spawn. Traps can be placed in rivers during the spawning season to catch some of the returning fish.

5   "Ocean ranching" is a good name for this method of mariculture. Ranchers send herds of animals out to pasture to graze. Similarly, fishermen can send young salmon out to sea to grow to maturity without any cost to the producer. The fishermen can then trap the salmon when they

FIGURE 4–1   Feeding time for young salmon being raised in captivity. (Source: National Oceanic and Atmospheric Administration)

return to spawn. In addition, they can control the numbers of salmon by restricting the catch or by releasing more salmon into the ocean. The cost to the industry and therefore to the consumer will decrease because of the reduction in equipment and labor.

6   **Mussel mariculture.** Mussels, which are a species of shellfish, also have the potential for producing large crops. They grow in cold-water regions that are relatively free of shellfish diseases and predators. Mussels are suited in many ways to mariculture. In particular, they tend to attach themselves to ropes dangling in the water. In this way they can grow in three-dimensional plots. The Lummi Indians of Washington State grow mussels and typically harvest more than 168,000 kilograms of mussel protein per hectare. In Canada and the United States, mussels are used mainly in animal feeds. Although mussels are not yet a widely popular source of food for people in North America, they are favored in many parts of the world, especially in Europe. An effective advertising campaign could probably make them an important part of the North American diet as well. Mussels are among the most economical and ecologically efficient products of mariculture. However, they are extremely sensitive to certain kinds of chemical pollution. Although such chemicals may be relatively harmless to the mussels themselves, they may affect the consumer. Therefore, one must be careful to farm mussels in clean water far removed from any toxic spills.

7   **Kelp mariculture.** The marine analogy to vegetable farming is the farming of kelp. Kelp is a kind of seaweed, rich in nutrients and especially popular in Japan. Kelp farming would be perhaps the strangest of all maricultural techniques. A frame several hundred meters wide would be suspended about twenty meters beneath the surface of the ocean. This frame, like an upside-down umbrella, would support a large nylon net on which the kelp could grow. These kelp farms would float far off the west coast of North America in the California Current. If the technique proved economically feasible, a number of kelp farms could be linked together. Such kelp plantations could be several kilometers across and would drift slowly in the ocean currents. A kelp plantation could be planted in the North Pacific and drift in the California Current until the kelp matured. Workers on floating platforms would tend the crops, and tugs would steer the plantation away from shipping lanes and islands (Culliney, 1979, pp 359–68).

The Bioeconomics of Mariculture

8 Most forms of mariculture are at present economically unprofitable. However, greater demand for food will produce greater profits. Mariculture is the feeding, raising, harvesting, processing, and marketing of a marine crop, and several simple bioeconomic° models of the mariculture process have been constructed (cf. Hanson, 1974; Bardach et al., 1972). A simple bioeconomic model of mariculture is shown in Figure 4–2. Each step in this model shows a controlled storage and conversion process. Money converts to nutrients at the beginning of the process. Nutrients in turn convert to energy and matter (for example, growing fish). The crop, through harvesting, converts to a concentrated state. Processing converts the raw, concentrated crop to a product that people will buy. Finally, marketing converts this product to money. At this point the cycle can begin again.

referring to the economics of a biological process

9 In practice, all of these storage and conversion processes except marketing represent an expenditure of money and are thus economic negatives. The mariculturist° must try, therefore, to reduce the cost of each storage or conversion process as much as possible. The ocean ranching technique mentioned earlier can reduce the cost of the nutri-

A physicist is a person who works in physics. Therefore a mariculturist is _____ .

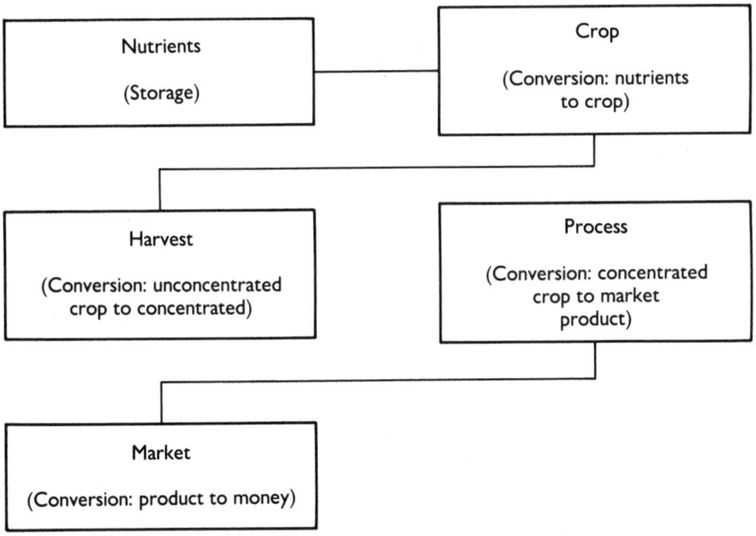

FIGURE 4–2 A bioeconomic model of mariculture: The storage and conversion process. (*Source:* Joe A. Hanson, ''Open Sea Mariculture in Bioeconomic Perspective,'' in Joe A. Hanson, (Ed.), *Open Sea Mariculture: Perspectives, Problems, and Prospects* (p. 10). New York: Van Nostrand Reinhold, 1974.

ents and crop to zero in salmon mariculture. In typical maricultural operations, however, money changes hands at every step in the process, as shown in Figure 4-3. A detailed model would have to include transportation costs and other expenses that are missing from this simplified diagram.

10   In Figure 4-3, overhead includes miscellaneous operating expenses, interest, the amortization costs of facilities, and the purchase cost of equipment. The maruculturist can reduce these costs by using "free" ocean space if possible.

11   Next, control of the biological environment includes the costs of protecting the crop from predators and disease. Selecting hardy species, breeding disease-resistant species, and finding relatively disease-free sites will reduce costs in this part of the operation.

12   A third concern is control of the physical environment. Light, water chemistry, and other physical factors

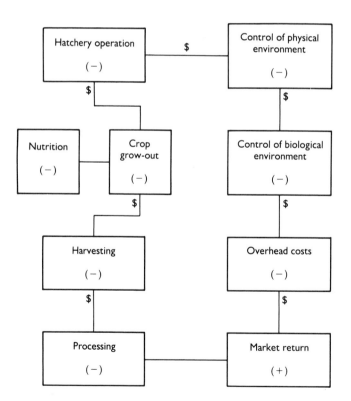

FIGURE 4–3 A bioeconomic model of the flow of money in mariculture. (*Source:* Joe A. Hanson, "Open Sea Mariculture in Bioeconomic Perspective," in Joe A. Hanson, (Ed.), *Open Sea Mariculture: Perspectives, Problems, and Prospects* (p. 10). New York: Van Nostrand Reinhold, 1974.

must be conducive to the health and growth of the crop. The cost of controlling the physical environment is likely to be lower on shore than in the open ocean. Again, careful site selection can help reduce these costs.

13   Another cost relates to the hatchery operation. The condition of the physical and biological environment is especially crucial at this stage in the development of the crop. It is difficult, therefore, to save much money at this stage.

14   Next, nutrition can range from cost-free open-sea ranching (as in the salmon example) to feeding with prepared foods. It may be possible in some operations to grow the food along with the crop, thus saving costs. In fact, this may be the most economically efficient type of maricultural operation. It could lead to the marketing of several crops.

15   The harvesting and processing operations require energy and are consequently costly. In a nonmaricultural fisheries operation, these are the only costs involved. The cost of these processes must be substantially lowered in a maricultural operation. Otherwise, the operation will not be able to compete successfully with commercial fishing. The mariculturist, of course, has a great deal more control over these operations than the fisherman has. He or she must make the maximum use of this advantage to compete with commercial fishing (Hanson, 1974, pp. 9–12; Bardach et al., 1972, pp. 1–28).

16   As the earth's human population increases, we shall have to think seriously about turning to the sea as a source of food. However, ocean fishing, like farming, is now pushed to its upper limit. Mariculture may indeed be the only solution to the world's food shortage. Through mariculture, land-based agriculture can now extend onto the continental shelves. The oceans can thus serve as an "open range" for marine animal and plant species.

References

Bardach, J. E., McLarney, W. D., & Ryther, J. H. (1972). General Principles and Economics. In J. E. Bardach, W. D. McLarney, J. H. Ryther (Eds.), *Aquaculture: The Farming and Husbandry of Freshwater and Marine Organisms* (pp. 1–28). New York: Wiley-Interscience.

Culliney, J. L. (1979). *The Forests of the Sea.* New York: Anchor Books.

Fishing, Commercial (1981). *Encyclopaedia Britannica,* (15th ed.). Vol. 7, pp. 360–361.

Hanson, Joe A. (1974). Open Sea Mariculture in Bioeconomic Perspective. In J. A. Hanson (Ed.), *Open Sea Mariculture: Perspectives, Problems, and Prospects* (pp. 9–12). New York: Van Nostrand Reinhold.

Checking Your Comprehension

1. Describe mariculture by comparing it with fishing and farming.
2. Explain how mariculture could be used in the salmon fishing industry.
3. What important problem could arise when growing mussels by mariculture?
4. What three specific analogies to land-based agriculture are mentioned in the passage?
5. Explain what conditions must exist for mariculture to be economically competitive with commercial fishing.

For Discussion

1. Explain how mariculture could be practiced on the high seas.
2. What uses of the sea has modern technology made possible? What additional uses could it make possible in the future?
3. Compare the conquest of the sea to the conquest of space. What do they have in common? How are they different?

Analyzing the Structure

1. Look at the introduction, and explain the way it is organized. Identify the thesis statement.
2. Look at the beginning of the second main part of the passage. What does the first sentence restate? What does the third sentence restate?
3. The first main part of the body uses enumeration. What set of items is being enumerated? After the first two items in the enumeration, what does the set of items seem to be? Does this prediction turn out to be correct or incorrect?
4. Find the description of the storage and conversion process. What are the signals that identify some of the steps in the process? Why are no signals required for the other steps?
5. Reread the conclusion of the reading passage. Does it echo, or restate, the thesis? If not, what is missing?

The Writing Process: The Thesis Statement

Now that you have practiced narrowing a topic, you can begin to think about communicating your ideas. There is no strict order to follow in organizing and developing your essay, but there are some results you will want to achieve. You will need to write a thesis statement that tells your readers how you have limited your topic; you will need to gather information on your topic and decide on a logical way to arrange it; and, to express that information, you will need to choose such ways as enumeration, classification, or comparison/contrast.

In this chapter we will look closely at formulating a thesis statement. You have already learned that a generalization is a statement about an issue. A thesis statement is a special kind of generalization. It will be the most important sentence in your essay. Simply stated, a thesis statement tells the reader the subject of the essay. It identifies the topic and the one or more aspects of the topic that you will discuss. For example, examine the following thesis statement for an essay:

> Civilized societies have begun to understand that war has harmful
> effects on society in both the social and the economic spheres.

It states a generalization on war—that war has harmful effects on society—and it identifies the two aspects of the generalization that will be discussed in the essay—the social and the economic effects.

Remember that not all generalizations make good thesis statements. For example, it would be difficult to write a meaningful essay on the generalization, ''A pencil has three important parts,'' because it is too specific. On the other hand, if the statement is too general, you could make it more specific by using the method for narrowing the topic discussed in Chapter 3.

How do you know whether a generalization is suitable? One consideration is how long the essay should be. Another consideration is how much information you can find to support that generalization. As we have suggested, a thesis statement is like a contract between the writer and the reader. The thesis statement tells readers what they can expect to read about in the essay. Therefore, writers should be careful not to promise more than they intend to write about in the essay. They should also avoid a thesis sentence that covers only a part of what they want the essay to contain.

In addition to being neither too specific nor too general, a thesis statement should not be an announcement. An announcement is a generalization that makes a simple statement of fact. The announcement says it all; nothing more can be said. An example of an announcement is ''At present, most nurses are women.'' It is usually not difficult to change an announcement into an acceptable thesis statement. The following thesis statements were made from the above announcement: ''Steps can be taken to make nursing an attractive profession for men as well as for women'' (process); and ''There are several reasons why more women than men are attracted to the profession of nursing'' (enumeration).

Another pitfall to avoid is the admonishment. An example of an admonishment is ''More men should go into nursing.'' Like announcements, admonishments are dead-end statements. Change them into thesis statements: ''There are several reasons why more men should go into nursing.''

While announcements and admonishments do not make good thesis statements, they can sometimes be used to introduce a thesis statement. For example, "At present most nurses are women. However, steps can be taken to bring more men into the nursing profession."

The thesis statement likewise should not be a statement of intent such as "This paper will discuss . . . ," or "In this paper I intend to show. . . ." If you have written a statement of intent such as "In this paper I plan to explain why most nurses are women," change it to a true thesis statement: "There are several reasons why most nurses are women."

Now let us look again at the narrowed topic chosen by the writer of the model essay in Chapter 1: "physical and social effects of destroying the Amazon rain forest." From it the writer generalized as follows: "Destroying the Amazon rain forest will result in physical and social effects," and "Destroying the Amazon rain forest could have harmful effects on living things." Choosing the second of these the writer reworked it into the thesis statement that will appear at the end of the introduction in the final version of the essay: "Destroying the Amazon rain forest could have serious consequences for all living things."

Exercises

1. Look again at the tree diagram in Chapter 3. Choose several issues shown on the diagram, or add some of your own. Then formulate a generalization that would make a suitable thesis statement for a short essay.

2. Write a short essay (three to five paragraphs) about mariculture from the viewpoint of a commercial fisherman. When you are ready to make a thesis statement, begin by writing several generalizations. Choose one and make it into a good thesis statement for your essay. If necessary, change the wording of the thesis statement to make it specific enough or general enough for what you want to write. If it is an announcement, an admonition, or a statement of intent, revise the thesis statement. Share your thesis statement with the class. Get the opinions of several of your colleagues and of the instructor before continuing with the writing process.

Writing About Reading

1. Write one paragraph explaining the steps in the storage and conversion process shown in Figure 4–2.

2. Write a short essay on the above topic. As an example for each of the steps, use salmon mariculture as it is described in the text. Divide the steps in the process so that they are contained in at least two body paragraphs. You might want to arrange the steps into two or more groups.

For example, the first group could include the first two steps (storage and crop), referring to the open-sea phase of salmon mariculture. Remember that the thesis statement should refer to the entire process, while each topic sentence should refer only to the steps contained in each paragraph.

3. Using the diagram in Figure 4–3 and the information on the life cycle of salmon in the reading passage, write a short essay on the economics of salmon mariculture. Arrange your information according to any methods that are appropriate.

4. Refer to "The Knowledge Economy" in Chapter 2 and "The New Luddites" in Chapter 3. Write an essay that explains how computers and information technology could be used in a mariculture operation. How might this technology affect the model shown in Figure 4–3?

Chapter 5

Cities in the Sea

CHAPTER FOCUS

As you study this chapter, you should focus on the following important points:

Arrangement of information: formal definition

Vocabulary: understanding new words

Signal words and phrases: *therefore, in spite of, nevertheless*

Sentence grammar: participles, hypothetical *would*

Writing: developing a strategy and gathering information

Content: the future construction of cities in the oceans

Arrangement of Information

Organization of the Content: Formal Definition

Often a writer must define a word or concept that the reader needs to understand. A definition may be as short as a single phrase or as long as a paragraph or several paragraphs. A long definition is called an extended definition. Regardless of length, a complete (formal) definition contains (1) the term or concept to be defined, (2) the class or group to which the term or concept belongs, and (3) characteristics that separate the term or concept from others in the same group or class.

For example, consider the term *chair*. The class or group to which *chair* belongs is *furniture*. The characteristics that separate a *chair* from other kinds of furniture are the following: (1) it is for sitting (unlike tables, chests, etc.); (2) it is designed to seat one person (unlike a sofa); and (3) it has a back (unlike a stool). With this information we can write a definition of *chair*.

A chair is a piece of furniture that has a back and a single seat.

Definitions such as this often use an adjective clause to list the characteristics. Notice that the present tense is used in both clauses and that the verb *be* is used in the independent clause. Like other adjective clauses of this type, definitions can be reduced:

A chair is a piece of furniture having a back and a single seat.

Sometimes an adjective clause is not necessary:

Anthropology is the study of human cultures.

Here, *anthropology* is the term to be defined, *study* is the class or group, and *of human cultures* is the characteristic that makes anthropology different from other studies.

It is often possible to put the characteristics before the class or group.

Water is an odorless and tasteless liquid.

Here *water* is the term to be defined, *liquid* is the class, and *odorless and tasteless* are the characteristics that make water different from other liquids.

Sometimes the concept, class, and characteristics are contained in different sentences. The reader has the job of recognizing them. For example, the definition of *anthropology,* given above, might appear like this:

In recent years there has been a growing interest in studying cultures and civilizations, including those that existed in the past. This study is called anthropology and is a popular subject in many universities.

Definitions of common or concrete things like chairs and water can often be written in one sentence. More complicated things or ideas may require several sentences. These extended definitions should begin with the term to be defined and the name of the class. The remaining sentences in the definition will describe characteristics or give examples of characteristics.

Mariculture is a type of agriculture that specializes in raising marine plants and animals. It makes use of hatcheries, or artificial ponds, where fish or seaweed can be raised under protected and controlled conditions. One type of mariculture makes use of the open oceans. In this type of mariculture, scientists send fish out into the ocean to find food. When the fish return to their home waters to spawn, they can be caught.

Here the term to be defined is *mariculture.* It belongs to the class of *agriculture.* Some of the special characteristics of mariculture that make it different from agriculture are then listed and described.

Exercises

1. Find the definition of *mercantilism* in paragraph 16 of "The Industrial Rev-olution" in Chapter 1. What are the class and characteristics of mercantil-ism? Rewrite this definition, using an adjective clause.

2. Find the definition of *kelp* in paragraph 7 of "Mariculture" in Chapter 4. What are the class and characteristics of kelp?

3. Find an extended definition of *mariculture* in the first paragraph of "Mari-culture." List the characteristics that belong to this definition.

Vocabulary Preview

Words in Context

The following words appear in this chapter's reading passage. Study them in their contexts and carry out the discussion tasks that follow.

	dense (adj.)
-ly (adv.)	densely
-ness (n.)	denseness
-ity (n.)	density

The *density* of the snow makes it hard to shovel. It is easier to re-move snow that is loose and fluffy. But only *densely* packed snow will make a good snowman.

What else can have density besides snow? Why does *dense* mean *stupid* or *uncomprehending* when it is used to describe a person's intelligence or under-standing?

> drawback (n.)

Traveling with very little luggage has advantages and disadvan-tages. One of the *drawbacks* is having to wash clothes every day or two.

Are there drawbacks to living in a big city? in a small town? on a farm? What are they?

	drift (n. or v.)
-er (n.)	drifter

After leaving home, I had trouble staying in one place. I *drifted* from one town to another. Because I was a *drifter,* I also changed jobs frequently. Finally I found a town and a job that I liked, and I stopped *drifting*.

Define the following:

1. driftwood
2. snowdrift
3. Do you get my drift? (slang)
4. The boat was adrift in a stormy sea.

encounter (n. or v.)

In many children's stories, the main characters *encounter* problems that they must overcome. They often meet difficult people or situations. At the end of the story the characters usually benefit from these *encounters.*

Have you ever encountered a difficulty? What was it?

	exert (v.)
-ion (n.)	exertion

Our town needed a new community center. I asked my brother, who knows many important people, to *exert* his influence on them. As a result of his *exertions,* our new community center is already in operation.

In addition to influence, what else could you exert on others? What is one way you could exert yourself physically?

	inspire (v.)
-ation (n.)	inspiration
-al (adj.)	inspirational
-ly (adv.)	inspirationally

The coach of the team *inspired* the football players to do their best. When they won the championship, the players thanked him for helping them to understand what they could do if they tried.

The *inspiration* for her new novel was the exciting story of her grandfather's sailing adventures.

When we say that someone "inspires confidence," what qualities does that person probably have?

Have you ever:

1. been inspired to do something difficult or unusual?
2. had an idea based on the work or ideas of someone else?

Explain.

look to (v.)

When people elect someone to high office, they *look to* him or her for leadership. They expect the person they have elected to produce new ideas and ways of doing things. Too often, however, people who have *looked to* others to help them are disappointed. They learn that they can rely only on themselves.

In what ways have you looked to others for help? Have you been satisfied or disappointed?

man (n. or v.)

The telephone counseling service operates twenty-four hours a day. The telephones are *manned* by volunteers. Sometimes, trying to counsel people in trouble is as difficult as *manning* the front lines in a battle.

Have you ever taken part in an effort that was manned by volunteers? What was your role in it?

monitor (n. or v.)

To detect certain illnesses, doctors can *monitor* body functions. For example, a doctor who wants to check on a patient's heartbeat may ask him or her to wear a *monitor* for a day.

What do you think is the function of a television monitor in a television broadcast studio? What might teachers use to monitor their students' progress?

	nourish (v.)
-ment (n.)	nourishment

It is not enough to *nourish* children physically by giving them enough food to eat. They need emotional, spiritual, and intellectual *nourishment* as well.

What do you think it means to nourish a friendship?

	prototype (n.)
-ical (adj.)	prototypical
-ly (adv.)	prototypically

The car I invented became the *prototype* for vehicles that use electric power. All such cars produced today use my basic design.

What do you consider to be the prototype of:

1. a science fiction movie?
2. a group that plays rock music?
3. an automobile?

	stress (n. or v.)
-ful (adj.)	stressful

He is often sad and lonely. The separation from his family has put great emotional *stress* on him.

Do you think that emotional stress could cause physical stress? If so, give a possible example.

tap (n. or v.)

Maple sugar comes from the trunk of the maple tree. The farmer *taps* the tree by boring a hole in the trunk and putting in a tube. The sap of the tree runs out through this tube, like water running out of the *tap* on the kitchen sink.

How can you tap the sources of knowledge? Can you think of anything else you could tap for your own benefit?

tow (n. or v.)

After the accident, my car was *towed* to the garage. On the way, the *tow* line broke, and my car blocked traffic for an hour.

What is a tow truck? Explain the meaning of the following: He went to the movies with his little brother in tow.

zone (n. or v.)

A temperate *zone* is an area of the world where the climate is not extremely hot or extremely cold.

What is a tropical zone? What is a reduced speed zone? a restricted zone?

Discovering Word Meanings

Use (1) context clues; (2) your knowledge of prefixes, suffixes, and roots; and (3) a dictionary, if necessary, to discover the meanings of the italicized words in the following sentences from this chapter's reading passage.

1. In the early 1970s, the Japanese began the construction of Aquapolis, the world's first semisubmersible floating city. They built it on the main Japanese island of Honshu and towed it south to Okinawa. There they displayed it at a 1975 *exposition*.

   (Use a dictionary to find the correct meaning of this word in this context. What is the root of this word?)

2. Aquapolis can be raised or lowered in the water as a protection against violent storms. When lowered, most of the structure rests beneath the surface. This protects it from rocking caused by high winds and surface *disturbances*.

   (Find the correct meaning of *disturbance* in this context. What word could you substitute for *surface disturbances*?

3. Aquapolis is a prototype of *futuristic* floating cities designed to run on solar, wind, and tidal energy.

> (What is the root of this word? How does the suffix *-istic* change the part of speech? What is another way to say *futuristic floating cities?*)

4. Its waste-water system is biological rather than chemical. It uses chlorella, a species of green *algae,* to dispose of sewage.

> (What do you know about the meaning of *algae* from the context? Notice the unusual ending of this word. Use your dictionary to discover its meaning and derivation.)

Signal Words and Phrases

Study the following signal words and phrases that appear in this chapter's reading passage.

1. therefore

This word modifies the entire sentence in which it occurs. It can be placed at the beginning, middle, or end of a sentence. Words and expressions with similar meanings include *consequently, as a result, for this reason/these reasons, accordingly,* and *so.*

> The land area of Hong Kong is small, but the population is large. *Therefore,* many of the city's poor are unable to find affordable homes in the city itself.

2. in spite of

The phrase containing this preposition can begin or end a sentence, or it can be inserted into the body of a sentence. *In spite of* carries a meaning contrary to or opposing the meaning of the sentence to which it is attached. A preposition with a similar meaning is *despite.*

> *In spite of* minor drawbacks, experiments like Conshelf and Sealab have proved the feasibility of living in the sea.

3. nevertheless

This word is a sentence modifier whose position in the sentence is flexible. *Nevertheless* follows a statement of fact that logically implies a certain result. But the result that follows *nevertheless* is unexpected. Words and phrases with a similar meaning are *nonetheless, but . . . anyway, however, in spite of that,* and *still.*

We read about the dangers and discomforts of a cruise to the Antarctic. *Nevertheless*, we decided to go.

Grammar Preview

Study the following passages, and work through the tasks.

1. Explain the meaning of the italicized terms in the following passage.

   The Japanese architect Kiyonori Kikutake has also suggested *floating containers* in his design of a town called Unabara (Ocean). Another Japanese architect, Hidezo Kobayashi, has proposed *building a city* in a bay or other natural enclosure. Supported on the continental shelf, it could extend *an existing city* from the shore into the ocean. It would use both structures that float and structures that are anchored to the bottom. Boats would pass over and around extensions of this city, and waves and tides would provide its energy. Kobayashi's city would also be a base for *exploiting mineral deposits* that lie beneath the continental shelf.

2. The following paragraph describes the advantages of a new subway system that already exists in Newtown. Now go back to the time before the subway system was built. Pretend that you are the designer of the system and that you have to convince a government committee to build the new subway. To do this, you have to explain the advantages of having a subway system. Use the paragraph below, but rewrite it to present the advantages a subway system would have if it were built. The first line of the rewritten paragraph has been started for you. It appears after the original paragraph.

   Newtown has a new subway system. It transports people quickly and cheaply from all parts of the city to the downtown center of the city. It stops at all major intersections, and it connects with buses and elevated trains. In this way it solves the problem of traffic congestion on downtown streets. It also makes the city convenient for tourists, because it is easy to travel to the city's major attractions.

   If Newtown had a new subway system, it _____

   _____

   _____

   _____

   _____

   _____ .

Getting Ready to Read

The reading passage in this chapter is about different kinds of futuristic cities that might be built in the sea. Such cities would make it possible for people who work in the seas to live with their families and be close to their place of work. Another use of such cities would be to provide more living space for our growing populations.

1. If you were designing a city in the sea, what necessities and conveniences would you provide? Would you provide a city on land with the same necessities and conveniences? Explain.

2. What problems do you think you would experience if you lived in a city in the sea?

3. Quickly scan the passage below to find the sentence that
   a. first mentions Aquapolis
   b. mentions a town called Unabara
   c. gives the date of the Conshelf I Habitat
   d. tells how many divers were in Sealab II
   e. refers to the design of New Venice

4. The title of the reading passage, ''Cities in the Sea,'' suggests that the topic is
   a. exploiting the sea to supply human needs
   b. making mariculture more profitable
   c. building cities in the oceans
   d. controlling human population and needs

5. Skim paragraph 1. What is the function of this paragraph? Its topic is:
   a. exploiting the sea to supply human needs
   b. making mariculture more profitable
   c. building cities in the oceans
   d. controlling human population and needs

6. What sentence or sentences state the thesis of this reading passage?

Now read the passage to the end. As you read, note different ways to build towns or cities in the oceans. Note also what important questions need to be answered before people can live easily under water.

READING PASSAGE

Cities in the Sea

1   As the earth's human population grows rapidly larger, satisfying basic human needs becomes more and more diffi-

cult. Among our primary requirements are living space
and shelter. Some parts of the world are simply running
out of room for their increasing populations, and people
are beginning to look to the sea for additional space. Other
basic requirements of human life are food and natural resources. It is no longer enough to farm and mine the lands
of the earth for foodstuffs and minerals. Consequently, we
have begun to tap some of the vast mineral and agricultural wealth of the oceans. In recent years, mining and
drilling in the sea have added to our stores of oil and gas.
In addition, deep sea exploration and mining will soon
give access to the rare minerals on the ocean floor. Another
developing technology is aquaculture, which extends techniques of farming from the land into the sea. Mariculture,
the branch of aquaculture that deals with saltwater species
above the continental shelves, may someday feed a starv-
ing world. There are therefore two reasons why it may become necessary to learn to live in the sea. First, we might
need some of its immense area for living space. Second,
we might need to exploit the resources that lie in its
depths. There are already a number of proposals and experiments that may help to achieve these goals.

2   In some coastal countries where there is not enough
land for an increasing population, living space can expand
into the sea. For example, the land area of Hong Kong is
small, but the population is large. Therefore, many of the
city's poor are unable to find affordable homes in the city
itself. They live in boats that are tied closely to each other
and moored to the shore. Such floating towns have inspired a number of architects. J. Dahinden (1972) points to
several futuristic designs for oceanic cities. One of these
designs, by Eckhard Schulze-Fielitz, is a huge city called
New Venice that would rest on floating containers. The
idea of floating cities has attracted special attention in Japan, which has an enormous population density. Like
Schulze-Fielitz, the Japanese architect Kiyonori Kikutake
has also suggested floating containers in his design of a
town called Unabara (Ocean). Another Japanese architect,
Hidezo Kobayashi, has proposed building a city in a bay
or other natural enclosure. Supported on the continental
shelf, it could extend an existing city from the shore into
the ocean. It would use both structures that float and structures that are anchored to the bottom. Boats would pass
over and around extensions of this city, and waves and
tides would provide its energy. Kobayashi's city would
also be a base for exploiting mineral deposits that lie beneath the continental shelf.

FIGURE 5–1 Living afloat: A view of junks and sampans in Aberdeen, Hong Kong. (Source: United Nations)

3   In the early 1970s, the Japanese began the construction of Aquapolis, the world's first semisubmersible° floating city (Planning of Aquapolis, 1975). They built it on the main Japanese island of Honshu and towed it south to Okinawa. There they displayed it at a 1975 exposition. Aquapolis can be raised or lowered in the water as a protection against violent storms. When lowered, most of the structure rests beneath the surface. This protects it from rocking caused by high winds and surface disturbances. In its normal raised position, the structure contains three main areas. The first is the top part of the structure, which is high above the water level, and includes residential, administrative, and exhibition zones. The middle level is at the water line. It contains transportation facilities, including its own harbor. Finally, beneath the water are storage and machinery zones. Aquapolis is a prototype of futuristic floating cities designed to run on solar, wind, and tidal energy. It uses a biological waste-water system, which dis-

When a submarine submerges, it goes under the water. If it goes only partly under the water, it is semisubmerged. Thus semisubmersible means

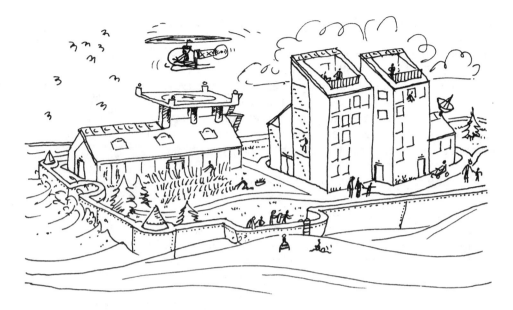

FIGURE 5–2   An artist's conception of a city in the sea.

poses of sewage by means of a species of green algae known as chlorella, rather than by chemical means. Adjacent to the city is a large maricultural ocean ranch that contains thousands of fish. Using equipment located in on-board laboratories, scientists monitor the movements and behavior of these fish.

4   The time may come when floating cities such as Aquapolis exist not only as permanent extensions of land-based habitats° but also as free-floating platforms. These would drift from continent to continent across the deep oceans. Such cities would permit deep sea miners and their families to live near their work places on the ocean floor. In this way they could enjoy the benefits of family life and the comforts of home. While all inhabitants of floating cities would experience difficulties, miners working on the ocean bottom would also encounter a different set of problems. One such problem would be the enormous pressure exerted by the ocean at great depths. Another would be the lack of easy access to air.

To inhabit *a place means to live in it. Thus a* habitat *is* ——————— .

5   To study these difficulties, and to test human adaptability to life beneath the sea, scientists have in recent years carried out several experiments (Life Support Systems, 1981). The first of these was the Conshelf I Habitat. A team directed by the French oceanographer Captain Jacques-Yves Cousteau used it successfully in 1962. The

team remained at a depth of ten meters in the Mediterranean Sea for seven days. The results of this experiment led to the building of the Conshelf II Habitat, where five oceanauts° lived successfully at eleven meters. Data from these experiments paved the way° for Conshelf III in 1964, when two men lived at a depth of 132 meters for forty-eight hours. A diving bell transported the men back and forth between the habitat and the ocean floor beneath them. In the same year the United States Navy tested Sealab I, in which four men lived at a depth of nearly 60 meters for nine days. The men breathed a mixture of gases consisting of 79 percent helium, 17 percent nitrogen, and 4 percent oxygen. They found the environment comfortable at a temperature of twenty-nine degrees Celsius and a relative humidity of 72 percent. This experiment made possible the construction of a larger habitat called Sealab II. It was manned by twenty-eight divers rotating in fifteen-day shifts.° From these experiments, scientists learned that daily swimming at these depths caused oceanauts to show symptoms of stress. Undersea miners, of course, would also have to engage in such activity to do their jobs.

6   In spite of minor drawbacks, experiments like Con-

An astronaut explores space on a spaceship. An oceanaut _____ .

Paving *means putting a hard surface on a road to make it smooth and easy to travel. Therefore, when we say that data from Conshelf II paved the way for Conshelf III, we mean* _____ .

Rotating in shifts *means taking turns. Here, each turn lasted fifteen days.*

FIGURE 5–3 Underwater research being conducted on the sea bed in the Gulf of Honduras. (Source: UN Photo 153977/Rick Sammon)

shelf and Sealab have proved the feasibility of living in the sea. Their success has encouraged the architect Warren Chalk to design an entire underwater city (Dahinden, 1972). This three-dimensional structure would make maximum use of space, and it would enable entire human populations to live safely and comfortably far beneath the sea for long periods.

7   Obviously, deep sea living has its physical dangers. It also has psychological drawbacks such as being in isolation and being out of one's element.° Nevertheless, the concept of the city in the sea may be coming of age.° Great underwater cities may someday be connected by elaborate systems of communication and transportation; and they might nourish whole new industries that exploit the resources of the sea. Perhaps our grandchildren will live in what futurist Alvin Toffler (1970, p. 168) calls "The New Atlantis."

In ancient times, the four elements were thought to be air, water, fire, and earth. Human beings are in their element when they live in air. They would be out of their element when _____.

Children who have reached the age when they are legally permitted to perform certain acts are said to have come of age. Thus a concept comes of age when _____.

References

Dahinden, J. (1972). *Urban Structures for the Future.* Translated by Gerald Onn. New York: Praeger.

Life Support Systems: Ambient Pressure Systems (1981). *Encyclopaedia Britannica* (15th ed.). Vol. 10, pp. 924–27.

Planning of Aquapolis (1975, October–November). *Japan Architect*, pp. 43–44, 46.

Toffler, A. (1970). *Future Shock.* New York: Random House.

Checking Your Comprehension

1. Name three ways of using the sea that are already in operation.
2. Describe the structure of Aquapolis.
3. In what ways is Aquapolis designed to preserve the environment?
4. What would be the purpose of building cities that float across the oceans?
5. What information did scientists get from the five experiments mentioned in the reading passage?
6. Look at Figure 5–2. If you were the architect of a city in the sea, what would you do to make it a pleasant living environment?

For Discussion

1. do you think the first prototype of a floating city was built in Japan?
2. Do you think the idea of floating cities is a good one for deep sea workers? Can it be compared to any land-based situation?

3. What political, military, and economic difficulties might arise from the existence of floating cities?

Analyzing the Structure

1. Locate all definitions that you can find in the text.
2. Find the topic sentences in paragraphs 3, 4, and 5.
3. "Cities in the Sea" mentions some real cities and habitats, and some that are not real. List both the real and the unreal examples. Explain how the verbs used show the difference between the real and the unreal. Now turn back to paragraph 7 of "Mariculture" in Chapter 4. How do you know what is already true about kelp and what is not yet true?
4. To what two major parts of "Cities in the Sea" does its thesis refer? Find the words in the text that connect these two parts.

The Writing Process: Gathering and Arranging Information

An important part of the writing process is gathering and arranging information. You might encounter many kinds of information in researching a topic. These include facts, examples, statistics, reasons, description, narration, history, or some combination of these. (For detailed information on how to gather information in a library, see the Appendix at the end of this book.) Since some of this information may turn out to be irrelevant to your final topic, you will have to decide which items to include and which to discard.

When you have collected your information, you must arrange it. Arranging, or organizing, information means deciding which items belong together and what order will best express your ideas. To achieve an order in which items of information fit together logically, you will usually need to find a principle of organization. Often more than one principle is possible. For example, suppose you have collected a large amount of information about the importance of trees. You might decide to arrange your information so that your essay discusses the relative importance of different aspects of trees. In other words, your principle of organization is degree of importance. Or you might arrange your information to show in what ways trees are important. Then some of it might refer to the products of trees, some to other uses that are not products, and some to the contribution of trees to natural cycles.

Even after you have chosen a principle of organization, you may have to use that principle to make choices about the order of your facts, examples, and the like. It is important to be flexible when you are arranging your information, for you may often have to experiment with different schemes before you find one that satisfies you. You may need to reorganize some of your material even while you are writing your essay.

At this point in your writing you will find it useful to make some notes—

usually called an outline—to indicate how the information will be arranged. These notes will act as a kind of road map, showing how you plan to get from the beginning to the end of your topic. At this point, too, you may begin to see the divisions in your topic that will suggest how many paragraphs the essay could have and what information might appear in each paragraph.

Let us see how the writer of the rain forest essay in Chapter 1 gathered and arranged his information, and how his notes on the arrangement suggested the paragraphs of his essay.

First he gathered information related to his general topic—effects of destroying the Amazon rain forest—and jotted down the following facts from his reading:

- Species found nowhere else
- Destroy rain forest, destroy species; extinction of species
- Ways of destroying rain forests: burning, building dams, and flooding land
- Need dams for electric power
- Building dams creates large lakes, stagnant water. Therefore, increase in mosquitoes that live in stagnant water and cause malaria: more malaria
- Other tropical diseases, but malaria is important example
- Brazil government encourages use of rain forest land for development.
- Strained political and economic relations between Brazil and industrialized countries
- Brazil government is building roads; makes it easier to get to forests.
- Rubber trees are important source of income; destroying them removes source of income.
- People who live in rain forests get new diseases. Natives and other poor people, no money for medicine
- Brazil has very large international debt.
- Rain forest absorbs carbon dioxide.
- No rain forest would make greenhouse effect worse problem.
- Native hunter-gatherer tribes must move to escape disease; must find other places to live if forest disappears. Will die of starvation because they cannot get food by hunting and gathering.
- Destruction of cultures
- Amount of oxygen in atmosphere may show significant decrease.

Next, he noticed that there were several logical ways to divide this information. He decided that he want to write a short essay without too much detail. To do this, he chose a principle of organization for his essay. In other words, he put the list of consequences of destroying the rain forest into two groups. One group included information on the physical and biological consequences of harming the rain forest. The other group included information on the social and economic effects of the destruction. While doing this, he realized that several items of information were irrelevant to this principle of organization; therefore, he removed them. He arranged the remaining information as follows:

Notes for Group 1 (Physical and Biological Consequences)

- Million species, plant and animal, in Amazon rain forest
- Species found nowhere else
- Destroy rain forest, destroy species; extinction of species
- Ways of destroying rain forests: burning, building dams, and flooding land
- Need dams for electric power
- Building dams creates large lakes, stagnant water. Therefore, increase in mosquitoes that live in stagnant water and cause malaria: more malaria
- Other tropical diseases, but malaria is important example
- Rain forest absorbs carbon dioxide.
- No rain forest would make greenhouse effect worse problem.
- Amount of oxygen in atmosphere may show significant decrease.

Notes for Group 2 (Social and Economic Consequences)

- Rubber trees are important source of income; destroying them removes source of income.
- People who live in rain forests get new diseases. Natives and other poor people, no money for medicine
- Native hunter-gatherer tribes must find other places to live to escape from diseases, and if forest disappears. Will die of starvation because they cannot get food by hunting and gathering.
- Destruction of cultures

Having divided the information into two groups, the writer tried to clarify the organization within each group. He did this by combining related information and eliminating repetition. He revised his notes as follows:

Notes for Group 1 (Physical and Biological Consequences)

- One million species of plants and animals, which live nowhere else on earth, would become extinct if the Amazon rain forest were destroyed.
- Burning the rain forest would accelerate the greenhouse effect, since the rain forest absorbs a lot of the carbon dioxide that causes this effect.
- The construction of hydroelectric dams causes the formation of large stagnant lakes. Malarial mosquitoes live in these lakes. This causes an increase in tropical diseases such as malaria.
- Killing the rain forest will reduce the amount of oxygen in the atmosphere.

Notes for Group 2 (Social and Economic Consequences)

- Killing the rubber trees in the rain forest will deprive many people of a way to make a living.
- Poor people, who cannot get medicines, will be badly affected by the increase in local diseases caused by destroying the rain forest. They will have to move to escape diseases.
- Destruction of the forest will force hunter-gatherer tribes to move. They will not be able to survive in unfamiliar territories, so they will die. This will also mean the end of their cultures.

Exercise

1. In this exercise, you are given a list of factual statements.[1] They are not arranged in order from general to more specific statements, nor are they arranged in groups. However, included among the statements is a thesis statement for an essay based on the information provided. Using this information, do both of the tasks below:
   a. Find the thesis statement and arrange the remaining statements so that each group will become one paragraph. Eliminate any statements that do not support the thesis.
   b. In each group, arrange the statements into a logical order. Since each group can be made into one paragraph, write a topic sentence for each paragraph.

Statements

- The last episode of the bubonic plague in Britain occurred in 1665–1667.
- The decline of typhus as a fatal disease was directly linked to an improvement in hygiene.
- Traditional ways of life were disrupted, so an increase in illegitimate births contributed to population growth.
- Cheap cotton clothing and bedding were easy to obtain as a result of the Industrial Revolution.
- Syphilis was a disease that began in England in 1500 but declined in the 1600s.
- After 1760, inoculation against smallpox became available.
- Public hygiene, such as garbage disposal and sewers, improved.
- The bubonic plague (the Black Death) killed one-third of the population of Europe in the fourteenth century.

---

[1]The source of the information in these statements is Eric Pawson (1979). *The Early Industrial Revolution: Britain in the Eighteenth Century* (pp. 28–31). London: B. T. Batsford, Ltd.

- Typhus was spread by fleas and lice.
- In preindustrial times, people used layers of woolen clothes and blankets to keep warm, and fleas and lice multiplied in these cloths.
- The increase in population that led to Britain's industrial revolution in the eighteenth and nineteenth centuries resulted partly from improvements in health and hygiene.
- The populations of towns grew because people left the farms to work in factories.
- Cotton cloth could be washed and boiled, so the typhus louse could not breed in it.
- Children often died of diseases such as scurvy and rickets that resulted from a lack of vitamins.
- Common illnesses like colds, measles, mumps, and dysentery caused the deaths of many children.
- People could afford to buy soap because their incomes rose and because soap became cheaper to manufacture.
- There were two categories of diseases, those that recurred regularly causing high death rates, particularly among children, and those that struck periodically as epidemics.

2. Working in groups of three or four, use brainstorming, the information in the reading passage, and group discussion to gather information for a short essay of three to five paragraphs on "Community Life in a Floating City." Decide what principle of organization your group will use and whether the information you have is relevant. Arrange your information according to the principle you have chosen and report your results to the class.

Writing About Reading

1. Write one paragraph in which you list and briefly describe the ocean habitats mentioned in the reading passage, and describe their purposes.

2. Write a short essay on the above topic using enumeration. If possible, divide the habitats into groups. Write one body paragraph for each of the groups.

3. Write an essay in which you define and describe the concept of "cities in the sea." Use any method of organization that is appropriate.

4. Describe in detail a maricultural operation that could be used successfully in a floating city like Aquapolis. Refer to the reading passage in Chapter 4 for information.

Chapter 6

Oceans of Death

CHAPTER FOCUS

As you study this chapter, you should focus on the following important points:

Arrangement of information: informal definition

Vocabulary: understanding new words

Signal words and phrases: *some . . . others, still, as we have seen, furthermore, in this way, still another*

Sentence grammar: reduction of adverb clauses, reduction of adjective clauses, past tense

Writing: arranging information and writing topic sentences

Content: the destruction of the world's oceans through man-made pollution

Arrangement of Information

Organization of the Content: Informal Definition

Definitions in a text are often given informally as brief explanations or restatements. As the examples below show, there are a number of ways of doing this. Note that some of them are interchangeable. Having choices makes it possible to vary the style and structure of sentences.

1. **that is**

   This expression can be used to explain or restate a word or expression either within the sentence where it occurs or at the beginning of the next sentence.

He won the election by demagoguery, that is, by using fear, prejudice, and emotion to influence voters.

He won the election by demagoguery. That is, he used fear, prejudice and emotion to influence voters.

2. i.e.

This is an abbreviation for the Latin term *id est*, which means *that is*. It is used to restate something within the sentence where it occurs.

A number of years ago there was a popular movement called ZPG, i.e., zero population growth.

3. or

This means the same as *i.e.* and is used to restate something within the sentence where it occurs.

An exciting technology recently proposed to combat the impending global food crisis is mariculture, or marine agriculture.

4. appositive

A word or concept is explained by immediately following it with an *appositive*, which is a single word, several words, or a phrase restating its meaning. An appositive is set off from the rest of the sentence by commas.

In the next stage, industrial society, people made things by using machines.

5. punctuating with dashes

This method is used in the same way as appositives. Dashes are sometimes preferred in long sentences or sentences that already contain commas. Note, however, that dashes also have other uses.

The mining industry is experimenting with organisms—very small forms of life—that will eat metals or ores.

6. parentheses

This method can be used like appositives or dashes. Note, however, that parentheses also have other uses.

The mining industry is experimenting with organisms (very small forms of life) that will eat metals or ores.

7. a form of the verb *to mean*

This indicates that a specific definition of a word or expression is being given. Note that it could also indicate that a more general interpretation is being given.

Information means collecting, storing, finding, spreading, and applying knowledge.

8. a form of the verb *to refer*

This can be used to signal that a definition is being given. Note that *to refer* also has other meanings.

The word *biotechnology* refers to a combination of biology with technology.

9. a form of the verb *to be known as*

This verb can be used to define. The verb *to be called* can also be used in this way. Note, however, that both of these verbs can be used in other senses.

A combination of biology with technology is known as *biotechnology*.

Exercises

1. Change the formal definition below into informal definitions according to the methods given in parentheses. Also use additional information in any definition for which it is provided.

   The Industrial Revolution was a period of great change that had important long-term effects on the economies of Western nations.

   a. (appositive)

   New information: The Industrial Revolution was also a time of social upheaval.

   b. (refers to)
   c. (to be called, to be known as)

2. Use the information in each of the following pairs of sentences to write an informal definition. Use the method given in parentheses.
   a. (i.e.) One species of shellfish is particularly suited to mariculture. That species is mussels.
   b. (that is) Mussels are a species of shellfish. Shellfish are aquatic creatures protected by shells.

Vocabulary Preview

Words in Context

The following words appear in this chapter's reading passage. Study them in their contexts and write the correct forms of the words in the blanks in the exercises that follow. In some cases you may have to include another word, such as a preposition.

	abrupt (adj.)
-ly (adv.)	abruptly
-ness (n.)	abruptness

When he looked out the window, the smile vanished _____

from his face. This sudden change in his expression was caused by

something he saw outside.

	ancestor (n.)
-y (n.)	ancestry
-al (adj.)	ancestral

She came from famous _____. One of her _____

had been a president of the United States. Another, her great-

grandmother, had been a well-known reformer.

	art (n.)
-ist (n.)	artist
-ic (adj.)	artistic
-ally (adv.)	artistically
-ry (n.)	artistry

One of the world's greatest _____ was Michelangelo, who

lived during the Italian Renaissance. Many of his paintings and

sculptures are located in the Vatican. One of the finest examples of

his _____ is the paintings that grace the ceiling of the Sis-

tine Chapel.

	avoid (v.)
-ance (n.)	avoidance
-able (adj.)	avoidable
un- (= *not*)	unavoidable

Death is _____. Nothing can prevent it. All living things

must die.

	block (n. or v.)
-age (n.)	blockage

We called a plumber because there was a _____

_____ one of our water pipes. The plumber found that a dead

mouse was _____ the flow of water through the pipe.

	compose (v.)
-ite (n.)	composite
-ition (n.)	composition
de- (= *not*)	decompose

When an animal dies, chemicals, bacteria, and other animals help the dead body to break down, or _____ _____ its basic chemical parts.

	cripple (v.)

Rick Hansen is a famous Canadian athlete who was _____ _____ an accident and could no longer use his legs. Unable to walk or run, he went around the world in a wheelchair to demonstrate the abilities of disabled people.

	descend (v.)
	descent (n.)
-ant (n.)	descendant

If we do not begin to take better care of our planet, our children and grandchildren will suffer. Our _____ will have no resources, and their air and water will be poisoned with pollution.

	devastate (v.)
-ion (n.)	devastation

California frequently experiences earthquakes. When the ground moves, buildings are often damaged and people are injured. Such _____ is painful and frightening. Fortunately, however, recent California earthquakes have not been as _____ _____ the extremely destructive one in 1906.

	digest (n. or v.)
-ion (n.)	digestion
-ive (adj.)	digestive
-ible (adj.)	digestible
in- (= *not*)	indigestible

The _____ system includes the stomach, the intestines, and the other organs that are necessary for processing food in the body. Good _____ depends on keeping these organs healthy.

	extinct (adj.)
-ion (n.)	extinction
-ish (v.)	extinguish
-able (adj.)	extinguishable
in- (= *not*)	inextinguishable

Many kinds of plants and animals have disappeared from the earth.

The dinosaurs have been _____ _____ millions

of years. Pollution is causing the _____ _____

many other species. Perhaps people will soon become

_____.

	generate (v.)
-ion (n.)	generation
-ive (adj.)	generative
de- (= *not*)	degenerative

His doctor told him that he was suffering from _____ heart

disease. His heart would only get worse and worse; it

would _____ until it stopped working. His only hope was

to get a new heart through a heart transplant operation.

	magnify (v.)
-cation (n.)	magnification

A microscope is used to enlarge the images of very small objects.

A _____ _____ one hundred makes an object ap-

pear one hundred times larger than it is.

	tolerate (v.)
-ance (n.)	tolerance
in- (= *not*)	intolerance
-ant (adj.)	tolerant
in- (= *not*)	intolerant

Some plants cannot _____ cold climates. They will die if the

temperature falls below freezing.

Discovering Word Meanings

Use (1) context clues; (2) your knowledge of prefixes, suffixes, and roots; and (3) a dictionary, if necessary, to discover the meanings of the italicized words in the following sentences from this chapter's reading passage.

1. Another group of nonbiodegradable pollutants consists of the toxic chemicals that are dumped into the sea as wastes from factory production. Among these chemicals are the *insecticide* DDT and a class of industrial chemicals called PCBs.

   (Use your dictionary to find the meaning of this word. What is the meaning of the suffix? What do the following words mean: *infanticide, patricide, genocide, suicide,* and *homicide?*)

2. In his book *After Man: A Zoology of the Future,* Dougal Dixon used his scientific knowledge and artistic imagination to picture the earth millions of years from now.

   (Look up *zoology* in your dictionary. From what language is it derived? What are the meanings of the parts of the word? What other words can you name that use the same suffix?)

3. Was there a nuclear war or a worldwide *epidemic* of some deadly, uncontrollable disease?

   (Which other words in the context help you to understand the meaning of *epidemic?* Is it used here as a noun or as an adjective? Use your dictionary to find the derivation of this word. What do the parts of the word mean?)

Signal Words and Phrases

Study the following signal words and phrases that appear in this chapter's reading passage.

1. **some . . . others**

   These words contrast two or more groups.

   Some wastes are eaten by fish. *Others* decompose in seawater.

2. **still**

   This word introduces unexpected information. Words and phrases with a similar meaning are *nonetheless, but . . . anyway, however, in spite of that,* and *nevertheless.*

   As civilizations grew, more pollutants were dumped into the seas. *Still,* this pollution did not threaten the marine environment.

3. **as we have seen**

   These words introduce a brief review of an important point that was mentioned earlier.

   As we have seen, one of the major ways we pollute the seas is . . . .

4. furthermore

This word may introduce the next item in an enumeration. Alternatively, it may also introduce more important or more specific information about the previous item. Words and phrases with a similar meaning include *in addition* and *moreover.*

Toxic chemicals can kill fish. *Furthermore,* such chemicals can harm people too if people eat fish that have been chemically poisoned.

5. in this way

These words refer back to an action or process that has just been described. They then introduce a consequence of this action or process.

Small marine creatures absorb poisonous chemicals in the sea. One fish may eat many such creatures. One person may eat many such fish. *In this way,* ocean pollution can be even more harmful to people than to marine life.

6. still another

These words may be used to introduce a later item in an enumeration. They may follow an item that was introduced with the word *another.* A phrase with a similar meaning is *yet another.*

One form of marine pollution is oil pollution. Another type is pollution caused by plastics. *Still another* kind of pollution is heavy metal pollution.

Grammar Preview

Study the following excerpts or paraphrases from this chapter's reading passage, and work through the tasks.

1. Rewrite the following sentences, being careful to preserve the meaning. Follow the instructions given in parentheses.
   a. By preventing the food from entering the bodies of these creatures, the small particles cause them to die.
   (First, use *because.* Then find as many other ways of rewriting this sentence as you can.)
   b. Two or more toxic substances, when acting together, produce more harmful effects than they can produce individually.
   (Find as many ways of rewriting the sentence as you can.)
2. Explain the meaning of the italicized phrase in each of the sentences below. Express this meaning in another way.
   a. One of the major ways we pollute the seas is to throw into them various types of waste and materials *foreign to the marine environment.*

b. The many thousands of poisonous materials *already in the oceans* can lead to countless hazards.

c. Kelp, a seaweed *eaten by the Japanese,* can concentrate cadmium in huge amounts.

d. Although oil leaks naturally into the sea from sources beneath the ocean bottoms, the quantities *produced by this natural leakage* are small.

3. Imagine that you are an environmentalist writing about the past. In an old notebook you have found the text that appears below. You decide to report this information in an essay that you are writing about the early industrial period. The first sentence has been done for you.

As civilizations grow, more and different pollutants are being dumped into the seas. Still, this pollution does not really threaten the marine environment. The seas seem capable of coping with anything that people can throw at them. This situation is changing, however, with the onset of industrialization. Now, factories are beginning to dump enormous quantities of materials into the seas. Especially in some coastal areas near large cities, ocean pollution is beginning to threaten marine life. For the first time, the oceans are beginning to fail in their ability to recycle humanity's wastes.

As civilizations grew, more and different pollutants were dumped into the seas. _____

_____

_____

_____

_____

Getting Ready to Read

The reading passage in this chapter is about some of the types of pollution that are damaging the world's oceans.

1. What does the title suggest about the content of the reading passage?

2. What are some of the ways in which you, as an individual, contribute to the pollution of the seas?

3. What in your opinion is the major cause of ocean pollution today, and what can be done to reduce this pollution?

4. Glance quickly through the reading passage and note the numbers of the paragraphs that enumerate types of ocean pollution.

Now read through this chapter's reading passage, "Oceans of Death." Look for information about the following: (1) the period in history when ocean pollution began to become a serious problem; (2) the categories and types of pollution; (3) the kinds of damage that can be caused by different pollutants; and (4) a way to predict where ocean pollution is likely to be most serious.

READING PASSAGE

Oceans of Death

1 The pollution of the earth's soil and water has become an issue of great concern. Until recently, most of that concern has focused on the land portion of the planet, where pollution directly affects people in their daily lives. Now, however, we have begun to realize that marine pollution is equally important. According to S. A. Patin (1982, pp. 3–4), marine pollution is the condition that results when people introduce into the seas substances harmful to life, health, resources, activities, or comforts.

2   Marine pollution is far from new. For over a million years, people have thought of the sea as a convenient place to throw their garbage. And it is true that the sea has a great capacity for absorbing organic wastes. Some of these wastes are eaten directly by the larger fishes. Others quickly decompose in sea water, i.e., they dissolve into a kind of organic soup that provides food to countless species of single-celled plant and animal life.

3   As civilizations grew, more and different pollutants were dumped into the seas. Still, this pollution did not really threaten the marine environment. The seas seemed capable of coping with anything that people could throw at them. This situation changed abruptly, however, with the onset of the Industrial Revolution. Suddenly, factories began dumping enormous quantities of materials into the seas. Especially in some coastal areas near large cities, ocean pollution began to threaten marine life. For the first time, the oceans began to fail in their ability to recycle humanity's waste.

4   It is becoming clear that marine pollution is a threat not only to marine life but to human life as well. As we have seen, one of the major ways we pollute the seas is to throw into them various types of waste and materials foreign to the marine environment. It is important to identify

FIGURE 6–1 Industrial pollution. (Source: U.S. Environmental Protection Agency)

these different types of pollutants and to understand the effects of each on marine and human life.

5   Marine pollutants fall into two major categories: biodegradable and nonbiodegradable substances. Biodegradable substances are materials that can be taken apart by natural processes within a short time. Such materials are usually not very harmful. One common biodegradable pollutant in the oceans is human waste from sewage. Marine

biologist John L. Culliney (1979, pp. 119–20) explains that in small quantities, it does not threaten the environment. In larger quantities, however, it provides a habitat for bacteria, which use up all the available oxygen in the area. As a result, all the fish in the region die. Sewage also contains viruses that are harmful to humans. Shellfish, particularly clams and oysters, accumulate these viruses in large quantities. When people eat shellfish, they increase their chances of getting certain diseases. One such disease is polio, a viral disease causing paralysis and sometimes death. Another is hepatitis, a serious disease of the liver.

6   A greater threat to marine life and eventually to human life are various types of nonbiodegradable substances. These are materials that cannot be quickly broken down into basic natural parts. One such material comes from plastic containers that are dropped overboard in large quantities from cruise ships. These containers break into tiny particles in the surf. The particles get stuck in the digestive systems of baby fish and one-celled° creatures called plankton. By preventing the food from entering the bodies of these creatures, the small particles cause them to die (Culliney, 1979, pp. 124–25). This has an effect on larger marine animals that depend on plankton for their food.

Something that has only one cell. A cell is the smallest unit of life.

7   Another group of nonbiodegradable pollutants mentioned by Culliney consists of the toxic chemicals that are dumped into the sea as wastes from factory production. Among these chemicals are the insecticide DDT and a class of industrial chemicals called PCBs.° All these chemicals have been closely linked with cancers in humans. In addition, small quantities of these chemicals affect the growth rate of many species and also make them less adaptable to normal environmental changes. In time, these effects could kill off entire species. In larger quantities, these toxic chemicals cause immediate death. Furthermore, the chemical poisoning of marine species can result indirectly in the poisoning of human beings. Some one-celled marine organisms readily absorb dangerous chemicals. As Culliney (1979, p. 193) observes, "In laboratory experiments, 98 percent of the DDT or PCB stirred into a jar of seawater was absorbed by plankton in six seconds." At first glance, the poisoning of plankton may not seem a cause of concern for humans. However, the very important process of food magnification is at work in the seas as elsewhere. In this process, the smallest forms of life, such as plankton, absorb dangerous chemicals from the sea. Larger animals eat

polychlorinated biphenyls: *a group of several highly toxic chemicals used as lubricants and heat-transfer fluids*

the plankton over a wide area. These animals are in turn eaten by still larger predators over a much wider area. And the process continues right up the food chain to humans, who catch and eat the larger fishes. Any one of these fishes may contain poisons that were originally spread over many hectares of the ocean (Culliney, 1979, p. 194). In this way, toxic chemicals in the seas may be even more dangerous to people than to marine plants and animals. Furthermore, two or more toxic substances, when acting together, produce more harmful effects than they can produce individually. Hence, the many thousands of poisonous materials already in the oceans can lead to countless hazards (Culliney, 1979, p. 204).

8   A third type of nonbiodegradable substance that causes serious pollution is oil. Although oil leaks naturally into the sea from sources beneath the ocean bottoms, the quantities produced by this natural leakage are small. Humans, however, are responsible for the dumping of ten times as much oil into the seas (Culliney, 1979, pp. 256–57). Some areas, such as the Gulf of Mexico and the waters off the coast of southern California, have become badly polluted as a result of offshore oil drilling. And major oil spills, such as the *Exxon Valdez*° disaster in Alaska in March 1989, destroy entire ecosystems.° These may take decades or even centuries to recover. As Culliney (1979, pp. 268–69) points out, oil can seriously weaken fish, especially at critical periods in their lives. In addition, oil can

the name of a ship that ran into some rocks in Alaska and spilled a large quantity of the oil it was carrying

The prefix eco *means* ecological. *Therefore an* ecosystem *is* _____.

FIGURE 6–2 Fish in the food chain.

change the normal behaviors of fish and thus reduce their chances for survival. There is also a limit to the amount of oil fish can tolerate without dying.

9   Still another category of nonbiodegradable pollutants is heavy metals such as cadmium, mercury, and lead (Patin, 1982, pp. 56–61). This type of marine pollution has had the most immediate and devastating effects on people. Kelp, a seaweed eaten by the Japanese, can concentrate cadmium in huge amounts. Cadmium has been linked to a degenerative bone disease in Japan. In Japanese, the disease is called *itai-itai,* meaning "ouch-ouch," because of the extreme pain it causes (Culliney, 1979, p. 281). And in 1965, six people in Nigata, Japan, were killed and forty-one were crippled from eating fish that contained mercury. Of course, these metals affect fishes as well. Even low levels of heavy metal pollution appear to be harmful to almost all species of marine life (Patin, 1982, p. 148).

10   Recognizing the types of marine pollution and understanding their effects on marine and human life are essential. The next step is to identify areas where marine pollution disasters are most likely to occur. According to chemist and oceanographer Edward D. Goldberg (1976, pp. 142–46), the greatest risks will be in countries with large populations and large ratios of gross national product to area. Chances are even greater for island countries or for countries where most of the population lives near the ocean. It is no surprise, therefore, that the most serious ocean poisoning incidents to date have occurred in Japan and the United States. Other high-risk areas include Hong Kong, Singapore, and the Netherlands. At the bottom of the list are the developing countries of the Third World.

11   All nations, but especially high-risk countries, must consider how to solve the problem of marine pollution. Their solutions may determine the fate not only of marine plants and animals but of all humankind. In his book *After Man: A Zoology of the Future,* Dougal Dixon (1983) used his scientific knowledge and artistic imagination to picture the earth millions of years from now. His world consists of a wonderful variety of plants and animals that have evolved far beyond their ancestors that are living today. Only one animal is missing from the scene: people. Why did our species finally vanish from the earth? Was there a nuclear war or a worldwide epidemic of some deadly, uncontrollable disease? According to Dixon, the extinction of our species was unavoidable and without glory. Our descendants died from a lack of the resources that they had wasted and from the poisons of their own garbage and pollution.

References

Culliney, John L. (1979). *The Forests of the Sea.* New York: Anchor Books.

Dixon, Dougal (1983). *After Man: A Zoology of the Future.* New York: St. Martin's Press.

Goldberg, Edward D. (1976). *The Health of the Oceans.* Paris: The Unesco Press.

Gross, M. G., & Palmer, H. D. (1979). Waste Disposal and Dredging Activities: The Geological Perspective. In H. D. Palmer & M. G. Gross (Eds.), *Ocean Dumping and Marine Pollution* (pp. 1–7). Stroudsburg, PA: Dowden, Hutchinson & Ross.

Patin, S. A. (1982). *Pollution and the Biological Resources of the Oceans.* Translated by Freund Publishing House. London: Butterworth.

Checking Your Comprehension

1. List the main marine pollutants.
2. Why was ocean pollution not a serious problem before advanced technology?
3. What is the difference between biodegradable and nonbiodegradable pollution?
4. Look at Figure 6–2. Use it to explain the impact of marine pollution on the food chain.
5. From what you have read here and in "Mariculture" in Chapter 4, can you think of a way to use a living species to test the degree of pollution in water?

For Discussion

1. What are some steps that individuals could take to help reduce ocean pollution?
2. Discuss the statement, "There is only one pollution . . . people"[1]
3. What human activities would be affected by extreme pollution of the oceans?

Analyzing the Structure

1. Which paragraphs in the reading passage contain the introduction, the body, and the conclusion?

[1] J. E. Lovelock (1982). *Gaia: A New Look at Life on Earth* (p. 122). Oxford: Oxford University Press.

2. Identify the thesis statement of the passage. In what way does it fulfill the requirements of a thesis statement?
3. Find the definitions of the following terms and identify the class and characteristics of each:
   a. marine pollution (paragraph 1)
   b. biodegradable substances (paragraph 5)
   c. *itai-itai* disease (paragraph 9)
      Note that paragraph 9 contains two definitions of *itai-itai*. One defines the disease; the other defines the word.
4. Rewrite the definition of the word *itai-itai* in one sentence, including the class and characteristics.

The Writing Process

Writing Topic Sentences

You have already learned that a thesis statement is a generalization that is broad enough to cover everything that your essay contains. Now we will look at another generalization that covers a more limited part of the essay, i.e., the topic sentence.

A topic sentence does for a paragraph what a thesis statement does for an essay or any other long piece of writing: It tells the reader the content of the paragraph. The writer then builds the rest of the paragraph with ideas and information connected to the topic sentence.

The topic sentence usually appears at the beginning of a paragraph, but it could be placed elsewhere. In example 1 below, the topic sentence is at the beginning of the paragraph. In example 2, the same paragraph has been rewritten to show how the topic sentence could appear at the end of the paragraph. The topic sentences are italicized.

Example 1

An important concern in mariculture is control of the physical environment. Light, water chemistry, and other physical factors must be conducive to the health and growth of the crop. The cost of controlling the physical environment is likely to be lower on shore than in the open ocean. Careful site selection can help reduce these costs.

Example 2

In mariculture, light, water chemistry, and other physical factors must be conducive to the health and growth of the crop. The cost of controlling the physical environment is likely to be lower on shore than in the open ocean. Careful site selection can help reduce these costs. *Thus we can see that control of the physical environment is an important factor in the success of a mariculture operation.*

Sometimes a topic sentence may be placed several sentences into the paragraph. The reason for this may be that introductory material precedes the topic sentence. Often this introductory material is a link to the preceding text. You will learn more about this kind of link in Chapter 11.

There are sometimes intermediary statements in an essay that are not broad enough to be thesis statements but are too broad to be topic sentences. Such statements can cover sections of the writing, and are used to divide the writing into logical groupings. This kind of statement will appear at the beginning of the paragraph that introduces the section, and the topic sentence of the paragraph will typically follow.

As an example, examine the italicized sentences in the following paragraph from this chapter's reading passage:

> *Marine pollutants fall into two major categories: biodegradable and non-biodegradable substances. Biodegradable substances are materials that can be taken apart by natural processes within a short time. Such materials are usually not very harmful. One common biodegradable pollutant in the oceans is human waste from sewage.* Marine biologist John L. Culliney explains that in small quantities, it does not threaten the environment. In larger quantities, however, it provides a habitat for bacteria, which use up all the available oxygen in the area. As a result, all the fish in the region die. Sewage also contains viruses that are harmful to humans. Shellfish, particularly clams and oysters, accumulate these viruses in large quantities. When people eat shellfish, they increase their chances of getting certain diseases. One such disease is polio, a viral disease causing paralysis and sometimes death. Another is hepatitis, a serious disease of the liver.

The writer used the first sentence to tell the reader that at least a portion of the rest of the essay will deal with two categories. The next two sentences introduce and define one of these categories. The fourth sentence is the topic sentence of the paragraph.

Now let us look once again at the rain forest essay in Chapter 1. The writer examined his notes and his thesis statement, and wrote a topic sentence for each paragraph as follows:

Thesis statement: Failure to preserve the Amazon rain forest could
                  have serious consequences for all living things.

Paragraph 1: Some consequences are physical or biological.
Paragraph 2: There are social and economic effects.

The thesis statement and the topic sentences, like all the other sentences in the essay, can be changed at any time. Writers often find ways of improving them as they write.

Writing the First Draft

The first draft is the writer's first attempt to write the body of the essay, which consists of the paragraphs that support the thesis statement. At this stage the writer does not need to be concerned about introductions or conclusions. His or her main concern is to write down the information according to the outline.

The writer of the rain forest produced the following first draft:

> Failure to preserve the Amazon rain forest could have serious consequences for all living things.
>
> Some consequences are physical or biological. One million species of animal and plant life depend on the rain forests and on each other to survive. Without the rain forests, species that live nowhere else on earth would quickly become extinct. The greenhouse effect might be the cause of an increase in the earth's temperature. It is increasing at an alarming rate. Scientists think that it might happen because of an increase in carbon dioxide. A large amount of carbon dioxide is absorbed by the rain forest. So destroying the rain forest would mean that there is more carbon dioxide in the air. Destroying the rain forests causes an increase in diseases like malaria. Forests are cleared to make room for hydroelectric dams, and large stagnant lakes are formed. Malarial mosquitoes breed in stagnant water. Without the earth's large forests, we might soon run out of air to breathe. The loss of the Amazon forests might cause a significant reduction in the amount of oxygen in the atmosphere.
>
> There are social and economic effects. Rubber trees are a major source of income for people who live in the area. The Amazon forests contain many of the world's rubber trees. People would have to find other ways to make a living if the forest disappeared. The introduction of previously unknown diseases into the region affects the local people. One of them is malaria. Poor people often have no protection against diseases. They cannot easily get medicines. Native peoples have lived for centuries in the area. Their tribes are now being forced to move. They are moving to escape disease. They will also need to find new sources of food as the forests disappear. Many of the native peoples are hunters and gatherers who are unable to change their way of life. They cannot find food in the areas where they must live. They are dying from disease and starvation. Also their cultures are disappearing.

Exercise

The focus of this exercise is topic sentences. Write a short essay about the impact that large scale construction of cities in the sea could have on ocean pollution. When you have chosen your organizing principle, make an outline that identifies your planned paragraphs. Then write topic sentences for these paragraphs. Exchange your outline and topic sentences for those of a partner to give and get suggestions for improvements. Then continue with the writing process. (*Hint:* Consider the extent of possible environmental damage and the ways in which it could be minimized. An example could be the energy and waste-disposal systems of Aquapolis, described in the reading passage of Chapter 5.)

Writing About Reading

1. In one paragraph define and give examples of nonbiodegradable ocean pollutants.

2. Write a short essay on the above topic. One way to do this is to include a definition of nonbiodegradable substances and then to divide the examples into groups.

3. Write an essay on your view of the steps that should be taken to reduce ocean pollution. Use any methods of organization that are appropriate.

4. Write an essay explaining how the following quotation relates to the information contained in the reading passages in Chapters 4–6: "We may find that the vital organs in the body of [the Earth] are not on the land surfaces but in the estuaries, wet lands, and muds of the continental shelves. . . . Until we know much more about the Earth and the role of these regions . . . we had better set them outside the limits for exploitation."[2]

---

[2]J. E. Lovelock (1982). *Gaia: A New Look at Life on Earth* (pp. 130–31). Oxford: Oxford University Press.

Rats used in genetic testing. (Source: USDA Photo by Murray Lemmon)

UNIT THREE

Genetic Engineering

The color of our hair and eyes, our sex, the shape and size of our bodies—these and many other characteristics and traits are passed from parents to children. Genetics is the science that studies how these characteristics and traits are transmitted. In recent years, scientists have begun to learn how to change this transmitted information. The techniques that they have developed to make such changes belong to a new science called genetic engineering.

Chapter 7 discusses the recent history of genetics and the birth of genetic engineering. It explains how biological information is transmitted from parents to children and how this information can be changed.

Chapter 8 describes what genetic engineering can do today and what it will be able to do within the next few years. The reading focuses on the fields of agriculture, manufacturing, and medical science.

Chapter 9 discusses the ethical issues involving genetic engineering. It asks whether we have the right to change nature and life. It suggests that we may do more harm than good if we try to change the genetic inheritance of people and animals.

Chapter 7

Genetic Engineering: A New Revolution in Technology

CHAPTER FOCUS

As you study this chapter, you should focus on the following important points:

Arrangement of information: paragraph structure, unity, and coherence

Vocabulary: understanding new words

Signal words and phrases: *like, unlike, instead, among others*

Sentence grammar: interpretation of noun clauses, past perfect tense, passive voice, participles, gerunds

Writing: getting feedback

Content: new genetic techniques for changing life

Arrangement of Information

Organization of the Text: Paragraph Structure

In Unit 2 you studied the main parts of an essay and how to recognize them. You also studied the correct formation and use of topic sentences in body paragraphs. In this unit you will learn more about the structure of a paragraph and see how to link the sentences smoothly and logically within a paragraph. In Unit 4 you will see how to link paragraphs smoothly and logically to each other in an essay.

A body paragraph in an essay has two parts: (1) a topic sentence that indicates the general topic of the entire paragraph; and (2) the supporting sentences of the paragraph. Supporting sentences may refer to the topic sentence directly. In this case these supporting sentences are *unified* with the topic sentence. This means that they are on the same topic as the topic sentence. If all the sentences in the paragraph refer to the topic sentence, then the paragraph is completely unified. It is also possible that some of the sentences refer to the sentences immediately preceding them. In this case, these sentences are *coherent.* This means that they add more information to the previous sentence. If every sentence in a paragraph refers to the ·sentence that came immediately before it, then the entire paragraph is coherent. Generally, a body paragraph is partly unified and partly coherent.

As an example, look again at ''Oceans of Death,'' the reading passage in Chapter 6. Paragraph 8 is about oil pollution. The topic sentence of this paragraph is the first sentence, ''A third type of nonbiodegradable substance that causes serious pollution is oil.'' This sentence tells the reader that oil pollution is the topic of the entire paragraph. If you look carefully at the whole paragraph, you will see that it is highly unified. Most of the sentences really give more information about the topic sentence. In fact, the word *oil* is in almost all the sentences. Only sentence 6 does not fit this pattern. In fact, sentence 6 is not unified with the topic sentence. Instead, it is coherent with the sentence that comes before it. Sentence 5 states that oil spills destroy entire ecosystems. Sentence 6 gives additional information about that destruction of ecosystems.

One way to understand the meaning of coherence is to consider why we choose the particular order of sentences in a paragraph. Every meaningful sentence can generate questions, i.e., it can cause the reader to ask certain questions. Look at sentence 1 in the following example:

> The factory in Newtown provides a major source of income for people living in the area. These people would have to find other ways to make a living if the factory moved.

This sentence could lead to such questions as, ''What sort of factory is it?,'' ''Who are the people who live in the area?,'' and ''What would the people do without their main source of income?'' Any sentence that answers such a question achieves coherence with the original sentence. Sentence 2 answers the last question, and since it follows sentence 1, the two sentences are coherent. In general, any sentence that answers a question that could be generated from the sentence that precedes it is *coherent* with that sentence. Any sentence that answers a question that could be generated from the topic sentence is *unified* with the topic sentence. A well-written paragraph that is both interesting and easy to understand should have both unified and coherent elements.

There are four main ways in which writers achieve coherence between sentences in a paragraph. As the examples below show, they (1) repeat key words, use synonyms, or use words that restate a previous idea; (2) use pronouns to refer to nouns in previous sentences or occasionally in a subsequent sentence; (3) use logical connecting words (e.g., *but, therefore, and*); and (4) use parallel constructions.

1. key words or synonyms

> The factory in Newtown provides a major source of income for *people* living in the area. *These people* would have to find other ways to make a living if the factory moved. Another serious *consequence* would be the loss of corporate taxes.

Sentence 2 begins with the words *these people,* which refer back to *people* in sentence 1. The word *consequence* in sentence 3 summarizes and refers to the meaning of sentence 2. (If the factory disappears, a *consequence* will be that the people will have to find other ways to make a living. Sentence 3 mentions another *consequence* of the closing of the factory.)

2. pronouns

> The main *buildings* in this university were built a hundred years ago. Some say that *they* add to the university's charm, but others say that *they* add only to the cost of maintenance.

The word *they* is used twice in sentence 2 to refer back to *buildings* in sentence 1. Writers who use pronouns in this way must be careful to ensure that there is one and only one antecedent. An antecedent can be a noun, pronoun, gerund, or any phrase or clause that can be substituted for a noun. Furthermore, the pronoun should be as close as possible to its antecedent.

3. logical connecting words

> The graduation ceremony was scheduled to take place outdoors. *However,* the weather forecast yesterday predicted rain. *As a result*, the ceremony was rescheduled to take place in the auditorium.

However and *as a result* both express logical relationships. Sentence 2 follows unexpectedly from sentence 1. Sentence 3 shows a result of the weather forecast mentioned in sentence 2.

4. parallel constructions

> Architecture based on lines and angles emphasizes strength and authority. Architecture based on curves emphasizes flexibility and compromise.

The almost identical grammatical structure of the two sentences suggests a relationship of coherence between them. Here, in addition, repeating some of the same words contributes to this effect.

Exercises

1. Look ahead to paragraph 10 of the reading passage of this chapter. Is this paragraph mainly unified or mainly coherent? Explain.

2. Look at paragraph 6 of the reading passage of this chapter. What is the topic sentence of this paragraph? How does this paragraph show unity and coherence at the same time?

Vocabulary Preview

Words in Context

The following words, arranged in groups, appear in this chapter's reading passage. Study the words in their contexts. Then complete the exercise that follows each group by writing the correct words in the blanks. Be sure to use the appropriate form of each word.

1. complexity, conceivably, decipher, pre-eminent, feat, heredity

	complex (adj. or n.)
-ity (n.)	complexity

Parents often tell their children that some things are too difficult for children to understand. When the children grow into adults, they learn that there are many *complexities* of life that even adults cannot understand.

	conceive (v.)
-able (adj.)	conceivable
in- (= *not*)	inconceivable
-ly (adv.)	conceivably

Only a few years ago, most people could not imagine many of the new inventions and ideas of science. These ideas and inventions were completely *inconceivable* to them. For example, many people could not *conceive* of the idea that anyone would ever walk on the moon.

	decipher (v.)
-able (adj.)	decipherable

Two friends invented a secret code so that they could send private messages to each other. Some of their classmates tried to *decipher* the code in order to be able to read the messages. However, they failed to discover how the code was constructed.

	eminent (adj.)
-ly (adv.)	eminently
-ce (n.)	eminence
pre-	pre-eminence
(= *ahead of*)	pre-eminent

One of the most famous American scientists of the 1940s was Barbara McClintock. She became *pre-eminent* in the field of genetics when she won the Nobel prize.

feat (n.)

The policeman risked his life to enter the burning house and rescue a young child. Everyone admired his act of strength and courage. For this *feat* he was awarded a gold medal by the city government.

	heredity (n.)
-ary (adj.)	hereditary
in- (= *in*)	inherit (v.)
-ance (n.)	inheritance

The biological laws of *heredity* were discovered by Gregor Mendel in 1866. These laws explain why individuals *inherit* certain physical characteristics from their parents and grandparents.

In recent years, _____ scientists have _____ the

biological code of _____. This remarkable _____

could _____ lead to the eventual understanding of many of

the _____ of life.

2. **exploitation, fermenting, fertilization, inherent, mechanized, phenomenal**

	exploit (n. or v.)
-ation (n.)	exploitation

During the period of colonization, many powerful countries took resources and wealth from smaller countries and gave little in return. This *exploitation* eventually caused the smaller countries to rebel and seek their independence.

	ferment (n. or v.)
-ation (n.)	fermentation

Centuries ago people learned how to make beer, wine, cheese, and other products by *fermenting* the foods from which they are made. This *fermentation* is caused by adding living substances called yeasts, which produce gas bubbles and change the chemistry of the original foods.

	fertile (adj.)
-ity (n.)	fertility
-ize (v.)	fertilize
-er (n.)	fertilizer
-ation (n.)	fertilization

To produce a better crop, a farmer must *fertilize* the fields where the food grows. *Fertilizers* consist of chemicals that are necessary for life. The high cost of *fertilization* is one reason that many Third World countries have poor crops.

	inherent (adj.)
-ly (adv.)	inherently

Danger is a natural part of the job of a police officer. In other words, danger is *inherent* in the job.

	mechanic (n.)
-al (adj.)	mechanical
-ly (adv.)	mechanically
-s (n., sing.)	mechanics
-ism (n.)	mechanism
-tic (adj.)	mechanistic
-ally (adv.)	mechanistically
-ize (v.)	mechanize

Much of the recent history of Western society has been a development from manual labor to labor aided by machines. But as more and more jobs become *mechanized,* many workers are threatened with loss of work.

	phenomenon (n.), phenomena (pl.)
-al (adj.)	phenomenal
-ly (adv.)	phenomenally

Her brother is so strong that he can lift up one end of a car. I never realized that he had such *phenomenal* strength. The ability to lift such a heavy weight is a most unusual *phenomenon.*

The young couple had often made wine at home as a hobby. Eventually they decided to buy a small winery so that they could make enough wine to sell. The winery they bought suffered from a number of problems, including unfair _____ of the workers, poor grapes, and faulty equipment. The new owners improved the working conditions of the workers. They also grew better grapes by improving the _____ of the fields, and they found better ways of _____ the grape juice to produce alcohol. They also bought new and better _____ equipment for pressing the juice out of the grapes. Eventually they succeeded in removing all the problems that had been _____ in the business when they bought it, and their winery went on to enjoy _____ success.

3. creation, hurling, inanimate, poised, surround, visualize

	create (v.)
-or (n.)	creator
-ion (n.)	creation
-ive (adj.)	creative
-ly (adv.)	creatively
-ity (n.)	creativity

The famous fashion designer brought out a new collection of clothes for the summer. Buyers came from around the world to look at his newest *creations*.

hurl (v.)

The boy was standing on the shore *hurling* small stones into the lake. Every now and then he threw a flat stone so hard that it skipped across the surface of the water.

	animate (v. or adj.)
in- (= *not*)	inanimate
-ion (n.)	animation

When the first explorers arrive at distant planets, will they find life forms that are quite different from what they know on earth? Perhaps something that appears to be *inanimate* will turn out to be alive.

poise (n. or v.)

Our daughter often places things where they can easily fall and break. Just today she *poised* an expensive vase on the edge of the table. We were able to catch it just as it was about to fall.

	surround (v.)
-ings (n., pl)	surroundings

A small group of discontented farmers staged a rebellion against the government. They had to give up their rebellion, however, when they found themselves *surrounded* by soldiers. Since there were soldiers on every side, there was no way to escape.

	visual (adj.)
-ly (adv.)	visually
-ize (v.)	visualize
-ation (n.)	visualization

She asked me to imagine what her new house looked like. She said that the second floor was twice as big as the first floor. I could not form a mental image of such a house. In fact, nobody I know can *visualize* it.

Try to _____ an _____ object the size of a football

field, being _____ through space. Imagine that it is made

almost entirely of ice and is _____ by gas and dust. Such is

the description of the typical comet. Thousands of these have

been _____ on the outer limits of our solar system since

its _____.

4. **immune, recombine, replicate, reproduction, sexuality, synthesize**

	immune (adj.)
-ity (n.)	immunity
-ize (v.)	immunize
-ation (n.)	immunization

The vaccines of Doctors Salk and Sabin provide *immunity* against the dangerous disease polio. Without this protection, many children would be crippled or even killed each year by this disease.

	combine (v.)
-ation (n.)	combination
re- (= *again*)	recombine

The large company split into two smaller companies. When business declined, the directors of the two companies voted in favor of a merger. Thus, the two companies *recombined* into one.

	replica (n.)
-ate (v.)	replicate (v.)
-ion (n.)	replication

Art forgers are talented criminals who make copies of famous paintings and sell them as originals. Sometimes a forger can *replicate* a painting so accurately that the original and the copy appear to be identical.

	produce (n. or v.)
-t (n.)	product
-ion (n.)	production
re- (= *again*)	reproduction

I am glad that you like the painting. It has been years since I saw the original, but I think that this is a very accurate copy. Many people have told me that this is the best *reproduction* that they have seen.

	sex (n.)
-ual (adj.)	sexual
-ly (adv.)	sexually
-ity (n.)	sexuality

Sex is nature's way of passing characteristics from parents to children and at the same time giving children a greater variety of possible traits. In this way children can be both similar to and different from their parents.

	synthesis (n.), syntheses (pl.)
-ize (v.)	synthesize
-tic (adj.)	synthetic
-ally (adv.)	synthetically

Ancient chemists, called alchemists, tried for centuries to make gold out of less valuable materials. Modern chemists can make many *synthetic* materials that do not exist in nature, but nobody has succeeded in *synthesizing* gold.

Genetic engineering is a science that began when scientists first learned how the basic chemicals of life were able to _____, or make copies of themselves. At first, scientists could only watch the processes of life. Gradually, however, they began to learn how to change some of these processes. They learned to change some of the chemicals of life and make them combine again, or _____, in different ways. This new technology has made great advances in such fields as agriculture, manufacturing, and the medical sciences. For example, medical science may soon make it possible for parents to decide which _____ their baby will be. Genetic engineering will also eventually provide entirely new methods of _____, such as cloning—the exact replication of a living organism. Many other possible benefits are expected from genetic engineering. Among these are ways to _____ new drugs and ways to change our bodies to make us _____ to many diseases.

Discovering Word Meanings

Use (1) context clues; (2) your knowledge of prefixes, suffixes, and roots; and (3) a dictionary, if necessary, to discover the meanings of the italicized words in the following sentences from this chapter's reading passage.

1. As one industrial revolution comes to an end, another is poised to begin. Unlike its *predecessor,* however, the coming industrial revolution will not be based on petroleum energy and mechanized production.

   (What is the *predecessor* of the coming industrial revolution? How does the prefix *pre-* help you to understand this meaning?)

2. Yeasts are capable of fermenting *carbohydrates,* converting them to carbon dioxide and alcohol.

   (Use your dictionary to find the roots that combine to form this word. From what language(s) are they derived? Give some examples of carbohydrates.)

3. When Watson and Crick discovered the structure of DNA in 1953, they knew that they were studying the molecule that contained the *blueprints* for life. The DNA molecule contains all the information necessary for the construction, growth, and reproduction of living organisms.

   (What does the second sentence tell you about the meaning of *blueprints* in this context? Use your dictionary to find the literal meaning of *blueprints.* Explain the connection between the two meanings.)

4. In 1961 Nirenberg noticed that the base units along the double helix of DNA are arranged in groups of three. He isolated one of these *triplets,* called codons, and observed what protein it produced.

   (What do the words *tricycle, trilogy, tripod, trinity,* and *trimester* have in common? Use this information to determine the antecedent of *triplet* in this context.)

5. The computerized gene machine enables scientists to build a gene out of the basic materials of DNA. It links DNA *subunits* in any desired order at the rate of about two per hour.

   (What are the parts of this word, and what do they mean? What other words do you know that start with the same prefix?)

Signal Words and Phrases

Study the following signal words and phrases that appear in this chapter's reading passage.

1. like, unlike, instead

When used as signal words, *like* introduces a comparison, and *unlike* introduces a contrast. *Like* indicates that the following item will be similar in some way to another item in the sentence. The item that follows *like* is already known to the reader or has already been explained in the text. The other item is not yet known to the reader, has not been described, or is more difficult to understand. An expression that has a meaning similar to that of *like* is *similar to.*

The moon is an airless world. *Like* the moon, Mercury has no atmosphere and, therefore, no clouds or weather patterns.

The moon is an airless world. Mercury, *like* the moon, has no atmosphere and, therefore, no clouds or weather patterns.

Unlike shows at least one significant difference between two items. If the sentence with *unlike* also contains *no, not, never,* etc., the word *instead,* often appears a sentence or two later. *Instead* means *in place of that.*

Unlike Mercury, Venus has a thick atmosphere and is covered by clouds.

Unlike universities, community colleges are not concerned with research. *Instead,* they concentrate on teaching and practical training.

Note that *instead* often appears by itself without other signal words such as *unlike.*

2. among others

These words indicate that the item being discussed is one of a group of similar items.

Scientists have discovered, *among others,* the gene that determines sex.

Grammar Preview

Study the following excerpts or paraphrases from this chapter's reading passage, and work through the tasks.

1. Read the following paragraph and answer the questions that follow. Use your own words to show that you understand the meaning of the paragraph. Begin each answer with the words given.

By 1960, scientists already knew that the ability of organisms to grow and reproduce depends on their ability to manufacture proteins. In addition, the fact that the manufacture of proteins is controlled by the structure of the DNA molecule was becoming obvious. Then, in 1961, Marshall W. Nirenberg noticed that the base units of the DNA molecule are arranged in groups of three. This led eventually to an understanding of the genetic code—the patterns that control the chemistry of life. Today, most scientists agree that the genetic code has not changed throughout the period of life on earth.

   a. What did scientists already know by 1960? The growth _____

   _____.

   b. What effect does the DNA molecule have on the manufacture of proteins? The shape of the DNA molecule _____.

   c. What did Nirenberg notice in 1961? Triplets _____.

   d. What do most scientists agree about today? Since _____

   _____.

2. Supply the correct tense and voice (active or passive) of the verbs in parentheses in the paragraph below. Explain your choices.

   In October 1980, the Genentech Corporation offered over a million shares of stock. The company, which (form) only a short time earlier by genetic researchers, was already worth nearly half a billion dollars. Already by the beginning of the decade, investors knew that scientists (acquire) enough knowledge about the chemistry of life to change life itself. Using new techniques, they could manufacture valuable products cheaply. Therefore, in one day of stock trading, investors increased the value of the company by $36 million. Amazingly, the company (not yet market) even one product!

3. Rewrite the following passage in your own words to show that you understand its meaning.

   Scientists have successfully built a living cell, using parts from other cells. They have, in addition, fused cells from two separate species, creating life forms that have never before existed. They have discovered the gene that triggers the sexuality of an infant, to determine whether a fetus will become a boy or a girl. Beginning in the early 1970s, scientists began mapping the locations of the one hundred thousand human genes to learn their positions on the chromosomes. Knowing the location of genes is essential to being able to replace them to fight disease and birth defects, or to manipulate heredity for whatever purposes.

Getting Ready to Read

The reading passage in this chapter is about the chemistry of life and ways to change living things in order to make new products.

1. In your opinion, will scientists ever learn how to create life? Why, or why not? Explain why you think human beings should or should not try to create life.

2. Have you ever considered a career in the biological sciences, such as agriculture, medicine, or genetics? What do you see as the advantages and disadvantages of such a career?

3. What new discoveries do you hope the biological sciences will soon provide?

4. Quickly glance through the article, "Genetic Engineering: A New Revolution in Technology," until you find a formal definition of genetic engineering. Without reading the article, explain what you think this definition means.

Now read the passage carefully from beginning to end. As you read, note how living things can be changed and the ways in which genetic engineering can be used to improve human life.

READING PASSAGE

Genetic Engineering: A New Revolution in Technology

1 As one industrial revolution comes to an end, another is poised to begin. Unlike its predecessor, however, the coming industrial revolution will not be based on petroleum energy and mechanized production. Instead, it will be a revolution in biotechnology. Biotechnology may be defined as a technology that uses biological, rather than mechanical, processes and techniques to produce materials for industry, agriculture, medical science, and other fields.

2   In some ways biotechnology is not new at all. For centuries, basic biotechnological processes have been used to make beer, wine, bread, and cheese with the help of single-celled organisms called yeasts. Yeasts are capable of fermenting carbohydrates, converting them to carbon dioxide and alcohol. Without them, as bakers and vintners have always known, bread would not rise, and wine would merely be grape juice. As these techniques were applied over the centuries, people gradually learned more about yeasts and how they worked. Although scientists learned how to choose the best yeasts and make them work efficiently, they had to be content with the products

FIGURE 7–I   The first stage of the wine-making process: hand picking grapes in the Santa Cruz Mountains in Calfornia. (Source: © Alexander Lowry, 1985)

that existing microorganisms could produce. Because the key to the mystery of life remained hidden, it was not possible to change the microorganisms and force them to produce new and more desirable products. Then, in 1953, two biochemists—James Watson and Francis Crick—discovered the structure of DNA (deoxyribonucleic acid), the basic molecule of life, and provided the key to the second industrial-technological revolution. Their work led to further scientific discoveries about the building blocks of life and on to the beginnings and continuing development of genetic engineering.

3   Genetic engineering is an enormously powerful new technique for changing life. To understand this process and what it can do, it is first necessary to understand something about life's basic chemistry. Living organisms consist of cells, which are the smallest units of life. The center of a cell, the area known as the nucleus, contains DNA and the other chemicals necessary for life. When Watson and Crick discovered the structure of DNA in 1953, they knew that they were studying the molecule that contained the blueprints for life. The DNA molecule contains all the information necessary for the construction, growth, and reproduction of living organisms. Watson and Crick found that DNA molecules consist of two chains of chemicals called nucleotides. Nucleotides are made of the sugar deoxyribose and four other chemicals called adenine, cytosine, guanine, and thymine. These four chemicals are known as the bases. The two chains twine around each other in the shape of a twisted ladder. At certain points along the chain, hydrogen bonds fasten the two chains together. This twisted shape is known as a double helix. To visualize the shape of the DNA molecule, think of a spiral staircase. The two deoxyribose chains are the railings on each side of the staircase; the bases, linked by hydrogen bonds, are the stairs that separate the railings and fasten the structure together (Fig. 7–2).

4   Knowing the structure of the DNA molecule, however, did not explain how it worked. The first important step toward understanding its operation was made by Arthur Kornberg in 1957. Kornberg showed that DNA replicates—forms an exact duplicate of itself—by separating into two strands. To visualize this, imagine our spiral staircase being cut right down the center. Each of the strands then picks up the necessary chemicals from its surroundings to manufacture an exact duplicate of its original form. There are now two spiral staircases—each one exactly like the original.

5   At this point in the mystery, two important facts were clear. First, scientists knew that the ability of organisms to grow and reproduce depended entirely on their ability to manufacture precisely the right proteins at precisely the right time (Prentis, 1984, p. 35). Second, it was becoming obvious that the manufacture of complex proteins was

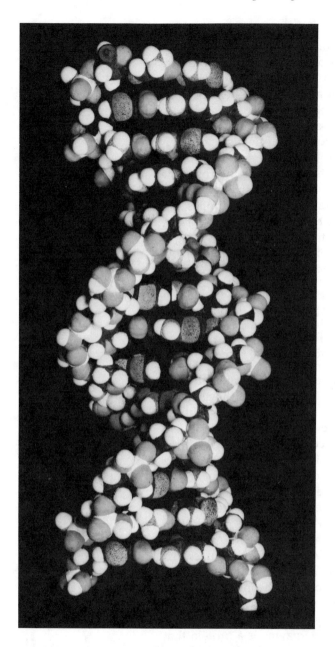

FIGURE 7-2 Model of a DNA molecule. (Source: Abbott Laboratories)

controlled in some way by the structure of the DNA molecule. It remained for another biochemist, Marshall W. Nirenberg, to decipher the DNA code and to explain the relationship between these two facts. In 1961 Nirenberg noticed that the base units along the double helix of DNA are arranged in groups of three. He isolated one of these triplets, called codons, and observed what protein it produced. This paved the way for other scientists to determine the proteins produced by each of the sixty-four possible combinations of DNA base codons. For the first time scientists knew the language of the chemistry of life—the genetic code (Table 7–1). The genetic code applies not merely to a single species but to virtually all forms of life. And most scientists agree that this code has not changed throughout the entire evolution of life on this planet. As Francis Crick (1986, p. 8) observed:

> The four-letter language of the nucleic acids,° the   *The nucleic acids are DNA*
> twenty-letter language of protein, and the little   *and RNA.*
> dictionary which relates the two languages—the
> genetic code—are, with minor exceptions, the
> same throughout nature, from viruses to humans.

6   Knowing the genetic code enabled scientists to predict which proteins a cell would produce, but they still did not understand how the DNA molecule sends its instructions to the cell. At about the same time that Nirenberg was deciphering the genetic code, other scientists were discovering a new molecule of life, RNA (ribonucleic acid). RNA is similar in many ways to DNA, but the sugar unit in the RNA molecule is ribose rather than deoxyribose. Furthermore, in RNA the base uracil takes the place of thymine. Finally, RNA forms a single strand, rather than a double helix. There are several kinds of RNA. One of these is messenger RNA (mRNA), which is manufactured by the DNA molecule and sent out into the cell to a specific location. The DNA molecule programs the mRNA with the information to produce a certain protein when it arrives at that location. An important function of these specific proteins is to serve as enzymes. An enzyme is a protein that helps to speed up a chemical reaction. It does this by helping to bring together the chemicals that are needed in the reaction.

7   Against the backdrop of these revolutionary breakthroughs, scientists were making other equally important discoveries. In 1956 researchers discovered that human cells contain forty-six chromosomes, and they have

TABLE 7–1 The Genetic Code

First position	Second position				Third position
	U	C	A	G	
U	Phe	Ser	Tyr	Cys	U
	Phe	Ser	Tyr	Cys	C
	Leu	Ser	Stop	Stop	A
	Leu	Ser	Stop	Trp	G
C	Leu	Phe	His	Arg	U
	Leu	Phe	His	Arg	C
	Leu	Pro	Gin	Arg	A
	Leu	Pro	Gin	Arg	G
A	Ile	Thr	Asn	Ser	U
	Ile	Thr	Asn	Ser	C
	Ile	Thr	Lys	Arg	A
	Met/ start	Thr	Lys	Arg	G
G	Val	Ala	Asp	Gly	U
	Val	Ala	Asp	Gly	C
	Val	Ala	Glu	Gly	A
	Val	Ala	Glu	Gly	G

*Each code of three bases, called a codon, determines a specific amino acid. The amino acids combine to form proteins. The four bases of mRNA are A (adenine), G (guanine), C (cytosine), and U (uracil). The first codon on the chart—UUU—specifies the formation of the amino acid phenylalanine (Phe). If the mRNA contains this codon, phenylalanine will be produced. If the mRNA contains the codon UCU, serine (Ser) will be produced, and so on. As the amino acids are produced, they are added to the protein chain, thus forming a complex protein. Three codons—UAA, UGA, and UAG—indicate that the protein chain is complete. When one of these codons appears, the cell stops adding amino acids to the protein chain. One codon—AUG— can signal the beginning of a protein chain or can cause the production of the amino acid methionine (Met). The other amino acids are alanine (Ala), arginine (Arg), asparagine (Asn), aspartic acid (Asp), cysteine (Cys), glutamic acid (Glu), glutamine (Gln), glycine (Gly), histidine (His), isoleucine (Ile), leucine (Leu), lysine (Lys), proline (Pro), threonine (Thr), tryptophan (Trp), tyrosine (Tyr), and valine (Val).

learned the functions of each of them. Chromosomes are structures that consist of DNA molecules and that contain the genes—the smallest units of heredity. Armed with this knowledge, doctors can now take chromosome samples from an unborn human fetus to determine its chances of getting certain genetic diseases in later life.

8   In other related developments, scientists have successfully built a living cell, using parts from other cells. They have, in addition, fused cells from two separate species, creating life forms that have never before existed. They have isolated pure human genes and in this way

have discovered, among others, the gene that triggers the sexuality of an infant, to determine whether a fetus will become a boy or a girl. Beginning in the early 1970s, scientists began mapping the locations of the one hundred thousand human genes to learn their positions on the chromosomes (Gene Research, 1986, p. 58). By the mid-1980s over two hundred genes had been mapped. Knowing the location of genes is essential to being able to replace them to fight disease and birth defects, or to manipulate heredity for whatever purposes. Another remarkable feat of genetic research was the work of Har Gobind Khorana, who in 1976 successfully constructed a human gene. He inserted the artificial gene into a living cell, where it worked perfectly. The work of Khorana and his predecessors proved that genetic science was crossing a new frontier—from a mere understanding of the processes that governed life to the deliberate manipulation of those processes. By 1980 geneticists had acquired sufficient knowledge of the chemistry of life to reach inside the nuclei° of cells and change life itself. Thus the new science of genetic engineering was born.

plural of nucleus, *the central part of something, such as a living cell*

9   Genetic engineering, also called recombinant DNA technology, may be defined as the procedures or techniques for changing the nature or function of an organism by altering its genetic structure. When an organism's DNA is changed in this way, it is called recombinant DNA because its parts are recombined, i.e., put together in a different way. This is done by replacing one or more genes of an organism with genes taken from a different organism. A restriction enzyme is used to capture the foreign genes, and a protein called a plasmid (also consisting of DNA) is used to carry the new genes into the cell and add them to the existing DNA. The foreign gene will use the cell to produce the protein that it produced in its natural host organism before it was transferred.

10   A famous and early example of genetic engineering involves the manufacture of human insulin. Insulin is a hormone—a chemical that controls natural functions of the body. The function of insulin is to regulate the amount of sugar in the blood. One of the human genes oversees the production of insulin in the human body. For reasons not entirely clear to modern medical researchers, some people's bodies do not produce the required amount of insulin. The result is diabetes, a potentially fatal blood-sugar disease. To control diabetes, doctors have learned to inject insulin directly into the bloodstream. However, before

1980 insulin was available only in small quantities and at a very high price. Most of the supply came from animals and was not the best for human use. In 1980 a team of researchers at Guy's Hospital in London, England, successfully isolated the human gene that governs insulin production and inserted it into the DNA of bacteria. The bacteria began producing human insulin in large quantities. This pure, inexpensive, and readily available insulin was the first commercially marketed product manufactured by techniques of genetic engineering.

11   Using genetic engineering, researchers can create organisms that will readily produce many substances of value to science, medicine, and technology. The process can be divided into four main stages: (1) obtaining the gene that carries the program for the desired product; (2) inserting the gene into the organism that will be the factory to make the product; (3) causing the organism to start producing; and (4) harvesting the product (Prentis, 1984, p. 37). Remarkable difficulties surround each of these stages, but scientists have developed, and are continuing to develop, methods to overcome these difficulties. One recent invention—the computerized gene machine— simplifies the first step in the process. This device enables scientists to build a gene out of the basic materials of DNA. It links DNA subunits in any desired order at the rate of about two per hour. In 1982 the gene machine successfully arranged 514 DNA bases to synthesize a gene to produce interferon, an immune-system protein that combats viral° infections and cancer (Prentis, 1984, p. 57).

adjective related to virus

12   Among the benefits that we may soon expect from the biotechnological revolution are methods to diagnose diseases; to cure or prevent AIDS,° cancer, and Alzheimer's disease°; to choose the preferred sex of unborn babies; to improve cereal crops and other plants by making them disease-resistant and self-fertilizing; to improve milk yields; and to understand the aging process and slow its effects. Farther into the future we may find ways to correct genetic defects, to enhance the strength and intelligence of unborn children, and to improve our understanding of the human brain and how it works. Already biotechnology has made possible artificial insemination° and in vitro° fertilization (Crick, 1986, p. 9). These breakthroughs give us barely a hint of what awaits us. As Jeremy Rifkin (1984, p. 7) writes,

a deadly disease of the immune system

a degenerative disease of the brain

in sexual reproduction insemination is the insertion of the male seed, or sperm, into the female egg

Latin for in glass, such as in a test tube. It refers to any process that occurs outside the living body.

> The recombinant DNA process is the most dramatic technological tool to date in the growing bio-

technological arsenal. The biologist is learning
how to manipulate, recombine, and reorganize living tissue into new forms and shapes, just as his
craftsmen ancestors did by firing inanimate matter. The speed of the discoveries is truly phenomenal. It is estimated that biological knowledge is
currently doubling every five years, and in the
field of genetics, the quantity of information is
doubling every twenty-four months. We are virtually hurling ourselves into the age of biotechnology.

13   Commercial exploitation of biotechnology will not be
left behind. Already, hundreds of major corporations in
every industrialized nation are lining up to seize their
share of the biotech market. Typical among them is Genentech, which began its existence in October 1980 by offering
more than a million shares of stock. The value of the stock
rose so greatly in a single day of trading that the company's assets increased by $36 million. The company,
worth over half a billion dollars, had not yet marketed
even one product (Rifkin, 1984, p. 11)! The *Encyclopaedia
Britannica*'s conservative view that ''genetic engineering
may, conceivably, become the pre-eminent form of engineering'' (Heredity, 1980, p. 816) may turn out to be one
of the greatest understatements of our time, for without
doubt a new and enormously powerful industrial revolution has begun.

References

Crick, Francis (1986, July–August). The Challenge of Biotechnol-
      ogy. *The Humanist, 46*(4), 8–9, 32.
Gene Research: Gains and Goals (1986, July 28). *U.S. News and
      World Report, 101*(4), 58.
Heredity (1980). *Encyclopaedia Britannica* (15th ed.), vol. 8, p. 816.
Prentis, S. (1984). *Biotechnology: A New Industrial Revolution.* Lon-
      don: Orbis.
Rifkin, Jeremy (1984). *Algeny: A New Word—A New World.* Har-
      mondsworth, England: Penguin.

Checking Your Comprehension

1. What is genetic engineering?
2. What was the first known use of genetic engineering?
3. Give the main discoveries in the historical development of genetic engi-
    neering.

4. What is DNA? Describe its structure and function. What is its relationship to RNA?
5. What is the gene machine, and what is its purpose?
6. What are some of the ways in which genetic engineering can be used?

For Discussion

1. What advances do you expect from genetic engineering in the immediate future? What fields or industries are likely to benefit most from this technique?
2. How important, if at all, is it for today's students of engineering, law, computer science, and business to include genetics in their courses of study? Give reasons for your opinions. How do you expect the genetic revolution to affect you personally?

Analyzing the Structure

1. What is the thesis statement of this essay?
2. Describe the structure and organizing principle of the body of this essay. Find the place in the essay that gives this information.
3. Which body paragraphs, if any, are highly unified? Which are highly coherent? Which are both?
4. What are the topic sentences of paragraphs 3, 4, and 5?

The Writing Process: Getting Feedback

At any stage in the writing process you may wish to get feedback from a reader. A good time to do this is right after you finish writing the first draft.

It is important to ask the reader specific questions that will help you locate any confusing or ambiguous sections that your essay may contain. The following can be very helpful in achieving this result:

1. Ask the reader to read your essay carefully and to determine whether it is an argument or an exposition. Then ask the reader to identify the organizational principle and the thesis statement. If the reader cannot do this easily, find out why. You may need to rethink your organizing principle or to rewrite your thesis statement.
2. Ask the reader to look at each body paragraph. Does it develop the organizing principle? Next ask the reader to summarize each paragraph in one sentence. Do you agree with this summary? Does it say something similar to the topic sentence? If not, you may need to rewrite all or part of the paragraph.

3. Ask the reader to consider how you have developed each paragraph. Does it use such methods as enumeration, definition, classification, and comparison/contrast? Does it contain support for the topic sentence in the form of reasons, facts, examples, statistics, description, etc.? Does it present these in a unified and coherent way? Do the paragraphs need transitions or bridges? What suggestions can the reader offer for improvement?

You may wish to consult with more than one reader to get a clearer picture of how to improve your essay. When you are finished, make all necessary changes and show them to the reader(s) to find out if these changes make the writing easier to understand.

Let us look once again at the first draft of the rain forest essay in Chapter 6. The reader who provided feedback on this draft noted that the essay divides the consequences of destroying the rain forest into two groups, and then enumerates the consequences in each group. Thus the essay has a clear organizing principle, and fulfills the expectations raised by the thesis statement and the topic sentences. The reader identified the essay as exposition based on classification and enumeration. However, she pointed out that the writer might make the essay more forceful by including an argument when he writes his conclusion.

Her main criticism of the essay had to do with the coherence of the paragraphs. She suggested combining or reordering some of the shorter sentences to make the relationships between certain facts clearer. This would, for example, show which parts of sentences are more important or which action or event occurred first; it would also suggest the relationship between sentences by placing them next to each other.

Another suggestion was to use more pronoun reference. One example was adding the pronoun *these* to the topic sentence of the second paragraph:

> Some of these consequences are physical or biological.

A third suggestion was to use more synonyms or to repeat key words more often. For example, the sentence "One of them is malaria" in paragraph 3 is ambiguous, because *them* could refer to either *disease* or *people* in the previous sentence. She proposed rewriting it as follows:

> One of these diseases is malaria.

Some additional suggestions regarding transitions and bridging will be taken up in Chapters 8 and 11.

The writer's revisions of his first draft are shown below. Portions to be changed are underlined in the original text, and changes appear in the margin.

First Draft with Corrections

Failure to preserve the Amazon rain forest
could have serious consequences for all living things.

Some consequences are physical or biological. One million species of animal and plant life depend on the rain forests and on each other to survive. Without the rain forests, species that live nowhere else on earth would quickly become extinct. The greenhouse effect might be the cause of an increase in the earth's temperature. It is increasing at an alarming rate. Scientists think that it might happen because of an increase in carbon dioxide. A large amount of carbon dioxide is absorbed by the rain forest. So destroying the rain forest would mean that there is more carbon dioxide in the air. Destroying the rain forests causes an increase in diseases like malaria. Forests are cleared to make room for hydroelectric dams, and large stagnant lakes are formed. Malarial mosquitoes breed in stagnant water. Without the earth's large forests, we might soon run out of air to breathe. The loss of the Amazon forests might cause a significant reduction in the amount of oxygen in the atmosphere.

There are social and economic effects. Rubber trees are a major source of income for people who live in the area. The Amazon forests contain many of the world's rubber trees. People would have to find other ways to make a living if the forest disappeared. The introduction of previously unknown diseases into the region affects the local people. One of them is malaria. Poor people often have no protection against diseases. They cannot easily get medicines. Native peoples have lived for centuries in the area. Their tribes are now being forced to move.

Handwritten margin annotations:

Some of these consequences →

Destroying the forests would speed up the greenhouse effect, which may be causing the earth's temperature to rise at an alarming rate. The rain forests absorb a large amount of carbon dioxide. Scientists believe that this gas is partly responsible for the rising temperatures.

such as

The loss of the Amazon forests might cause a significant reduction in the amount of oxygen in the atmosphere. Without the earth's large forests, we might soon run out of air to breathe.

One of these diseases is malaria. Poor people, who cannot easily get medicines, often have no protection against these diseases.

Without this ecosystem, these species, which live nowhere else on earth, would quickly become extinct.

As forests are cleared to make room for hydroelectric dams, large stagnant lakes are formed. These provide breeding grounds for malarial mosquitoes

The Amazon forests contain many of the world's rubber trees which are a major source of income for people living in the area. These people

Native peoples, whose tribes have lived for centuries in the area, are now *being forced to move to escape disease and to find new sources of food as the forests disappear.*

They are moving to escape disease. They will also need to find new sources of food as the forests disappear. Many of the native peoples are hunters and gatherers who are unable to change their way of life. They cannot find food in the areas where they must live. They are dying from disease and starvation. Also their cultures are disappearing.

These people are dying from disease and starvation, and their cultures are vanishing.

Exercise

Using as a source the reading passage in Chapter 7, write a short essay on the effects genetic engineering could have on any one human problem such as food shortages, health, reproduction, or the environment. Exchange the first draft of your essay with that of one or more partners to give and receive feedback. The feedback should include both written comments and discussion.

Writing About Reading

1. Write a one-paragraph extended definition of genetic engineering. Refer back to Chapter 5 for help with definitions.

2. Write a short essay on the above topic. Your essay should explain what genetic engineering is and what it is capable of doing.

3. In a short essay, enumerate and describe the major scientific breakthroughs leading to our current understanding of genetics. Use any methods of organization that are appropriate.

4. Referring to "The Knowledge Economy" in Chapter 2, discuss why an economy based more on information exchange than on heavy machinery is a good economy for genetic engineering. Explain why, in your view, companies such as Genentech are enjoying great success in the new economy.

Chapter 8

Recent Advances in Biotechnology

CHAPTER FOCUS

As you study this chapter, you should focus on the following important points:

Arrangement of information: classification

Vocabulary: understanding new words

Signal words and phrases: *in fact, whereby*

Sentence grammar: parallelism, choice of verb tense, sentence structure, adjective clauses, articles

Writing: transition signals

Content: a description of present and future techniques and products from genetic engineering and biotechnology

Arrangement of Information

Organization of the Content: Classification

We have seen that enumeration is often combined with other types of organization. One of these is classification.

There is a strong relationship among enumeration, classification, and definition. A classification divides something into all its parts, showing their levels of generality and their relationship to each other. For example, the tree diagram below classifies computer systems into hardware and software. These are at the same level of generality. Hardware is further classified into the computer and its peripherals; software is further classified into system software and applications software. These four items are at the same level of generality. In general, any item in a classification can be further classified into items at the next, more specific level of generality. The tree diagram shows four levels of generality.

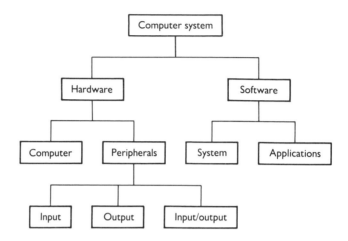

Any complete level of generality under one item in a classification forms an enumeration. For example, input devices, output devices, and input-output devices are an enumeration of the types of peripherals. It is possible to think of enumerations as horizontal slices of classifications.

Vertical slices of classifications yield definitions. The class of the definition is the level of generality immediately above the term to be defined. The characteristics are at the level of generality immediately below the term to be defined. For example, the following is a definition of *peripherals*, based on this classification of computer systems:

> A peripheral is a type of computer hardware that is used to input or output information.

Exercises

1. Make a tree diagram of the types of cities in the sea that are described in Chapter 5's reading passage.

2. The reading passage of Chapter 6 lists the following types of ocean pollution: sewage, plastics, toxic chemicals, oil, and heavy metals. The first of these is biodegradable, which means that natural processes can break it down quickly into less harmful substances. The other pollutants are non-biodegradable. Construct a tree diagram showing a classification of these substances. Then continue the classification as far as you can, using both the reading passage and your own knowledge.

Vocabulary Preview

Words in Context

The following words appear in this chapter's reading passage. Study them in their contexts and carry out the discussion tasks that follow.

cattle (n.)

The rancher bought ten new cows and a bull. His plan was to breed and sell *cattle*. He had to sell the animals when they were young, however. The cost of feeding fully grown *cattle* for a period of time can be significant.

Have you ever visited a ranch where cattle were raised? What is the meaning of the expression *to die like cattle*?

clone (n. or v.)

Nonsexual reproduction from a single parent is already possible with some species, such as frogs. Every *clone* produced in this way is absolutely identical to the parent.

Do you think that scientists should attempt to clone humans? Why or why not? Why do we sometimes say that some modern fashions, such as hair-styles, make people look like clones?

	correct (v. or adj.)
-ly (adv.)	correctly
-ive (adj.)	corrective
-ion (n.)	correction

There was something wrong with a valve in the patient's heart. The doctors decided that the problem had to be *corrected*. They performed *corrective* surgery to repair the valve.

Is it better for a teacher to correct all the mistakes in a student's paper, or to focus on a few serious mistakes? What is meant by *correct behavior*?

	desire (n. or v.)
-able (adj.)	desirable
un- (= *not*)	undesirable

Many medicines seem to have *undesirable* side effects. For example, some upset the stomach. Others make the patient sleepy. Still others can be habit-forming.

What is the thing you most desire?

device (n.)
devise (v.)

My grandfather was a talented tinkerer who liked to build useful machines to solve problems. Using an old vacuum cleaner, he once *devised* a trap that caught hornets as they flew in and out of their nest. Another time, he used two posts and a chain to *devise* a simple machine that was capable of lifting an automobile.

Have you ever devised a toy or a simple machine? What are some of your favorite devices?

	diverse (adj.)
-ity (n.)	diversity
-ify (v.)	diversify
-cation (n.)	diversification

I don't advise you to put all your money into the stock market. It might be better to *diversify*. Why not invest some of your money in stocks, some in real estate, and some in precious metals? That way you are probably less likely to lose everything.

Do you have only one hobby, or do you have several diverse hobbies? How similar or diverse are they?

	divide (v.)
sub-	subdivide
(=*under*)	
-sion (n.)	division
-ive (adj.)	divisive
-ly (adv.)	divisively
-ible (adj.)	divisible
in- (= *not*)	indivisible

The builder bought a large piece of land. Then he *subdivided* the land into a number of smaller pieces. He built houses on each of the smaller pieces and sold them for a large profit.

What is meant by *divide and conquer*?

	donate (v.)
-ion (n.)	donation
-or (n.)	donor

Former students collected money and *donated* it to the scholarship fund. This gift makes it possible for students without much money to attend the university. We are very grateful to the *donors* for their generous *donations*.

Should community organizations receive government money or private donations?

	ethics (n.)
-al (adj.)	ethical
-ly (adv.)	ethically

We depend on religion and philosophy to teach us the difference between right and wrong. In modern times, we often have to make *ethical* decisions about new advances in science.

Do you believe that people's ethical behavior can be changed by changing laws?

	mammal (n.)
-ian (adj.)	mammalian

Baby animals of many species get milk from their mothers' bodies. These are the *mammals,* and they include mice, cows, monkeys, and humans, among others.

Do you know any of the other characteristics of mammals? Name a mammal that lives in the sea.

	order (n. or v.)
dis-	disorder (n. or v.)
(= *undo*)	
-ed (adj.)	ordered
	disordered
-ly (adj.)	orderly
	disorderly

Everyone talks about how organized our neighbors are. They have such an *ordered* life that they do exactly the same things at the same time every day. Their garden has an *orderly* arrangement too. The plants are arranged according to size. The neighbors would be shocked to see the *disorder* in my house. But what can you expect in a house where there are six children and a dog?

What does it mean to *call a meeting to order*?

	parasite (n.)
-ic (adj.)	parasitic
-al (adj.)	parasitical
-ly (adv.)	parasitically

Large trees often have small plants growing out of them. These *parasitic* plants derive their water and nutrients from the large tree.

What do we mean when we refer to a person as a parasite?

	plant (n. or v.)
trans-	transplant (n. or v.)
(= *across*)	

We *planted* the small peach tree in back of the house, but it did not get enough sunlight there. So we dug it up and *transplanted* it to the front of the house.

Do you know anyone who has had a transplant operation?

	receive (v.)
	receipt (n.)
-ient (n.)	recipient

Every year the Nobel Prize is awarded to people who have made contributions to science, literature, and peace. The *recipients* are honored at special ceremonies in Sweden and Norway.

Have you ever been the recipient of a prize or award?

	succession (n.)
-ive (adj.)	successive
-or (n.)	successor

After Elizabeth I, there was a *succession* of unpopular kings in England. James I was considered to be weak. His son, Charles I, was put to death at the start of the civil war. Later Charles II became king, but he was forced to flee the country.

Have you ever had examinations on three successive days?

Discovering Word Meanings

Use (1) context clues; (2) your knowledge of prefixes, suffixes, and roots; and (3) a dictionary, if necessary, to discover the meanings of the italicized words in the following sentences from this chapter's reading passage.

1. These included the human growth hormone, which is helpful in treating certain kinds of growth defects in children, and an improved version of the *antibiotic* penicillin.

   (Use a dictionary to find the meanings of the parts of this word. What does an antibiotic do?)

2. Doctors use cortisone to treat *arthritis* and several other disorders.

   (From what language is the root of this word derived? What is the meaning of the suffix? Name other words that have the same suffix and discuss their meanings.)

3. Hemophilia is an often fatal disease in some men that prevents *blood clotting*.

   (Where will you look in the dictionary for the meaning of this phrase?)

Signal Words and Phrases

Study the following signal words and phrases that appear in this chapter's reading passage.

1. in fact

This phrase indicates that more specific or more emphatic information is being added to the immediately preceding statement or statements. Expressions with a similar meaning include *indeed*, and *as a matter of fact*.

> Many companies that have used genetic engineering have begun to make significant profits. *In fact*, genetic engineering is rapidly becoming the most important form of engineering.

2. whereby

This word introduces an explanation or tells how something is done. Expressions with a similar meaning include *by means of which* and *according to which*.

> Amniocentesis is a process *whereby* cells of an unborn human embryo are removed from the mother and tested for genetic defects.

Grammar Preview

Study the following excerpts or paraphrases from this chapter's reading passage, and work through the tasks.

1. The following sentences from the text contain parallel structures. Break each sentence into shorter, simpler sentences so that each contains only one of these structures.
   a. These techniques include treatments for diseases, methods for preventing diseases, and ways to aid the process of reproduction.
   b. Scientists have found ways not only to improve the use of yeasts but also to create new sources of nutrition.
   c. Processes similar to those used in food production and agriculture can also benefit the manufacturing industry by creating new products as well as new techniques for production.

2. Note the tense of each verb in the following paragraph from the text. Explain the reasons for the writer's choices of tense.

> Genetic engineering is such a new field that its potential is only beginning to be understood. Ever since the first product of genetic engineering—human insulin—was tested in 1980, the new technology has reached into many diverse fields. Many companies that have used genetic engineering have begun to make significant

profits. In fact, genetic engineering is rapidly becoming the most important form of engineering. Great advances are already being made in such fields as food production, industry, and medicine.

3. Punctuate the following texts correctly.
    a. Eventually new antibiotics such as tetracycline appeared in addition geneticists have learned how to use biotechnology to produce cortisone cheaply and in large quantities.
    b. Amniocentesis is a process whereby cells of an unborn human embryo are removed from the mother and tested for genetic defects by studying the chromosomes of these cells scientists can predict the chances that the unborn baby will suffer from certain genetic diseases in later life.

4. Break the following sentences into smaller sentences, according to the model.

    Another technique is cloning, which farmers and scientists may eventually use to produce offspring.

    Another technique is cloning. Farmers and scientists may eventually use cloning to produce offspring.

    a. Genetically engineered species will also benefit fruit and vegetable farming, which has made use of cloning and species mixing for many years.
    b. This technique brought about the Green Revolution, which greatly increased the food production of many Third World countries.
    c. Already they have created a nutritional substance called single-cell protein, which is commonly added to animal feeds.

5. Note each article (*a*, *an*, or *the*) in the following text, and explain why it is used in this context.

    However important genetic engineering may be for industry, its effects are likely to be still greater in the field of medicine. Medical biotechnology is providing both new medical substances and new medical techniques. Among the substances, the most important have been drugs, enzymes, and hormones. Human insulin, a hormone produced by genetically engineered bacteria, became, in 1982, the first genetically engineered product to be licensed for human use. The engineering of insulin was followed in quick succession by other genetically produced hormones and drugs. These included an improved version of the antibiotic penicillin.

Getting Ready to Read

The reading passage in this chapter is about the newest advances in the fields of biotechnology and genetic engineering. Some of these advances are available now. Others may be available in the near future. These advances are intended to benefit many fields, but the greatest benefits may be to agriculture, manufacturing, and medical science.

1. Think about the physical, mental, and emotional characteristics of the members of your extended family. What combination of these characteristics would you like your children to have? If a shopping list of these characteristics were available, would you want to design your children? Why or why not?

2. Is there a new medicine or medical technique available today that could have helped a member of your family or one of your friends if it had been available a few years ago?

3. Can you think of any dangers that could result from the discoveries or techniques that you mentioned in questions 1 and 2 above?

4. Scan the text to find the name of a painkiller that is more powerful than morphine.

5. Quickly skim through the reading passage looking for the beginnings of the main sections. Try to find these sections as quickly as possible. What are they?

Now read the passage to the end. As you read, note the different products and techniques that can be created by biotechnology and genetic engineering.

READING PASSAGE

Recent Advances in Biotechnology

1 Genetic engineering is such a new field that its potential is only beginning to be understood. Ever since the first product of genetic engineering—human insulin—was tested in 1980, the new technology has reached into many diverse fields. Many companies that have used genetic engineering have begun to make significant profits (Prentis, 1984, p. 14). In fact, genetic engineering is rapidly becoming the most important form of engineering. Great advances are already being made in such fields as food production, industry, and medicine.

2 The use of biogenetic° technology in food production can be divided roughly into two main categories: genetic agriculture and genetic food processing. The application of genetic engineering to agriculture can be further subdi-

Bio- *means life. Therefore,* biogenetic *is an adjective that means* _____.

vided into land-based techniques and techniques of aqua-
culture° and mariculture. Many of the most recent techniques of land-based agriculture are important in animal
farming, but some apply mainly to vegetable farming. A
few techniques are useful to both. Animal farming already
uses the process of in vitro fertilization to increase the
number of offspring. In this process, scientists remove the
egg from the female's body and fertilize it with sperm from
the male. After a few days, the egg is placed in the uterus
of the mother or of another female. In due time, the fetus
grows to term and has a normal birth. Another process
that farmers and scientists may eventually use to produce
offspring is cloning. In cloning, offspring develop from the
cells of one parent only and become physically identical to
that parent. Although it may be many years before it becomes possible to clone mammals, it is already possible to
clone some simpler creatures such as frogs. Farther into
the future, researchers hope to use a process called cell fu-
sion, or selfing, to produce offspring in a way that rapidly
identifies any undesirable genetic traits. Such traits could
then be corrected by genetic engineering. And research is
already producing new or improved species of cattle and
other farm animals (Office of Technology Assessment,
1982, pp. 177–79).

3   Genetically engineered species will also benefit fruit
and vegetable farming, which has made use of cloning and
species mixing for many years. The relatively simple process of grafting enables farmers to clone plants or to produce hybrids (mixtures) that are ideally suited to local conditions. This technique brought about the so-called Green
Revolution, which greatly increased the food production
of many Third World countries. The next major genetic
breakthrough in cereal crop production will perhaps be a
new species of wheat that does not require expensive fertilizers. Scientists are attempting to create wheat that is able
to absorb nitrogen directly from the air. This type of wheat
could grow in Third World countries that are too poor to
afford imported fertilizers (Prentis, 1984, p. 120).

4   Unlike genetic agriculture, genetic food processing
has used biotechnology for centuries. People have used
yeasts to ferment foods for at least six thousand years. Today genetic food technology has two main purposes: (1) to
create the modern sweeteners, flavors, and fragrances of
mass-produced convenience foods; and (2) to develop new
kinds of foods (Prentis, 1984, p. 141). Scientists have
found ways not only to improve the use of yeasts but also

*Aqua- means fresh water
in Latin. Therefore
aquaculture is similar to
mariculture, except
that _____.*

to create new sources of nutrition. In the near future, scientists expect to use the new technology to create completely new kinds of food. Already they have created a nutritional substance called single-cell protein, which is commonly added to animal feeds (Office of Technology Assessment, 1982, pp. 109–14).

5   Processes similar to those used in food production and agriculture can also benefit the manufacturing industry by creating new products as well as new techniques for production. Genes are used to make enzymes, and these in turn stimulate the chemical reactions that produce alcohol, methane, and many other substances, including plastics, fibers, rubber, leather, paper, starch, textiles, fertilizers, and pesticides. As techniques improve, the cost of producing such substances genetically will, in most cases, be lower than the costs of producing them by conventional methods (Prentis, 1984, pp. 157–62; Office of Technology Assessment, 1982, pp. 93–95).

6   Genetic techniques have found applications in at least two other important fields: the mining industry and pollution control. Miners could use genetically produced bacteria with appetites for heavy metals and oil to extract these minerals from mines and wells. Environmentalists could use such bacteria to clean up oil spills and other pollution (Prentis, 1984, pp. 166–68; Office of Technology Assessment, 1982, pp. 117–19).

7   However important genetic engineering may be for industry, its effects are likely to be still greater in the field

FIGURE 8–1   Making a meal of an oil slick.

of medicine. Medical biotechnology is providing both new medical substances and new medical techniques. Among the substances, the most important have been drugs, enzymes, and hormones. Human insulin, a hormone produced by genetically engineered bacteria, became, in 1982, the first genetically engineered product to be licensed for human use. The engineering of insulin was followed in quick succession by other genetically produced hormones and drugs. These included the human growth hormone, which is helpful in treating certain kinds of growth defects in children, and an improved version of the antibiotic penicillin. Eventually, new antibiotics such as tetracycline appeared. In addition, geneticists have learned how to use biotechnology to produce cortisone cheaply and in large quantities. Doctors use this substance to treat arthritis and several other disorders. To control pain, genetic engineering has yielded a group of chemicals called endorphins. These are twelve hundred times more powerful than morphine, but, unlike morphine, they are very safe to use. More recently, geneticists have learned how to produce an improved version of the enzyme L-asparaginase, a chemical used to treat leukemia (Prentis, 1984, pp. 57–63; Office of Technology Assessment, 1982, pp. 59–60).

8   Some of the most exciting work of biotechnologists, however, extends beyond the production of drugs, enzymes, and hormones into areas that science has only recently begun to understand. As scientists have learned more about the body's immune system, they have found new ways to engineer some of the human immunoproteins.° Among these are the interferons, which have been used successfully to treat some viral infections and cancers (Prentis, 1984, pp. 84–85; Office of Technology Assessment, 1982, pp. 70–71). Perhaps most promising of all, however, are the monoclonal antibodies, which are produced from identical, cloned cells. These antibodies are highly specific, and can seek out and destroy foreign viruses without attacking healthy parts of the organism. They may provide a way of transporting lethal anticancer chemicals to cancerous cells without harming nearby healthy cells (Crick, 1986, p. 8; Prentis, 1984, pp. 78–79). Monoclonal antibodies also allow scientists to make safe antiviral vaccines from the shells of viruses rather than from the viruses themselves.[1]

proteins produced by the body's immune system to attack diseases

[1] When a foreign invader such as a virus enters the body, the body's immune system produces cells called antibodies that attack and destroy the invader. Even if the virus is already dead, the immune system will pro-

9   Cyclosporin is another substance that genetic engineering may soon produce in large quantities. Doctors use it to modify the body's immune reaction to foreign proteins and viruses. It has been used successfully to treat auto-immune disease—a disorder in which the body's immune system attacks the body itself rather than a disease. Another use of cyclosporin is to prevent the bodies of organ transplant recipients from rejecting donor organs.

10   Even more revolutionary than the substances that genetic engineering has produced for the treatment of disease are the new genetic techniques. These techniques include treatments for diseases, methods for preventing diseases, and ways to aid the process of reproduction. In the near future, genetic engineering may provide weapons against many of the most terrible diseases of the Third World. Scientists are working on treatments for parasitic diseases, malaria, sleeping sickness, and even leprosy; they are also trying to find a genetic cure for sickle-cell anemia, a blood disorder that kills many black people every year (Prentis, 1984, pp. 88–95; see Figure 8–2).

11   In addition to fighting diseases, genetic engineering can help correct or prevent some of the mistakes of nature. A genetic engineering technique that holds great promise is the *planting* of corrective genes. Scientists have already successfully planted corrective genes in laboratory animals and in laboratory samples of human tissues. This technique uses harmless viruses to carry healthy genes to parts of the body, where they replace damaged genes. There is great hope that gene planting will soon be used to treat many genetic disorders, including hemophilia, an often fatal disease in some men that prevents blood clotting (Gene Research, 1986, p. 58).

12   One of genetic engineering's major contributions to health science is in the area of human reproduction. Amniocentesis is a process whereby cells of an unborn human

duce the necessary antibodies to fight it. Vaccines are made from dead viruses and injected into the body. The body reacts by producing the correct antibodies for that virus. If the living virus later attacks the body, the antibodies will destroy the virus before it has a chance to do any harm. Vaccines can sometimes be dangerous, however. There is always a small chance that the vaccine will contain a few live viruses that will cause the patient to get the disease. Using genetic engineering, scientists are learning how to overcome this danger by making only the protein shell of viruses. Since this shell is the only part of the virus that the antibody recognizes, vaccines containing the shells of viruses would be just as effective as those that contain the entire virus. If only the shells are used, there is far less chance that a living virus could get into the vaccine (Prentis, 1984, pp. 86–87).

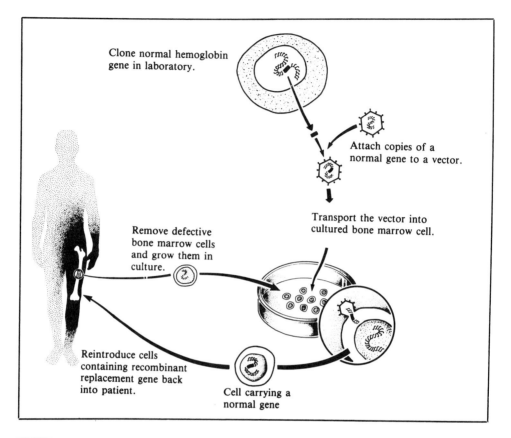

Clone normal hemoglobin
gene in laboratory.

Attach copies of a
normal gene to a vector.

Transport the vector into
cultured bone marrow cell.

Remove defective
bone marrow cells
and grow them in
culture.

Reintroduce cells
containing recombinant
replacement gene back
into patient.

Cell carrying a
normal gene

FIGURE 8–2   Basic steps in gene therapy for sickle-cell anemia. (Source: David Suzuki and Peter Knudtson (1988). *Genethics: The Ethics of Engineering Life.* (p. 195). Toronto: Stoddart Publishing Co. Limited. Reprinted with the permission of Stoddart Publishing Co. Limited, 34 Lesmill Rd., Don Mills, Ontario, Canada.)

embryo are removed from the mother and tested for genetic defects. By studying the chromosomes of these cells, scientists can predict the chances that the unborn baby will suffer from certain genetic diseases in later life. Another genetically devised process that has become useful in human reproduction is in vitro fertilization, mentioned earlier. By producing what have become known as "test-tube babies," the process has enabled some childless couples to have children of their own (Heredity, 1980).

13   As the advances in biotechnology occur at an ever-increasing rate, public attitudes toward recombinant DNA technology will have trouble keeping up with the latest knowledge. Polls indicate that a significant number of people have little understanding of current biotechnology (Mixed Views on Biotech, 1987). And the breakthroughs

are coming with such speed that education and the media will have difficulty keeping the public informed. A widening gap between scientific knowledge and public understanding could, at the very least, have serious ethical and legal consequences.

References

Crick, Francis (1986, July–August). The Challenge of Biotechnology. *The Humanist, 46*(4), 8–9, 32.

Gene Research: Gains and Goals (1986, July 28). *U.S. News and World Report, 101*(4), 58.

Heredity (1980). *Encyclopaedia Britannica* (15th ed.). Vol. 8, p. 816.

Mixed Views on Biotech (1987, June 5). *Science, 236,* 1179.

Office of Technology Assessment (1982). *Genetic Technology.* Boulder: Westview.

Prentis, S. (1984). *Biotechnology: A New Industrial Revolution.* London: Orbis.

_____

Checking Your Comprehension

1. According to some definitions, *agriculture* means the process of growing food on land. Compare this definition with the definition implied in paragraph 2 of the reading passage. Suggest a definition based on this paragraph.
2. Explain the process of in vitro fertilization.
3. Define *cloning* and *grafting*. How are they related?
4. How can genetic engineering be used to produce materials? What are the advantages of this technique? (Refer to Chapter 2.)
5. What are monoclonal antibodies, and how do scientists hope to use them?
6. How can genetic engineering help make safer vaccines?
7. What is gene planting?
8. Determine the level of importance that the author of the passage attaches to different areas affected by genetic engineering. Explain the reasons for your interpretation.

For Discussion

1. In the term *genetic engineering*, what is the significance of the word *engineering*? What does it have in common with other forms of engineering?
2. If you had the power to make the decision, would you prefer to encourage or to prevent advances in genetic engineering? Explain.

Analyzing the Structure

1. The thesis statement of this chapter's reading passage introduces a classification. What are the divisions and subdivisions of this classification? Show these in a tree diagram.
2. Analyze paragraph 3 in the reading passage in terms of unity and coherence. Refer specifically to each sentence of the paragraph. Identify the methods used to achieve unity and coherence, including the transition signals.

The Writing Process:
Transition Signals

We have seen that one of the ways to achieve coherence between the sentences in a paragraph is to use words that show a logical connection between two sentences. These words are often called *transitions* or *transition words*, and they include the signal words and phrases that appear in each chapter of this book. We shall refer to them here simply as *signals*. Notice how the coherence between the following two sentences is improved by the use of the signal *nevertheless*, which signals the contradiction between the two statements:

Without Transition

To prevent some of the dangers of genetic research, scientists have agreed to experiment only with relatively harmless substances. The potential for danger exists in every technological endeavor.

With Transition

To prevent some of the dangers of genetic research, scientists have agreed to experiment only with relatively harmless substances. *Nevertheless*, the potential for danger exists in every technological endeavor.

Signals may be used to show any of several different kinds of logical relationships between sentences. For example, the phrase *as a result* indicates that what came before the phrase is a cause of an event, action, or idea, and that what follows the phrase is a consequence of that cause. The following list indicates some of the most important relationships that can be shown by signals. Examples are included with each category.

Addition:	*moreover, furthermore*
Comparison:	*like, similarly*
Concession:	*despite, I admit that*
Condition:	*in that case, in that event*
Contrast:	*unlike, on the other hand*

Example: *for example, thus*
Inclusion: *among others, together with*
Interpretation: *apparently, it would appear*
Reference: *according to, as we have seen*
Restatement: *in brief, that is to say*
Result: *as a consequence, therefore*
Sequence: *first, a final*
Support: *indeed, as a matter of fact*
Time: *yesterday, soon*
Unexpected
  result: *however, nevertheless*

It is important to realize that the signals in any one category rarely have exactly the same meaning. Study the signal words and phrases in each chapter to find their meanings and to see how they are used in examples. A good dictionary will give you additional information and examples. You should also note that a signal can sometimes have more than one meaning and so can be included in more than one of these categories. For instance, *thus* can introduce an example, but it can also signal a result. When used to show a result, *thus* has a meaning similar to that of *therefore*.

An important part of the writer's task is to use signals effectively to help the reader proceed easily through the written text. Appropriate signals must, therefore, be placed wherever they are necessary. At the same time, however, the writer must be careful not to overuse them. Too many signals can be just as annoying or confusing to the reader as not enough. One of the best ways to find out how many signals you need and where you need them is to ask a reader. Therefore, when you are getting feedback about your first draft, you should ask specifically for feedback about signals.

As we have seen, the writer of the Amazon essay received feedback about his first draft to improve the essay's coherence (see Chapter 7). Now let us examine further improvements made by adding transition signals. In the version of the essay below, changes shown in the margin will replace the underlined passages.

> Failure to preserve the Amazon rain forest
> could have serious consequences for all living things.
>
> *It is estimated, for example, that one million*
> Some of these consequences are physical or biological. One million species of animal and plant life depend on the rain forests and on each other to survive. Without this ecosystem, these species, which live nowhere else on earth, would quickly become extinct. *would also speed up*
> Destroying the forests would speed up the

greenhouse effect, which may be causing the earth's temperature to rise at an alarming rate. The rain forests absorb a large amount of carbon dioxide. Scientists believe that this gas is partly responsible for the rising temperatures. Destroying the rain forests causes an increase in diseases such as malaria. As forests are cleared to make room for hydroelectric dams, large stagnant lakes are formed. These provide breeding grounds for malarial mosquitoes. The loss of the Amazon forests might cause a significant reduction in the amount of oxygen in the atmosphere. Without the earth's large forests, we might soon run out of air to breathe.

There are social and economic effects. The Amazon forests contain many of the world's rubber trees, which are a major source of income for people living in the area. These people would have to find other ways to make a living if the forest disappeared. The introduction of previously unknown diseases into the region affects the local people. One of these diseases is malaria. Poor people, who cannot easily get medicines, often have no protection against these diseases. Native peoples, whose tribes have lived for centuries in the area, are now being forced to move to escape disease and to find new sources of food as the forests disappear. Many of the native peoples are hunters and gatherers who are unable to change their way of life. They cannot find food in the areas where they must live. These people are dying from disease and starvation, and their cultures are vanishing.

A third consequence is the increase

A final physical consequence of the loss of the Amazon forests might be

There are social and economic effects as well.

An even more serious consequence is the introduction of previously unknown diseases, such as malaria, into the region.

In addition, native peoples,

However, many of the native peoples

The result is that these people are dying

Examine these changes carefully in order to understand why the writer made them and how they improve the coherence of the essay. Try to suggest other ways to improve the coherence by improving transitions.

Exercises

1. Study the above changes in the Amazon essay. Explain which ones mark enumerations, which one relates to the essay's organizing principle, and which ones clarify the meaning of one sentence in relation to another.
2. Write a short essay on the dangers to society of cloning human beings. After you finish the first draft, underline and review the transitions you have used. Exchange papers with another writer. Give and receive feedback about the transitions, and make any changes that are necessary.

Writing About Reading

1. In one paragraph, classify the main fields and genetic breakthroughs mentioned in the reading passage.

2. Write a short essay on the above topic. One way to do this is to allow each body paragraph to reflect one part of the classification.

3. Write an essay about the possible significance of genetic engineering for individuals or families faced with the following medical situations: AIDS, cancer, a hereditary disease, and reproductive problems. Make distinctions among these based on at least one of the following: degree of importance or difficulty, types of effects, differences in peoples' attitudes toward them, or any other distinction you think is valid.

4. Write an essay explaining how genetic engineering could revolutionize mariculture.

Chapter 9

Genetic Ethics

CHAPTER FOCUS

As you study this chapter, you should focus on the following important points:

Arrangement of information: language and patterns of classification

Vocabulary: understanding new words

Signal words and phrases: *clearly, meanwhile, of course, in other words, above all*

Sentence grammar: participles, transitions

Writing: introductions

Content: ethical questions related to genetic engineering

Arrangement of Information

Organization of the Content: Language and Patterns of Classification

Common Vocabulary and Expressions Used in Classification

Typically, a classification consists of three parts: (1) the items to be classified; (2) the group to which these items belong; and (3) a verb phrase that shows the relationship between the items and the group. Note the following example:

A computer system consists of hardware and software.

In this example, *computer system* is the group; *hardware* and *software* are the items; and *consists* is a verb showing the classifying relationship between the group and the items.

In addition to the parts of the classification, there are three things to consider when trying to express a classification: (1) Do you want to start with the separate items that are being classified or with the group to which these items belong? These are the two major kinds of classification. (2) Will you use the active voice or the passive voice? This will depend on the meaning of the verb you are using in your classification. (3) Is there a classifying agent either mentioned or implied; in other words, is there someone who is doing the classifying?

1. two main patterns of classification: starting with the items, or starting with the group

The following two patterns, and the examples after each, indicate the two main ways of structuring a classification. The first pattern begins with the items to be classified and shows their relationship to the group.

Pattern 1

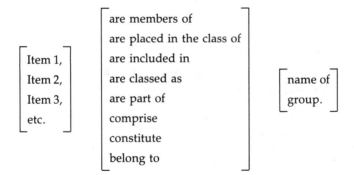

Example

Input devices, output devices, and input-output devices are classed as peripherals.

The second pattern begins with the group and shows its relationship to the items to be classified.

Pattern 2

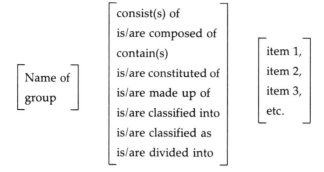

Example

Peripherals consist of input devices, output devices, and input-output devices.

2. use of active or passive voice

As you can see from the patterns given above, some expressions of classification use the active voice and some use the passive voice.

Active voice

Peripherals consist of input devices, output devices, and input-output devices.

Passive voice

Peripherals are divided into input devices, output devices, and input-output devices.

Clearly, for the purposes of classification it is important to understand the precise meanings of the classifying verbs. It is also important to know how to use the active and passive voices. Sometimes switching from active to passive voice makes it possible to change from pattern 1 to pattern 2.

Pattern 1

Input devices, output devices, and input-output devices comprise peripherals.

Pattern 2

Peripherals are divided into input devices, output devices, and input-output devices.

3. the classifying agent

The classifying agent is the person (or persons) doing the classification. There are three possibilities: (a) a classifying agent is clearly present; (b) a classifying agent is implied; or (c) there is no classifying agent.

a. A classifying agent is clearly present.

Botanists divide trees into deciduous and evergreen.

Botanists classify trees as deciduous and evergreen.

In these sentences the classifying agent is *botanists*. Note that this type of classification sentence belongs to pattern 2, since the group (trees) is mentioned before the types (deciduous and evergreen).

Pattern 1 may also indicate the presence of a classifying agent.

Pines, firs, and spruce, among others, are placed by botanists in the class of evergreen trees.

Pines, firs, and spruce, among others, are classed by botanists as evergreen trees.

b. A classifying agent is implied.

In many classifications, the classifying agent is implied but not named. Otherwise, these classifications are the same as the ones given above.

Pattern 1

Pines, firs, and spruce, among others, are placed in the class of evergreen trees.

Pines, firs, and spruce, among others, are classed as evergreen trees.

Pattern 2

Trees are divided into deciduous and evergreen.

Trees are classified as deciduous and evergreen.

If a classifying agent is named or implied, it is possible (but not necessary) to include the basis of the classification in the classifying sentence. The basis of the classification is the principle, rule, or method that was used to make the classification. It is usually expressed as a noun or noun clause. Pattern 2 is usually used.

| (Classification sentence, with agent named or implied) | $\begin{bmatrix} \text{in accordance with} \\ \text{on the basis of} \\ \text{according to} \\ \text{depending on} \end{bmatrix}$ | (Basis of the classification) |

Languages are classified into families *according to common roots of words.* (basis of classification = noun)

Trees are divided into deciduous and evergreen trees *on the basis of whether they lose their leaves in the winter.* (basis of classification = noun clause)

Computer scientists divide computer software into systems software and applications software *in accordance with the type of task it performs.* (basis of classification = nouns + adjective clause)

Note that these examples all imply or name a classifying agent.

c. There is no classifying agent.

In some classifications, a classifying agent is neither named nor implied. Classifications of this kind cannot include the basis of the classification. If there is no agent, the classifying verb will be *be* or some other verb that has the same meaning as *be* or *exist.* A precise knowledge of the meaning of the verb can help you decide whether it can have an agent.

Red, yellow, and blue are the primary colors.

Red, yellow, and blue constitute the primary colours.

The primary colors are red, yellow, and blue.

The primary colors consist of red, yellow, and blue.

Because of the meanings of the verbs in these classification sentences, no agent is possible. Therefore, no basis of the classification is possible. These sentences are stated as facts of nature, not as arrangements made by people.

Sentences beginning with *there are* can be used to classify. Because of the verb *be*, no agent is possible. Classification sentences beginning with *there are* belong to pattern 2. The names of the items often follow a colon or are listed in a second sentence.

There are three colors in the primary spectrum: red, yellow, and blue.

There are three colors in the primary spectrum. They are red, yellow, and blue.

Note that these sentences are equivalent to other pattern 2 sentences, such as the following:

The primary spectrum consists of three colors: red, yellow, and blue.

The primary spectrum consists of three colors. They are red, yellow, and blue.

The primary spectrum consists of red, yellow, blue.

Classification Terms

Learn the following words, which are often used to indicate larger and smaller groups within classifications: *family, group, subgroup, class, set, category, branch, division, subdivision, grade, rank, order, part, kind, type, variety, species.*

> English, Russian, Estonian, and many other languages of Europe belong to the family of Indo-European languages.

> Monkeys, apes, and man are included in the order primates.

Exercises

1. The following outline is a classification of types of ocean pollutants. Using this outline, write a classification sentence for each of the two main types of ocean pollution (Chapter 6). Rewrite each sentence so that you have one example from each of the two classification patterns.

   I. Ocean pollutants
   - A. Biodegradable
     1. Sewage
     2. Organic garbage
   - B. Nonbiodegradable
     1. Plastics
     2. Toxic chemicals
     3. Oil
     4. Heavy metals

2. The following outline is a classification of the main types of cities in the sea (Chapter 5). Using this outline, write classification sentences for each of the three main types of cities in the sea. Begin at least one of your sentences with *There are.*

   I. Marine Habitats
   - A. Free-floating
     1. Hong Kong houseboats
     2. New Venice
     3. Unabara
     4. Aquapolis
   - B. Attached
     1. Kobayashi's city
   - C. Submerged
     1. Conshelf I, II, III
     2. Sealab I, II
     3. Chalk's city

Vocabulary Preview

Words in Context

The following words appear in this chapter's reading passage. Study them in their contexts and write the correct forms of the words in the blanks in the exercises that follow. In some cases you may have to include another word, such as a preposition.

	apply (v.)
-cable (adj.)	applicable
-tion (n.)	application
mis-	misapplication
(= *faulty*)	

When the boy burned himself on the stove, his mother rubbed some medicine on the wound. Unfortunately, she did not _____ the medicine correctly. An infection was caused by this _____ , and the boy had to be treated by a doctor.

	critic (n.)
-al (adj.)	critical
-ally (adv.)	critically
-ize (v.)	criticize
-ism (n.)	criticism

Whenever you write something, it is a good idea to let another reader _____ it. Such an analysis of its strengths and weaknesses can help you to improve it. A person who can give good, constructive _____ is valuable to every writer.

	cure (n. or v.)
-able (adj.)	curable
in- (= *not*)	incurable
-ly (adv.)	incurably

One of the most terrible diseases of modern times is the AIDS virus, which leads to death within several years. Although some drugs are helpful in relieving certain symptoms of the disease, there is no effective _____ _____ AIDS. However, many previously _____ diseases can now be treated. Medical research-

ers hope to find a treatment for AIDS as well.

	dominate (v.)
-ion (n.)	domination
-ant (adj.)	dominant
-ance (n.)	dominance

All of history seems to have been a struggle for _____ .

Each country wanted to control all the others. History should teach

us that countries, like people, do not want to be

_____ _____ others.

	expect (v.)
-ant (adj.)	expectant
-ation (n.)	expectation

During the months of pregnancy, when a woman is _____ a

baby, she must be particularly careful about her own health. Choices

that _____ _____ mother makes can affect the

health of the baby.

	foresight (n.)
	foresee (v.)
-able (adj.)	foreseeable
-ly (adv.)	foreseeably
un- (= *not*)	unforeseen

If we could look into the future, we could _____ many

advances that will be made in the years ahead. But of course we

cannot see into the future. There is really no such thing as

"the _____ future."

	institute (n. or v.)
-ion (n.)	institution

Our city has two universities and four community colleges.

These _____ _____ higher learning receive most

of their funds from taxes. Unfortunately, these schools do not have

enough money to pay all their bills. Therefore, they will have

to _____ some new procedures designed to cut costs.

	law (n.)
out-	outlaw (n. or v.)
(= *out-*	legal (adj.)
side)	
il- (= *not*)	illegal
-ly (adv.)	legally
-ize (v.)	legalize
-ation (n.)	legalization

During the 1920s alcohol was _____ _____ the
United States. People caught buying or selling alcohol had to pay
fines or go to jail. The _____ against alcohol did not stop
people from drinking, however. After a few years, the government
again _____ the use of alcohol.

	mutate (v.)
-ant (adj.)	mutant
-ion (n.)	mutation

One reason it is so difficult to cure or prevent colds is that the viruses
that cause colds are always changing. These _____ are
very rapid and allow one kind of virus to become a slightly different
kind of virus. As a result, there are many kinds of colds.

	perfect (v. or adj.)
-ly (adv.)	perfectly
-ion (n.)	perfection

All people make mistakes. We are not _____. However, we
are all capable of striving for _____.

	pose (n. or v.)

Children usually do not like to _____ for a photograph. They
are too restless, and they get bored standing still. Yet a good photog-
rapher has ways to achieve an attractive _____.

	prison (n.)
-er (n.)	prisoner
im- (= *in*)	imprison (v.)
-ment (n.)	imprisonment

The criminal was tried and convicted in a court of law and

_____ for ten years. At the end of the period

_____ _____, the _____ was

allowed to leave _____ and go home.

	race (n.)
-ial (adj.)	racial
-ly (adv.)	racially
-ist (n.)	racist
-ism (n.)	racism

The color of the skin, the height of the jawbone, and the shape of the

eyes are often characteristics of one's _____ .

_____ similarities are usually much more evident than indi-

vidual differences.

	rapid (adj.)
-ly (adv.)	rapidly
-ity (n.)	rapidity

Many technologically advanced countries have high-speed rail trans-

portation. The trains move _____ _____ one city

to another. In general, the _____ _____ modern

travel does not allow us to relax and to enjoy the trip.

	revoke (v.)
-able (adj.)	revocable
ir- (= *not*)	irrevocable
-ation (n.)	revocation

If a driver causes accidents, his or her license to drive may

be _____. This _____ _____ the license

may be for a specified period of time, or it may be permanent.

	spontaneous (adj.)
-ly (adv.)	spontaneously
-ness (n.)	spontaneousness
-ity (n.)	spontaneity

Never leave oily rags lying around. Sometimes they begin to burn

without any obvious cause. Such _____ combustion, as it

is called, is the cause of many house fires. Some people plan everything in advance. This lack _____ _____ removes
the uncertainty but also much of the joy of life.

trait (n.)

We admire many of the characteristics of our friends. Some of
these _____ may include helpfulness, generosity, and
sympathy.

undergo (v.)

She told us about her experiences during the war. She was forced
to _____ a long, difficult march across the country with
several other women prisoners. She and the other prisoners
_____ many hardships.

Discovering Word Meanings

Use (1) context clues; (2) your knowledge of prefixes, suffixes, and roots; and
(3) a dictionary, if necessary, to discover the meanings of the italicized words
in the following sentences from this chapter's reading passage.

1. "The developments are having an impact on the whole *spectrum* of life
   processes, including forestry, agriculture, dentistry and medicine."

   (What is the origin of this word? What is its literal meaning? What is the
   meaning in this context?)

2. Transplant surgery involving many different organs is now possible and
   can often extend the patient's *lifespan*.

   (Look up the word *span* in a dictionary. Which of its several meanings
   combines with *life* in this context?)

3. Genetic engineering will eventually enable scientists to create *humanoids*
   that could be used as a source of spare organs.

   (What meaning does the suffix *-oid* have in the word *spheroid*? How does
   this suffix change the meaning of *human*?)

Signal Words and Phrases

Study the following signal words and phrases that appear in this chapter's reading passage.

1. clearly

The idea that follows *clearly* is considered to be very easy to understand or to solve. A word with a similar meaning is *obviously*.

Food production is increasing linearly. Population is increasing exponentially. *Clearly*, we must control population or find new sources of food, or many people will starve.

2. meanwhile

This signal, which appears between statements about two events, shows that the events are happening, or have happened, at the same time. A phrase with a similar meaning is *in the meantime*.

Educators and governments are trying to inform people about AIDS in an effort to prevent it. *Meanwhile*, medical researchers are trying to find a cure for this dreaded disease.

3. of course

This signal may mean *clearly* or *obviously* as explained in example 1 above. Otherwise, it may introduce a well-understood concession that seems to contradict the main idea. A word with a similar meaning is *naturally*.

Every year taxes are raised higher and higher until the average person is no longer able to maintain a comfortable life style. *Of course*, we recognize that taxes are necessary. But they should be reasonable and within the means of the taxpayer.

4. in other words

This signal is usually used to restate an important point more simply, so that it will be easier to understand. It may also be used to introduce an interpretation or an example relevant to the previous point. Other phrases with a similar meaning include *that is* and *that is to say*.

Soon doctors will be able to give us a list of all our genetic weaknesses. *In other words*, they will be able to tell us what genetic diseases we are most likely to get.

5. above all

This signal is used to introduce the most important (and usually the last) item in an enumeration. A phrase with a similar meaning is *most importantly*.

Suzuki lists several ethical guidelines for genetic engineers. *Above all,* he recommends that we should always be open to new ideas about life.

Grammar Preview

Study the following excerpts or paraphrases from this chapter's reading passage, and work through the tasks.

1. Explain the meaning of each italicized passage in the following sentences.

   Some critics worry that *mutating* organisms, *created by science,* could get out of control, *spreading new, incurable diseases* or *destroying agricultural crops.*

   A risk of genetic agriculture is that genetically *engineered* species may mix with natural species.

   Microorganisms can be altered to perform *desired* functions.

   Transplant surgery *involving* many different organs is now possible.

2. Explain the meanings of the italicized words in this context. How do these words improve the coherence of the passage?

   In some Third World societies, boys are prized more highly than girls. When amniocentesis shows that a fetus is female, parents sometimes prefer to end the pregnancy. *As a consequence,* some governments have outlawed amniocentesis. *However,* nothing prevents the expectant mothers from going elsewhere to have the test performed. *It is likely* that algeny will soon provide a solution to this problem by allowing parents to decide what sex the baby should have. *Again, however,* this practice would present serious ethical concerns that must be dealt with before such a procedure could be permitted.

Getting Ready to Read

The reading passage in this chapter is about some of the ethical concerns that many people have about genetic engineering.

1. What dangers or disadvantages do you see in genetic engineering? Can these dangers or disadvantages be overcome?

2. Should genetic engineering be controlled by governments, industries, scientists, churches, or others? Or should it be abolished?

3. Scan the article quickly to find: (a) the names of the experts whose views form the conclusion of the passage; (b) the author and date of *Frankenstein;* (c) the profession of Louis Siminovitch; and (d) the profession of Robin Marantz Henig.

4. The reading passage discusses some of the possible negative effects of genetic engineering on several fields. Quickly skim through the article to find out what fields these are.

5. Approximately what proportion of the references for this reading passage is to newspaper articles? How recent is most of the information?

Now read through this chapter's reading passage, "Genetic Ethics." Note: (1) the disadvantages of genetic engineering in several fields; (2) the ethical concerns that many people have about genetic engineering; and (3) recommendations for meeting some of these concerns.

Genetic Ethics

1 The promises of genetic engineering seem almost limitless. In only a few years scientists have developed methods for improving agricultural yields, producing valuable new substances and materials, and predicting which diseases a person is likely to get in later life. Even more remarkably, medical researchers have been able to locate the genes responsible for nearly six hundred genetic diseases (Mallovy, 1988, p. 17). Locating these genes is the first step toward repairing or replacing them and thus preventing the diseases they cause. As Louis Siminovitch, director of Toronto's Mt. Sinai Research Institute, observes,

> We are in the midst of a golden age of biological and medical research. Advances are occurring with amazing rapidity, and the opportunities and challenges are unprecedented. The developments are having an impact on the whole spectrum of life processes, including forestry, agriculture, dentistry and medicine (Mallovy, 1988, pp. 16-17).

2 Together with the many benefits of genetic research, however, are the dangers and risks involved whenever scientists tamper with the basic structures of life. In the early days of recombinant DNA technology, many books and movies appeared that warned of the dangers of genetic ex-

periments gone wrong. They depicted creatures that were half-human and half-animal, gigantic mutant insects, and new strains of deadly viruses that resisted all treatment. Nor was this fear of genetic havoc restricted to the science fiction of the twentieth century. As early as 1818 Mary Shelley wrote *Frankenstein,* the book that became the most famous genetic horror story of all time. In it, a genetically created human monster attacks and destroys his own creator. All technologies have the capacity to produce evil as well as good, and genetic engineering is no exception. In an attempt to limit the dangers of genetic research, scientists from all over the world have drafted a list of guidelines for recombinant DNA experiments. They have agreed to work only with relatively harmless substances and to develop strains of bacteria that cannot exist outside laboratory conditions. In this way they have prevented early fears from becoming reality. There can be no doubt, however, that the potential for danger exists in this, as in every technological endeavor. Together with benefits, genetic engineering brings with it a number of dangers and risks, and some of these lead to fundamental ethical concerns.

3   One of the most significant risks of genetic agriculture, for example, is the possibility that genetically engineered species will mix with natural species. Scientists are not able to predict the results of such a mixing, which could cause a fundamental change in the definition of life. Many genetically engineered species have already been produced, so the danger of such mixing is high (Gooderham, 1989, p. A14). For example, scientists have successfully engineered a new species of carp, a fish that is popular in many parts of the world. This new species contains a growth gene from another kind of fish, the rainbow trout. The new kind of carp grows twenty percent faster than ordinary carp. The same kind of technology can be used on many different species of fish, perhaps allowing scientists to turn entire bays, or even oceans, into mariculture farms (Schneider, 1989). What does the future hold for such "improved" species? Will they destroy all the other fish in the oceans? And when only the engineered species are left, will these die out from some genetic weakness that scientists had not foreseen? Clearly, it is dangerous to play such games with nature.

4   At least three serious objections may be raised against genetically altered species. First, the new species could force many farmers and fishermen out of business. Next, the existence of such species could have a harmful

effect on the balance of nature. Finally, genetic techniques could cause animals to suffer (Schmeck, 1988). An experiment in the United States that demonstrates some of these objections is the injection of an engineered growth hormone into cows to make them produce more milk. Such cows regularly produce three times as much milk as normal cows. If the government permits this technique to be used commercially, however, fewer cows will be needed, and many dairy farmers will lose their businesses. There are also indications that the technique may be harmful to the cows themselves and possibly even to the people who drink the milk that these cows produce (Schneider, 1988).

5   Another major user of genetic engineering techniques is the manufacturing industry. Genetic manufacturing, however, could pose even more serious threats than genetic agriculture. In agriculture, clearly identifiable species such as cows and carp are altered to make them more profitable. In manufacturing, on the other hand, microorganisms—very small forms of life—are altered so that they will produce desired substances or perform desired functions. Because these creatures are too small to be seen without microscopes, and because they tend to reproduce rapidly, their potential for creating hazards is great. Therefore, governments of such countries as the United States, where much genetic research is taking place, are establishing guidelines and appointing panels to control such research. Meanwhile, critics are questioning the efficacy of

FIGURE 9–1   Supercow corners the job market.

these guidelines and are pointing to the potential harm that genetically altered microbes might cause if they are released into the environment. One of the greatest dangers of modified microorganisms, the critics point out, is their tendency to undergo spontaneous mutations. When organisms mutate spontaneously, they change into different organisms without any outside influence. The changed organisms may be much more dangerous than the original, genetically altered ones. Some critics worry that mutating organisms, created by science, could get out of control, spreading new, incurable diseases or destroying agricultural crops (Field Test, 1989).

6   The area of greatest concern to critics of genetic engineering is, of course, medical science, for genetic medicine would affect people directly by altering human genes. Even critics who are not greatly concerned about the genetic manipulation of livestock or bacteria are likely to be worried about the possible effects of genetic engineering on people. Algeny, the use of genetic engineering to cure or prevent disease, is a new science, but there is no doubt that it will soon come of age. How will algeny affect medical practice and medical ethics? Two examples will illustrate some of the dangers and ethical concerns involved.

7   One of the fastest growing fields of medicine is transplant surgery, in which an organ from one person is placed into the body of another. Transplant surgery involving many different organs is now possible, and can often extend the patient's lifespan and improve the quality of life. As a result, there is a large demand for replacement organs. However, relatively few such organs are available. The shocking evidence suggests that in some countries children are being kidnapped and killed in order to provide an illegal source of organs. At the same time, to get desperately needed money, poor people in some Third World countries are selling spare organs, such as kidneys, from their own bodies (Taylor, 1989). Obviously, there are serious social, economic, and ethical concerns surrounding these activities. These concerns will be complicated by algeny and genetic engineering. For one thing, genetic techniques will enable doctors to predict the kinds of diseases that a person is likely to experience later in life. People will be able, therefore, to plan for these diseases. But even more remarkably, genetic engineering will eventually enable scientists to create humanoids that could be used as a source of spare organs. These creatures may contain human hearts, kidneys, lungs, and other organs. Such genet-

ically produced sources of human organs could eliminate the illegal trade in the body parts of children and the poor; however, this use of humanoids would present a completely new set of ethical problems to be debated and resolved.

8   Another example of a genetic technique that may soon have implications for genetic ethics is amniocentesis, a procedure for determining the sex of a fetus. In some Third World societies in which boys are prized more highly than girls, mothers who do not want to give birth to a girl occasionally use this technique to determine whether or not to have an abortion. As a consequence, some governments have outlawed amniocentesis. However, nothing prevents the expectant mothers from going elsewhere to have the test performed (Weisman, 1988). It is likely that algeny will soon provide a solution to this problem by allowing parents to decide what sex the baby should have. By changing the genes on a single chromo-

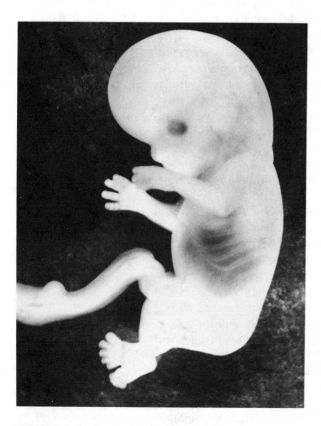

FIGURE 9–2 A two-month-old human fetus.

some, the sex of a baby could be changed while it is still in the womb. Again, however, this practice would present serious ethical concerns that must be dealt with before such a procedure could be permitted.

9   In dealing with the ethical concerns of algeny and genetic engineering, Jeremy Rifkin (1983) points to the branch of recombinant DNA technology called eugenics. Eugenics is concerned with using biotechnology to remove biologically undesirable characteristics and to make genetic changes that will improve an organism or species. Rifkin refers to the eugenics movement in the United States early in this century, long before genetic engineering was born. In the 1920s some federal and state laws were instituted that identified certain racial and genetic traits as being inferior to others. Under these laws thousands of American citizens were required to be sterilized so that they could not pass on these traits (Rifkin, 1983, p. 229). An even more drastic eugenics program was imposed by the government of Nazi° Germany in the 1930s and 1940s. Millions of Jews and others were treated as being racially inferior and were imprisoned and killed (Rifkin, 1983, p. 230). In addition, unspeakable° medical experiments were performed on many of these prisoners. In recent years, according to Rifkin, eugenics has once again become a popular idea. This new interest in eugenics is apparently more commercial than racial, however, and is directed at improved economic performance and quality of life (Rifkin, 1983, p. 231). It seems that every age and society has its own ideas about what is desirable and good. And if we do not know what perfection is, what will our moral obligations be when it lies within our power to alter the human species? Rifkin asks, for example, whether a parent will have the right to refuse genetic engineering of his or her unborn children. Will the parent be guilty of a crime if the children get a genetic disease that could have been prevented by biotechnology (Rifkin, 1983, p. 232)?

Nazi *refers to the government of Germany around the time of the Second World War.*

so bad that nothing could be worse and that it is almost impossible to mention

10   Soon, as medical writer Robin Marantz Henig (1989) points out, doctors will be able to give us a list of all our genetic weaknesses. In other words, they will be able to tell us what genetic diseases we are most likely to get and how we will probably die. Even before biotechnology provides us with treatments for these diseases, however, we will have ethical choices to make. Most importantly, society will have to decide who is allowed to use personal genetic information and for which purposes this information may be used. Henig (1989, p. 20) asks, ''Will the presence of a faulty gene be enough to prevent full access to school-

ing, health care, employment and the other rights and privileges of society?'' She notes further that genetic information about individuals poses two important concerns. ''The first is whether knowledge of the information is itself potentially hazardous to the individual; the second, whether institutions will misuse that knowledge to foster their own dominance and control.'' There is a very real fear that in the near future employers will demand to know the genetic profiles of their workers. They may fire or refuse to hire people with certain genetic weaknesses. Insurance companies may not sell insurance to people who have a high genetic risk of getting cancer or some other serious disease. Schools may refuse to admit children whose genetic profiles indicate behavioral problems or learning disabilities. Henig points out that such discrimination already exists. In one case, an insurance company refused to renew the policy of a driver whose genetic profile indicated the possibility of getting a rare nervous disease in later life. At the time the insurance policy was revoked, the driver had no symptoms of illness and had been driving for twenty years without accidents or tickets (Henig, 1989, p. 22).

11   In view of these and other ethical considerations involving eugenics, Rifkin asks society to consider seriously whether science should be thinking about genetic engineering of human beings at all. He wonders whether we have misplaced our values about life and have forgotten that being human means more than being a well engineered machine (Rifkin, 1983, p. 233). In an attempt to ensure that bioengineering can continue without posing a threat to people and societies, Suzuki and Knudtson (1988, pp. 345–348) have proposed ten ethical principles for dealing with genetic engineering. Among these principles are the need for understanding genes and what they do, the possible applications and misapplications of genetic techniques, and the need for privacy concerning an individual's genetic profile. In addition, they stress the importance of the diversity of living species, and insist that the genes that define a species and determine genetic traits are not the property of individuals and must not be changed without the consent of all members of the society. Above all, they indicate that we must always be ready to receive new ideas about life, ethics and humanity—not only from science, but also from art, philosophy, and religion. And we must look for these ideas not only in our own culture but also in all other cultures and throughout all periods of history.

References

Field Test of Gene-Altered Organisms Backed (1989, September 22). *New York Times*, p. 12.

Gooderham, M. (1989, October 23). Aquacultural Team Fishing for Pedigree Catch. *Toronto Globe and Mail*, p. A14.

Henig, Robin Marantz (1989, December 24). High-Tech Fortune Telling. *New York Times Magazine*, pp. 20–22.

Mallovy, N. (1988). A Golden Age of Biological and Medical Research. *University of Toronto Magazine, 16*(2), 14–17.

Rifkin, Jeremy (1984). *Algeny: A New Word–A New World*. Harmondsworth, England: Penguin.

Schmeck, H. M., Jr. (1988, December 27). Gene-Altered Animals Enter New Commercial Era. *New York Times*, p. C1.

Schneider, K. (1988, June 12). Biotechnology's Cash Cow. *New York Times Magazine*, pp. 44–47, 52–53.

Schneider, K. (1989, June 12). A Designer Fish Raises Fears for Nature As We Know It. *New York Times*, p. E4.

Suzuki, David, & Knudtson, P. (1988). *Genethics*. Toronto: Stoddart.

Taylor, P. (1989, August 22). Kidneys Sold by Poor for Transplants, MD Says. *Toronto Globe and Mail*, pp. A1, A15.

Weisman, S. R. (1988, July 20). State in India Bars Fetus-Sex Testing. *New York Times*, p. A1.

Checking Your Comprehension

1. Why do geneticists want to locate the genes that are responsible for a number of diseases?
2. How do the early fictional treatments of genetic engineering relate to the problems that we currently face?
3. What have scientists done to combat the dangers of genetic experiments?
4. What are the primary dangers inherent in creating new species and altering existing species?
5. How could genetic manufacturing be more dangerous than genetic agriculture?
6. What are spontaneous mutations, and how could such mutations pose a threat?
7. What is algeny, and what kinds of ethical concerns would it present? Explain the relationship of algeny to eugenics.
8. Describe the main ethical concerns of transplant surgery and amniocentesis. Indicate what new concerns could arise as a result of genetic engineering.

For Discussion

1. In your view, what steps should be taken to protect society from the possibly harmful effects of genetic research?

2. Suppose that you or a loved one were dying from a disease for which genetic engineering might soon provide a cure. How would this change the answer you gave to the previous question?
3. If you were an employer, what would be your attitude toward hiring people with genetic defects?
4. Do you think public money should be used to educate people who are going to die shortly after they finish school?
5. Which of the ethical problems discussed in this essay seems most serious to you? Why?

Analyzing the Structure

1. What is the thesis statement of the reading passage, and how does the introduction prepare the reader for this thesis statement?
2. How does the thesis statement relate to the information contained in the body of the essay?
3. What arrangement of information did the author of the reading passage use?
4. Explain the use of the following transitions: (a) *In this way* (paragraph 2); (b) *Clearly* (paragraph 3); (c) *however* (paragraph 5); and (d) *on the other hand* (paragraph 5).

The Writing Process: Introductions

After you have written your first draft of an essay and revised it with the help of a reader, it is time to write an introduction and a conclusion, or to improve the existing introduction and conclusion. You will learn more about writing conclusions in Chapter 10.

An introduction should do several things. First, it should show the relationship or relevance of the thesis statement to an issue or issues that are slightly more general. This places the subject of the essay in a context of facts or ideas. Another function of an introduction, which is really a part of the first function, is to show why the thesis statement is important. The introduction should also explain any words or ideas in the thesis statement that might be unfamiliar to the reader. Finally, the introduction should catch the reader's interest. The extent to which an introduction performs these functions depends on who the readers of an essay will be. The writer must keep in mind the reader's interests and what the reader already knows about the subject, and how to relate the essay to those interests and to that knowledge.

It is important to be clear about what belongs in the introduction rather than in the body of the essay. The introduction sets the stage by showing why the topic is interesting or important, and by giving background information necessary to understand the topic. It does not give specific information on the topic itself. The inclusion of such specific information is a signal that the structure of the essay might need revision.

Introductions can also vary in length, from a single introductory sentence to several paragraphs or pages. A sense of proportion is important here, as it would be strange to have a five-paragraph introduction to an essay with only two body paragraphs.

There are also several strategies that a writer can use to accomplish the purposes of an introduction. Among other things, an introduction can describe a problem, give a brief history of a situation, describe the situation, describe a place, define words, tell a story, or discuss a quotation. In any event, it must move smoothly from the slightly more general issues to the thesis statement. As a result, the thesis statement is often the last sentence or combination of sentences in the introduction.

Now let us look at the introduction to the rain forest essay (see Chapter 1). When the writer began to develop this essay, he began with the general idea of the environment and then narrowed it down until he arrived at his thesis statement. To write his introduction, he returned to several of the more general issues and moved step by step toward the thesis statement, as follows:

- How living things depend on each other in order to survive
- The ecosystems of tropical rain forests
- The Amazon rain forest
- The destruction of the Amazon rain forests
- The consequences of that destruction (thesis statement)

The writer also had to consider who the readers of his essay would be and how much they would know about the subject. High school and university readers would know where the Amazon is, but some general readers might not be sure. Both groups might lack knowledge about rain forests. The introduction, therefore, refers to ''the Amazon River Basin in Brazil,'' and contains a brief explanation of what rain forests are and what they do. The geographical reference is brief to avoid insulting the intelligence of knowledgeable readers.

The following is the final version of the introduction to the rain forest essay. This introduction, also shown in Chapter 1, was revised according to feedback from a reader.

> Living things often depend on each other to survive. In some places, such as the oceans and the tropical forests, thousands of species may be living together in this way. These living creatures also interact with the nonliving, or inorganic, things around them. Such areas of close interdependence in nature are known as ecosystems. These ecosystems, however, do more than support the plants and animals that live in them. They also influence the environment of the entire planet. The ecosystems of tropical rain forests, for example, protect the entire planet by returning water to the air as vapor and by providing much of the oxygen that we breathe. One of the largest of these is the rain forest of the Amazon River Basin in Brazil. This forest is almost as large as the United States. It protects many unique species, and it plays a major role in controlling the

earth's atmosphere and weather. However, it is being destroyed to provide farm land. Little is being done to prevent this destruction. Many people do not seem to understand that the failure to preserve the Amazon rain forest could have serious consequences for all living things.

Exercises

1. Explain whether you think that the introduction to the rain forest essay fulfills all the requirements and purposes of an introduction as outlined above. Be specific.
2. Write a short essay on the topic "Choosing Genes for Reproduction or Replacement." When you are ready to write an introduction to your essay, consider the information about introductions given above. Write the first draft of your essay, including the introduction. Then exchange your essay with your neighbor's, and give and get feedback in order to improve your introductions.

Writing About Reading

1. Sketch a simple tree diagram, classifying the kinds of problems that could arise from genetic engineering. Then write one paragraph based on your tree diagram.

2. Write a short essay on the above topic. One way to achieve this is to devote one body paragraph to each of the branches in your tree diagram.

3. Write a short essay on the topic "Advantages and Disadvantages of Genetic Engineering." (Note that this topic is very general. Therefore, narrow the topic before beginning to plan and write your essay. For instance, you could focus on the advantages and disadvantages of genetic engineering in medicine, in agriculture, etc.) Use any methods of organization that are appropriate.

4. Write an essay on the topic "Genetic Engineering and Exploitation of the Seas."

Children watching TV at Sears.

UNIT FOUR

Media

The speed and ease of communication in North American society are perhaps the greatest influences on its contemporary culture. Information—in words, pictures, and music—can travel with lightning speed around the world. This information is carried in various ways, and each of these ways, or channels, is called a *medium.*[1] Some of these channels carry public information, and these are referred to as *the media.* Included in the media are newspapers, magazines, books, radio, and television. The first three are sometimes called the print media, while the latter are called the electronic media.

This unit contains three chapters that focus mostly on the medium of television. The first two chapters are taken from *Amusing Ourselves to Death: Public Discourse in the Age of Show Business,* a book by Neil Postman. The third chapter is taken from an article by Susan Chira in the *New York Times* entitled "Reading, Writing and Broadcast News."

Chapters 10 and 11 present parts of the overall argument of Postman's book. Each of them illustrates how that argument affects an area of public discourse. Chapter 10 discusses television news programs as a form of entertainment. Chapter 11 argues that television has become the model for conducting classroom teaching as a form of entertainment. Chapter 12 reports on the introduction of television news programs to the classroom.

Although some paragraphs of the original publications have been omitted, as indicated by ellipses (. . .) in the texts, the language of the material presented here has not been altered. These selections will give you an opportunity to read and analyze material written for educated readers who are native speakers of English.

---

[1]*Medium* is the singular form of *media.* Thus we say, "The *media are* carriers of modern culture. The most important *medium* today *is* television."

Chapter 10

Television News: "Now . . . This"[1]

CHAPTER FOCUS

As you study this chapter, you should focus on the following important points:

Arrangement of information: making an argument

Vocabulary: understanding new words

Signal words and phrases: *as such, at the very least, in any case, then, in short*

Sentence grammar: parallelism; passive voice

Writing: conclusions

Content: how television news as entertainment influences public discourse and people's understanding of world events

Arrangment of Information

Organization of the Content: Argument

The word *argument* can be used in at least two senses. One can *have an argument*, or one can *present or make an argument*. When people have opposing ideas about a topic, they might have a heated and sometimes angry discussion about it, i.e., they might *have an argument* during which each participant tries to persuade the others that his or her ideas are the better ones. Often, however, *having an argument* has more to do with emotions than with ideas.

---

[1]The title and the reading passage of this chapter are taken from *Amusing Ourselves to Death* (Chap. 7, pp. 99–113) by Neil Postman. Copyright © 1985 by Neil Postman. Reprinted by permission of Viking Penguin, a division of Penguin Books USA, Inc.; London: Methuen.

To *make an argument* also means that one tries to persuade others to accept one's ideas or position on a topic. But the statement of these ideas or this position is usually more logical, carefully organized, and supported by relevant evidence.

It is not always easy to tell the difference between argument, which presents a point of view, and exposition, which presents information. One reason is that before someone can make an argument, he or she must explain the subject of the argument, that is, the person must use exposition. Another reason is that it is possible to use exposition to report an argument to a listener or reader without intending to persuade. Part of the process of understanding a text is being able to distinguish exposition from argument.

Giving Reasons

Essentially, argument involves giving reasons for a point of view. A simple statement of a position can be accomplished in a single sentence. For example, someone who opposes capital punishment might say, "I am against capital punishment because I believe that a civilized society should not kill even a murderer." Here the statement of position is "I am against capital punishment." The reason given is the belief of the speaker. To persuade a listener or reader, however, more extended argument is usually needed. This includes identifying reasons for taking a certain position and presenting information to support those reasons. As an example, below are five reasons and the kinds of supporting evidence that might be given in making an argument against capital punishment:

1. a. **Reason:** the wrong person may have been convicted of the crime
   b. **Supporting information:** examples of wrongful convictions for murder

2. a. **Reason:** capital punishment does not deter murderers
   b. **Supporting information:** statistics that show that the murder rate is the same with or without capital punishment, or even higher with capital punishment

3. a. **Reason:** capital punishment is an act of revenge
   b. **Supporting information:** quotations from interviews with courtroom spectators at murder trials

4. a. **Reason:** social conditions are the real cause of most crime
   b. **Supporting information:** statistics that show the murder rate under various social conditions; comments of social workers and prison psychiatrists

5. a. **Reason:** capital punishment is judicial murder
   b. **Supporting information:** comparison of capital punishment to premeditated murder, using legal definitions of murder

Kinds of Evidence

As the example above shows, several kinds of information constitute evidence to support a point of view on a topic. Among these are facts, statistics, personal observations, statements by authorities, and examples. These are the same kinds of information that support any thesis statement or topic sentence, but in an argument they are used to support the reasons that in turn support the speaker's or writer's point of view. Notice that while it is acceptable to use the opinions of authorities as supporting evidence, it is not acceptable to use unsupported opinions of the speaker or writer.

Although an argument may have been made by using supporting evidence, it is important to judge the quality of that evidence. For example, if facts or statistics are presented, they may have been selected because they support the argument, while other information that contradicts the argument may have been omitted; authorities who are quoted may not be prominent or respected in their fields; well-known personalities may be quoted on matters in which they have little or no expertise; or examples may be interesting but irrelevant to the point they are supposed to illustrate.

In addition to the improper use of supporting evidence, there are many faulty ways of constructing an argument. These are called logical fallacies. Here we can call attention to only a few of them.

Equivocation. The meanings of words change according to context. When the meaning of a word or phrase shifts from one part of an argument to another, the argument is likely to be faulty:

> Equality is said to be one of the great ideas behind democratic forms of government. But the fact that people are not born equal makes a mockery of this principle.

This argument is equivocal because the meanings of *equality* and *born equal* are not the same in this context. *Equality* here probably means being equal before the law, while *born equal* means having the same potential at birth.

Oversimplification: Black-or-White Fallacy. Oversimplification is a general category that includes several fallacies. All of these involve leaving out some kind of relevant information. The black-or-white fallacy consists in arguing that only extremes are important and that smaller differences can be ignored:

> Someone argues that A and B are equally objectionable because A's drinking is done to improve social relationships at parties, but B's drinking has caused him to lose several jobs.

This argument ignores differences of degree and insists that only the strict fact of being a drinker counts in each case.

Oversimplification: Straw Man Fallacy. The person who commits this fallacy knocks down his opponent's weakest argument and ignores the others:

Speaker A: The new Italian film is not worth seeing. In the first place, the subtitles are a nuisance. Secondly, the acting is childish. But worst of all, the story is trivial and even vulgar.

Speaker B: It's ridiculous to complain about a film because of its subtitles. You knew before you went that it was a foreign film. It shows a kind of laziness to blame the subtitles, when you don't want to make the effort to understand what the film was really about. Why, if we didn't have subtitles, we would miss seeing hundreds of good films.

The *straw man* strategy distracts attention from the main arguments and avoids dealing with them.

Ad Hominem Argument. This is an argument directed at the person making the argument rather than at what that person is saying. This distracts attention from the real point of the argument:

Speaker A: The government shouldn't reduce the funds it gives to universities. We won't be able to maintain our educational standards, and in a few years we will have a shortage of highly trained people.

Speaker B: Well, people like you who have children to educate would naturally think like that.

Speaker A: What do you mean? My children have nothing to do with my opinion.

Speaker B: It's just that you would have to pay higher tuition if the government gives the universities less money.

The focus of the argument has been changed from the original topic to the personal motives of Speaker A.

Fallacy of Hasty Generalization. Many of the generalizations we make are drawn from experience and observation. If we generalize on the basis of very few examples, we may say things about all members of a group that are true of only a few or some members of that group. For this reason, it is wise to limit our generalizations to some part of a class or group. For example, instead of saying that teenagers are irresponsible (all teenagers, about everything), we might say that some teenagers are irresponsible about handling money.

Fact and Opinion

We have already said that argument consists of giving reasons for statements. Not all statements, however, can become the topics of arguments. For example, the statement "Summer begins on June 21 in the Northern Hemisphere" is a statement of fact. We cannot say seriously that summer does not begin on June 21. Even statements of personal preference can be thought of as facts. For example, if someone says, "I like ice cream," that is a fact. What is not a fact is the judgment that the statement implies, i.e., "Ice cream is good." That statement is an opinion, and it is possible to give reasons to support or to refute that opinion. If we go back to the statement "I am against capital punishment," we see that is a statement of fact. The implication, however, is "Capital punishment is bad/wrong/unacceptable." This is a judgment, a statement of opinion, and we can give reasons to support or refute that opinion (refer to the section on forming generalizations in Chapter 4).

Exercise

In the blank before each sentence below, write *F* for fact, *O* for opinion, and *X* for other. Be prepared to explain your choice.

1. _____ Final examinations should be abolished.

2. _____ World government is essential for humankind's survival.

3. _____ Most lead pencils are really made of graphite.

4. _____ Stop at the red light.

5. _____ Movies are the best form of entertainment.

6. _____ My car ran out of gas.

7. _____ I think the president of student council has done a good job and should be reelected.

8. _____ You're stepping on my toe.

The Other Side of the Argument

If it is necessary to produce arguments to persuade a reader or listener to agree with your point of view, it is also necessary to assume that there are arguments for an opposing point of view. These are called counterarguments. When someone argues against a certain position, he or she tries to *refute* that position.

It is possible to make an argument without mentioning any counterarguments. However, it is usually best to assume that a reader or listener will be aware of at least some objections to your position. It is usually a good idea, therefore, to mention possible counterarguments and to try to refute them with your own arguments. A brief statement or summary of a counterargument is usually enough to show that you are aware of its existence. Often, this recognition of counterarguments can help to clarify and even strengthen your own position. Naturally, you will give much more attention to your own opinions than to opposing points of view.

Exercises:

1. Following the above example of reasons and possible supporting evidence for opposing capital punishment, suggest counterarguments, i.e., arguments in favor of capital punishment.

a. Reason: _____

Supporting information: _____

b. Reason: _____

Supporting information: _____

c. Reason: _____

Supporting information: _____

d. Reason: _____

Supporting information: _____

e. Reason: _____

Supporting information: _____

2. Now that you have a list of arguments and supporting evidence for both sides of an argument about capital punishment, choose a position on this issue. You may add arguments of your own and/or omit any of those given here. Then prepare an outline of your argument. Be sure to include references to opposing arguments. Write a thesis statement that would be suitable for an essay on this topic. Study the order of your arguments and divide them into preliminary paragraphs.

3. Conduct a debate on the topic of capital punishment, using the arguments you have listed. The debate can be conducted in several small groups simultaneously, or a single debate can involve the entire class. Try to avoid logical fallacies.

The Language of Argument

The essence of argument is the connection between the reasons supporting it and the conclusion that one can draw from those reasons. There are a number of signal words and phrases that point out that connection to the reader or listener. Among the signals that precede the statement of a conclusion are:

therefore
consequently
then
as a result
so
hence
for this/these reason(s), we can say that
this leads to/points to/suggests/proves that
this implies/requires/entails/shows/indicates/tells us that
from this we can see/understand/deduce/conclude that

Among the signals that precede reasons in an argument are:

because
for
since
as
as is shown/indicated/implied/proven by

Among the signals that refer to the reasoning process itself are:

if *X*, then *Y*
in the event that *X*, then *Y*
assuming *X*, then *Y*

Vocabulary Preview

Words in Context

The following words, arranged in groups, appear in this chapter's reading passage. Study the words in their contexts. Then complete the exercise that follows each group by writing the correct words in the blanks. Be sure to use the appropriate form of each word.

1. means, metaphor, perception

means (n., sing. or pl.)

I live in the center of the city, so I have various ways of getting to work. I can ride my bicycle, or I can take one of several other *means* of transportation, including my car, a taxi, the subway, or the bus. Going by public transportation, however, is a *means* of saving time and money.

	metaphor (n.)
-ical (adj.)	metaphorical
-ly (adv.)	metaphorically

She is a wonderful person. She is the center of her social group, and she radiates comfort and warmth toward everyone near her. In a poem I wrote about her, I used the sun as a *metaphor* to describe these qualities.

	perceive (v.)
	perception (n.)
-ive (adj.)	perceptive
-ly (adv.)	perceptively
-ible (adj.)	perceptible
-ly (adv.)	perceptibly

There are many different ways to understand his story, so your *perception* of its meaning might differ from mine.

One _____ of helping readers to understand how two things

are similar is to use a special type of comparison, or _____ .

For example, a writer can help a reader's _____ of how

strong and fierce a soldier is by saying that the soldier is a lion in battle.

2. *ad hominem* **argument, context, fallacy, impede, implications**

ad hominem argument (n. phrase)

Your opponent in the debate did not present any real argument for his point of view. Instead, he used an *ad hominem argument*. He suggested that you were in favor of minority rights only because you are a member of a minority group.

	context (n.)
-ual (adj.)	contextual

Why are bathing suits acceptable on the beach but not on city streets? It is because of the different *contexts* in which clothes are worn. At the beach, the combination of water, sun, and sand provides a reasonable *context* for minimal clothing. The *context* of city streets does not.

	fallacy (n.)
-ous (adj.)	fallacious
-ly (adv.)	fallaciously

Your argument would be good if it were based on facts. However, its *fallacy* is that it is based on incorrect information. Therefore, your argument is wrong.

	impede (v.)
-ment (n.)	impediment

When a car breaks down on a public road, it usually *impedes* traffic. Accidents and bad weather are also *impediments* to the smooth and rapid movement of traffic.

	imply (v.)
-icate (v.)	implicate
-ion (n.)	implication

Medical research has succeeded in helping people to live longer. One *implication* of this fact is that the population will have a larger percentage of old people. Another *implication* is that young people will have to plan ahead for longer periods of retirement. Often people do not understand the meanings for the future that simple facts *imply*.

There are a number of ways to present an argument illogically. One such _____ is using an _____ . The words _____ are Latin, meaning *to the man*. This kind of argument attacks an opponent instead of discussing the real subject of disagreement. In this way it _____ a clear understanding of the issues. In the _____ of politics, the common occurrence of this kind of _____ argument has serious _____ because it prevents many good candidates from seeking office.

3. nurtured, precedence, reinforced, tenets

nurture (v.)

Her garden was magnificent. She had carefully *nurtured* each tree and plant with water, fertilizer and careful cultivation of the earth.

	precede (v.)
-ent (n.)	precedent
-ence (n.)	precedence

I love to play tennis, but since my exams start next week, studying takes *precedence* over sports.

	enforce (v.)
re- (= *again*)	reinforce
-ment (n.)	enforcement
-able (adj.)	enforceable
-ly (adv.)	enforceably

I have always been afraid of horses. This fear was *reinforced* when my sister's new pony kicked me yesterday. Now I am more afraid than ever before.

tenet (n.)

All religious and cultural groups have sets of beliefs that they follow. These *tenets* can be written down formally, or they can be passed orally from one generation to another.

One of the _____ of educational psychology is that most children who are _____ in good physical and emotional environments have good learning potential. Their natural abilities are made stronger, or are _____ , by having enough food, physical activity, love, and encouragement. Unfortunately, some educators still give punishment _____ _____ praise.

4. anachronism, defuse, nuances, polls, prominence

	anachronism (n.)
-ic (adj.)	anachronistic
-ally (adv.)	anachronistically

The television cartoon show called "The Flintstones" is a good example of an *anachronism*. In this program, the characters resemble cave men who lived in prehistoric times. Yet their speech, ideas, and way of life as well as their tools and other equipment are those of our modern society. Even presenting such characters on television at all is *anachronistic*.

defuse (v.)

The children are about to get into a fight over the new toy we gave them. Let's try to *defuse* the situation by taking them on a picnic. Then maybe they will forget their argument and be friends again.

nuance (n.)

Husbands and wives usually know each other so well that they notice all the *nuances* of each other's behavior. They can interpret the shade of meaning of every word and action.

	poll (n. or v.)
-ster (n.)	pollster

Let's find out what people think about the new tax. We'll take a *poll* of one thousand people who represent the general population. How many *pollsters* will we need to *poll* that many people in one week?

	prominence (n.)
-ent (adj.)	prominent
-ly (adv.)	prominently

Every year the town's businesspeople choose a "Businessperson of the Year." He or she is chosen because of *prominence* in the community. The chosen individual is usually well known for participating in community activities or for promoting business opportunities.

The candidate disliked using _____ to measure public opinion. She also disapproved of conducting political campaigns by means of television. She felt that these practices would destroy the many different interpretations, or _____ , of opinion and policy. Her opponents called her an _____ because her ideas and actions were more like those of the past than of the present. However,

her _____ in the nation helped her to _____ these

attacks and to win the election.

5. introspection, juxtaposition, line of demarcation, surrealistic

	introspection (n.)
-ive (adj.)	introspective

She is a person who examines her own thoughts and behavior carefully. She has always had the habit of *introspection.*

juxtaposition (n.)

Jerusalem is a fascinating city because of the *juxtapositions* of ancient and modern ways of life. Wherever you look, you can see the old and the new side by side.

line of demarcation (n. phrase)

When the civil war ended, the *lines of demarcation* between the two sides gradually disappeared, and the citizens became reunited.

	real (adj.)
-ly (adv.)	really
-ist (n.)	realist
-ic (adj.)	realistic
-ally (adv.)	realistically
sur-	surreal
(= be-	
yond)	

The model of the city of the future was full of strange shapes and colors. This *surrealistic* vision contrasted sharply with the dull reality of today's industrial town.

The paintings we saw at the exhibition looked as though they had

come from the artist's dreams. These _____ works of art

showed strange _____ in which photographs of real objects

were placed next to fantasy figures. One image was placed partly on

top of another, so that there were no _____ between reality

and unreality. When I thought about my own dreams, my

_____ convinced me that my paintings would be very different from the ones this artist had created.

6. brevity, discrete, dissolution, embedded, paradigm

	brief (adj.)
-ity (n.)	brevity

Most people recognize the *brevity* of life. People usually feel that their lives have been too short to accomplish their goals.

	discrete (adj.)
-ion (n.)	discretion

He kept the parts of his life separate from one another. His professional life, his family life, and his religious life were *discrete* facets of his being.

	dissolve (v.)
-ion (n.)	dissolution

When the stock market crashed, several large business organizations broke apart. The *dissolution* of these companies caused much economic hardship.

	bed (n. or v.)
em- (= *to cause to be or have*)	embed (v.)

Fossils of ancient plants and animals have been found in rocks in some areas. For example, dinosaur bones have been removed from rocks in which they were *embedded* millions of years ago.

	paradigm (n.)
-tic (adj.)	paradigmatic
-ally (adj.)	paradigmatically

The union and the company have reached an agreement that should be a *paradigm* for worker-management relations. It is a model for solving disputes about pay, fringe benefits, and seniority.

The professor's lecture was remarkable for its _____ . Even though it was short, however, it succeeded in being a

_____ of good organization. In fact, if I ever give a lecture I will try to organize it in the same way. The content of the lecture was also interesting. He discussed the _____ of the Roman

Empire and the effects that its breakup had on European history. He
also discussed a number of _____ cultural groups that remained separate from Roman culture even though they had
been _____ within it for many years.

Discovering Word Meanings

Use (1) context clues; (2) your knowledge of prefixes, suffixes, and roots; and (3) a dictionary, if necessary, to discover the meanings of the italicized words in the following sentences from this chapter's reading passage.

1. And how do we decide that the performance lacks *verisimilitude?* Does the audience believe that the newscaster is lying, that what is reported did not in fact happen, that something important is being concealed?

   (Use your dictionary to find the roots of this word.)

2. . . . Americans are the best entertained and quite likely the least well-informed people in the Western world. I say this in the face of the popular *conceit* that television, as a window to the world, has made Americans exceedingly well informed.

   (Which meaning of this word can be used easily with *popular?*)

3. Viewers . . . expect the newscaster to play out his or her role as a character who is *marginally* serious but who stays well clear of authentic understanding.

   (Where are the margins on a page? If something is marginal, would you call it important or unimportant?)

4. . . . What possible interest could there be in a list of what the President says <u>now</u> and what he said <u>then</u>? It is merely a *rehash* of old news, and there is nothing interesting or entertaining in that.

   (Have you ever eaten hashed brown potatoes? If so, what do you think *hash* means? What part of speech is *rehash* in this sentence? As what other part of speech does your dictionary define *rehash?*)

Signal Words and Phrases

Study the following signal words and phrases that appear in this chapter's reading passage.

1. as such

This signal refers to a description or a definition that has been given in the previous sentence or sentences. It means "being the thing just described or defined."

He has spent his life as a benefactor of other people. *As such*, he deserves your respect.

2. at the very least

This signal, a more emphatic form of *at least*, indicates that the sentence in which it appears describes a minimum standard. The phrase can occur at the beginning, middle, or end of a sentence, and is separated from the sentence by commas.

When he was fired from his job, he sued his employer for wrongful dismissal. He hoped to win several thousand dollars as compensation. *At the very least*, he wanted to restore his professional reputation.

3. in any case

This signal means "whether something being discussed happens or is true." Other signals with a similar meaning include *anyway, anyhow,* and *in any event.*

The professor said that, if possible, she would schedule personal interviews before the spring vacation. *In any case*, she said that all essays would be marked and returned by that time.

4. then

Then may be used as a signal with a meaning similar to that of *therefore* and *in that case*. When *then* is used with this meaning, it is often separated by commas from the rest of the sentence.

They want to make their own decisions. The responsibilities, *then*, will be theirs as well.

5. in short

This phrase is used to signal a summary or restatement of an immediately preceding discussion or description. It is separated by commas from the rest of the sentence.

The ancient Greeks described Helen of Troy as having perfect physical characteristics: a slim, well proportioned body; graceful posture; and magnificent, shining hair. To the Greeks, she was, *in short*, the image of perfect beauty.

Grammar Preview

In many advanced-level texts, sentences are long and complex. Often, a list of grammatical structures such as several noun clauses or prepositional phrases will occur within one sentence. This can make the sentence difficult to understand. The first exercise below focuses on such multiple uses of various grammatical structures taken from the reading passage in this chapter. In the second exercise, a number of sentences using passive constructions are quoted from the reading passage. The focus here is on reasons a writer may have for using the passive voice.

1. The sentences below, taken from the reading passage in this chapter, contain parallel structures. Break each sentence into shorter, simpler sentences so that each contains only one of these structures. Study the following example.

   They expected a country with forests so thick, water so abundant, and soil so rich that it could supply their needs forever.

   They expected a country with forests so thick that it could supply their needs forever.

   They expected a country with water so abundant that it could supply their needs forever.

   They expected a country with soil so rich that it could supply their needs forever.

   a. There is no murder so brutal, no earthquake so devastating, no political blunder so costly—for that matter, no ball score so tantalizing or weather report so threatening—that it cannot be erased from our minds by a newscaster saying, "Now . . . this."

   b. The newscaster means that you have thought long enough on the previous matter (approximately forty-five seconds), that you must not be morbidly preoccupied with it (let us say, for ninety seconds), and that you must now give your attention to another fragment of news or a commercial.

   c. In part because television sells its time in seconds and minutes, in part because television must use images rather than words, in part because its audience can move freely to and from the television set, programs are structured so that almost each eight-minute segment may stand as a complete event in itself.

   d. . . . we are presented not only with fragmented news but news without context, without consequences, without value, and therefore without essential seriousness. . . .

   e. This means that you will exclude women who are not beautiful or who are over the age of fifty, men who are bald, all people who are overweight or whose noses are too long or whose eyes are too close together.

f. A suspected killer being brought into a police station, the angry face of a cheated consumer, a barrel going over Niagara Falls (with a person alleged to be in it), the President disembarking from a helicopter on the White House lawn—these are always fascinating or amusing. . . .

g. "You are required . . . to pay attention to no concept, no character, and no problem for more than a few seconds at a time."

h. He goes on to say that the assumptions controlling a news show are "that bite-sized is best, that complexity must be avoided, that nuances are dispensable, that qualifications impede the simple message, that visual stimulation is a substitute for thought, and that verbal precision is an anachronism."

i. The program abjures visual stimulation, consists largely of extended explanations of events and in-depth interviews (which even there means only five to ten minutes), limits the number of stories covered, and emphasizes background and coherence.

j. By television's standards, the audience is minuscule, the program is confined to public-television stations, and it is a good guess that the combined salary of MacNeil and Lehrer is one-fifth of Dan Rather's or Tom Brokaw's.

2. In the following sentences from the text, the author uses the passive voice. In each case, explain why he might have done so, according to the example below.

> Television did not invent the "Now . . . this" world view. . . . But it is through television that it has been nurtured and brought to a perverse maturity.

Here the author is saying that television was a passive instrument that allowed or made it possible for the "Now . . . this" world view to develop. There is no specific active subject available. In other words, there is no specific person or thing that made it possible for the "Now . . . this" world view to develop.

a. Viewers are rarely required to carry over any thought or feeling from one parcel of time to another.

b. She was accordingly hired in January 1981.

c. Does the audience believe that the newscaster is lying, that what is reported did not in fact happen, that something important is being concealed?

d. All television news programs begin, end, and are somewhere in between punctuated with music.

e. But as long as the music is there as a frame for the program, the viewer is comforted to believe that there is nothing to be greatly alarmed about; that, in fact, the events that are reported have as much relation to reality as do scenes in a play.

   f. It is simply not possible to convey a sense of seriousness about any event if its implications are exhausted in less than one minute's time.

   g. Viewers would be quite disconcerted by any show of concern or terror on the part of newscasters.

   h. For example, America's newest and highly successful national newspaper, *USA Today*, is modeled precisely on the format of television. It is sold on the street in receptacles that look like television sets.

   i. It has been demonstrated many times that a culture can survive misinformation and false opinion.

Getting Ready to Read

The reading passage in this chapter is taken from a book by Neil Postman entitled *Amusing Ourselves to Death: Public Discourse in the Age of Show Business*. Postman writes about the way we communicate with each other in public life under the influence of television. In "Now . . . this," Chapter 7 of his book, Postman analyzes how television news programs illustrate public discourse as entertainment.

1. Do you watch the news on television? What are your other sources of daily news?

2. Which television news programs do you prefer, and why?

3. Do you have any criticisms of television news programs? If so, what are they?

4. Discuss how you would handle the following if you were asked to produce a television news show:
   a. Hiring people to present the news
   b. Choosing the kinds of news items you would use
   c. Deciding how much time to spend on each item
   d. Choosing film footage and photographs to show in presenting the news items

5. Consider the following statement: "People who watch television news regularly are very well informed." Give at least one argument that supports this statement, and one argument that opposes it.

6. Scan the reading passage and find
   a. all references to specific newspapers and magazines
   b. the author's definition of *disinformation*
   c. the author's opinion of the "MacNeil-Lehrer Newshour"

Now read the passage carefully from beginning to end. As you read, note the ways in which television news can be misleading or inadequate.

READING PASSAGE

"Now . . . This"

1 The American humorist H. Allen Smith once suggested that of all the worrisome words in the English language, the scariest is "uh oh," as when a physician looks at your X-rays, and with knitted brow° says, "Uh oh." I should like to suggest that the words which are the title of this chapter are as ominous as any, all the more so because they are spoken without knitted brow—indeed, with a kind of idiot's delight. The phrase, if that's what it may be called, adds to our grammar a new part of speech, a conjunction that does not connect anything to anything but does the opposite: separates everything from everything. As such, it serves as a compact metaphor for the discontinuities in so much that passes for public discourse in present-day America.

When a person worries, he or she often wrinkles the forehead so that it looks like rows of knitted wool.

2 "Now . . . this" is commonly used on radio and television newscasts to indicate that what one has just heard or seen has no relevance to what one is about to hear or see. The phrase is a means of acknowledging the fact that the world as mapped by the speeded-up electronic media has no order or meaning and is not to be taken seriously. There is no murder so brutal, no earthquake so devastating, no political blunder so costly—for that matter, no ball score so tantalizing or weather report so threatening—that it cannot be erased from our minds by a newscaster saying, "Now . . . this." The newscaster means that you have thought long enough on the previous matter (approximately forty-five seconds), that you must not be morbidly preoccupied with it (let us say, for ninety seconds), and that you must now give your attention to another fragment of news or a commercial.

3 Television did not invent the "Now . . . this" world view. As I have tried to show,° it is the offspring of the intercourse between telegraphy and photography. But it is through television that it has been nurtured and brought to a perverse maturity. For on television, nearly every half hour is a discrete event, separated in content, context, and emotional texture from what precedes and follows it. In part because television sells its time in seconds and minutes, in part because television must use images rather than words, in part because its audience can move freely to and from the television set, programs are structured so

In Chapter 5, "The Peek-a-Boo World," of Postman's Amusing Ourselves to Death

that almost each eight-minute segment may stand as a complete event in itself. Viewers are rarely required to carry over any thought or feeling from one parcel of time to another.

4   Of course, in television's presentation of the *news of the day,* we may see the "Now . . . this" mode of discourse° in its boldest and most embarrassing form. For there, we are presented not only with fragmented news but news without context, without consequences, without value, and therefore without essential seriousness; that is to say, news as pure entertainment.

method of communication

5   Consider, for example, how you would proceed if you were given the opportunity to produce a television news show for any station concerned to attract the largest possible audience. You would, first, choose a cast of players,° each of whom has a face that is both "likable" and "credible." Those who apply would, in fact, submit to you their eight-by-ten glossies,° from which you would eliminate those whose countenances are not suitable for nightly display. This means that you will exclude women who are not beautiful or who are over the age of fifty, men who are bald, all people who are overweight or whose noses are too long or whose eyes are too close together. You will try, in other words, to assemble a cast of talking hair-do's. At the very least, you will want those whose faces would not be unwelcome on a magazine cover.

group of actors that performs in a play, film, etc.

shiny photographs measuring 8 × 10 inches

6   Christine Craft has just such a face, and so she applied for a co-anchor° position on KMBC-TV in Kansas City.° According to a lawyer who represented her in a sexism suit she later brought against the station, the management of KMBC-TV "loved Christine's look." She was accordingly hired in January 1981. She was fired in August 1981 because research indicated that her appearance "hampered viewer acceptance."[2] What exactly does "hampered viewer acceptance" mean? And what does it have to do with the news? Hampered viewer acceptance means the same thing for television news as it does for any television show: Viewers do not like looking at the performer. It also means that viewers do not believe the performer, that she lacks credibility. In the case of a theatrical performance, we have a sense of what that implies: The actor does not persuade the audience that he or she is the character being portrayed. But what does lack of credibility

An anchor *fastens or holds something in place. What is an anchorman on a TV news show? What is a co-anchor?*

a city in Missouri in the midwestern United States

[2]For a fairly thorough report on Ms. Craft's suit, see the *New York Times,* July 29, 1983.

FIGURE 10–1 Newscaster Walter Cronkite in the newsroom. (Source: CBS News Photo)

imply in the case of a news show? What character is a co-anchor playing? And how do we decide that the performance lacks verisimilitude? Does the audience believe that the newscaster is lying, that what is reported did not in fact happen, that something important is being concealed?

7   It is frightening to think that this may be so, that the perception of the truth of a report rests heavily on the acceptability of the newscaster. In the ancient world, there was a tradition of banishing or killing the bearer of bad tidings. Does the television news show restore, in a curious form, this tradition? Do we banish those who tell us the news when we do not care for the face of the teller? Does television countermand the warnings we once received about the fallacy of the ad hominem argument?

8   If the answer to any of these questions is even a qualified "Yes," then here is an issue worthy of the attention of epistemologists.° Stated in its simplest form, it is that television provides a new (or, possibly, restores an old) definition of truth: The credibility of the teller is the ultimate test of the truth of a proposition. "Credibility" here does not refer to the past record of the teller for making

Epistemology is the theory of knowledge. Therefore epistemologists _____.

statements that have survived the rigors of reality-testing. It refers only to the impression of sincerity, authenticity, vulnerability or attractiveness (choose one or more) conveyed by the actor/reporter.

9   This is a matter of considerable importance, for it goes beyond the question of how truth is perceived on television news shows. If on television, credibility replaces reality as the decisive test of truth-telling, political leaders need not trouble themselves very much with reality provided that their performances consistently generate a sense of verisimilitude. I suspect, for example, that the dishonor that now shrouds Richard Nixon° results not from the fact that he lied but that on television he looked like a liar. Which, if true, should bring no comfort to anyone, not even veteran Nixon-haters. For the alternative possibilities are that one may look like a liar but be telling the truth; or even worse, look like a truth-teller but in fact be lying.

Richard Nixon resigned as president of the United States after denying his knowledge of the criminal acts of members of his administration.

10   As a producer of a television news show, you would be well aware of these matters and would be careful to choose your cast on the basis of criteria used by David Merrick and other successful impresarios.° Like them, you would then turn your attention to staging the show on principles that maximize entertainment value. You would, for example, select a musical theme for the show. All television news programs begin, end, and are somewhere in between punctuated with music. I have found very few Americans who regard this custom as peculiar, which fact I have taken as evidence for the dissolution of lines of demarcation between serious public discourse and entertainment. What has music to do with the news? Why is it there? It is there, I assume, for the same reason music is used in the theater and films—to create a mood and provide a leitmotif° for the entertainment. If there were no music—as is the case when any television program is interrupted for a news flash—viewers would expect something truly alarming, possibly life-altering. But as long as the music is there as a frame for the program, the viewer is comforted to believe that there is nothing to be greatly alarmed about; that, in fact, the events that are reported have as much relation to reality as do scenes in a play.

managers of large-scale entertainments

musical theme that identifies characters or ideas

11   This perception of a news show as a stylized dramatic performance whose content has been staged largely to entertain is reinforced by several other features, including the fact that the average length of any story is forty-five seconds. While brevity does not always suggest triviality, in this case it clearly does. It is simply not possible to con-

vey a sense of seriousness about any event if its implications are exhausted in less than one minute's time. In fact, it is quite obvious that TV news *has* no intention of suggesting that any story has any implications, for that would require viewers to continue to think about it when it is done and therefore obstruct their attending to the next story that waits panting in the wings.° In any case, viewers are not provided with much opportunity to be distracted from the next story since in all likelihood it will consist of some film footage. Pictures have little difficulty in overwhelming words, and short-circuiting introspection. As a television producer, you would be certain to give both prominence and precedence to any event for which there is some sort of visual documentation. A suspected killer being brought into a police station, the angry face of a cheated consumer, a barrel going over Niagara Falls (with a person alleged to be in it),° the President disembarking from a helicopter on the White House lawn°—these are always fascinating or amusing, and easily satisfy the requirements of an entertaining show. It is, of course, not necessary that the visuals actually document the point of a story.

places on both sides of a stage where actors wait their turns to perform

Niagara Falls, located on the border between New York State and Ontario, Canada, is famous for being a high and extremely powerful waterfall.

The residence of the president of the United States is called the White House.

FIGURE 10–2 Diving into shallow waters.

Neither is it necessary to explain why such images are intruding themselves on public consciousness. Film footage justifies itself, as every television producer well knows.

12   It is also of considerable help in maintaining a high level of unreality that the newscasters do not pause to grimace or shiver when they speak their prefaces or epilogs to the film clips. Indeed, many newscasters do not appear to grasp the meaning of what they are saying, and some hold to a fixed and ingratiating enthusiasm as they report on earthquakes, mass killings and other disasters. Viewers would be quite disconcerted by any show of concern or terror on the part of newscasters. Viewers, after all, are partners with the newscasters in the "Now . . . this" culture, and they expect the newscaster to play out his or her role as a character who is marginally serious but who stays well clear of authentic understanding. The viewers, for their part, will not be caught contaminating their responses with a sense of reality, any more than an audience at a play would go scurrying to call home because a character on stage has said that a murderer is loose in the neighborhood.

13   The viewers also know that no matter how grave any fragment of news may appear (for example, on the day I write a Marine Corps general has declared that nuclear war between the United States and Russia is inevitable), it will shortly be followed by a series of commercials that will, in an instant, defuse the import of the news, in fact render it largely banal. This is a key element in the structure of a news program and all by itself refutes any claim that television news is designed as a serious form of public discourse. Imagine what you would think of me, and this book, if I were to pause here, tell you that I will return to my discussion in a moment, and then proceed to write a few words in behalf of United Airlines or the Chase Manhattan Bank. You would rightly think that I had no respect for you and, certainly, no respect for the subject. And if I did this not once but several times in each chapter, you would think the whole enterprise unworthy of your attention. Why, then, do we not think a news show similarly unworthy? The reason, I believe, is that whereas we expect books and even other media (such as film) to maintain a consistency of tone and a continuity of content, we have no such expectation of television, and especially television news. We have become so accustomed to its discontinuities that we are no longer struck dumb,° as any sane person would be, by a newscaster who having just reported

Dumb *means speechless.*
Therefore struck dumb
means _____.

that a nuclear war is inevitable goes on to say that he will be right back after this word from Burger King: who says, in other words, "Now . . . this." One can hardly overestimate the damage that such juxtapositions do to our sense of the world as a serious place. The damage is especially massive to youthful viewers who depend so much on television for their clues as to how to respond to the world. In watching television news, they, more than any other segment of the audience, are drawn into an epistemology based on the assumption that all reports of cruelty and death are greatly exaggerated and, in any case, not to be taken seriously or responded to sanely.

14   I should go so far as to say that embedded in the surrealistic frame of a television news show is a theory of anticommunication, featuring a type of discourse that abandons logic, reason, sequence and rules of contradiction. In aesthetics, I believe the name given to this theory is Dadaism; in philosophy, nihilism; in psychiatry, schizophrenia. In the parlance of the theater, it is known as vaudeville.°

Vaudeville was a form of stage entertainment that was popular in the United States during the first part of the twentieth century. It consisted of a number of unrelated performances by comedians, acrobats, singers, and so on.

15   For those who think I am here guilty of hyperbole,° I offer the following description of television news by Robert MacNeil, executive editor and co-anchor of the "MacNeil-Lehrer Newshour." The idea, he writes, "is to keep everything brief, not to strain the attention of anyone but instead to provide constant stimulation through variety, novelty, action, and movement. You are required . . . to pay attention to no concept, no character, and no problem for more than a few seconds at a time."[3] He goes on to say that the assumptions controlling a news show are "that bite-sized is best, that complexity must be avoided, that nuances are dispensable, that qualifications impede the simple message, that visual stimulation is a substitute for thought, and that verbal precision is an anachronism."[4]

exaggeration

16   Robert MacNeil has more reason than most to give testimony about the television news show as vaudeville act. The "MacNeil-Lehrer Newshour" is an unusual and gracious attempt to bring to television some of the elements of typographic discourse. The program abjures° visual stimulation, consists largely of extended explanations of events and in-depth interviews (which even there means only five to ten minutes), limits the number of sto-

does not use

[3]Robert MacNeil, "Is Television Shortening Our Attention Span?" *New York University Education Quarterly* 14:2 (Winter 1983), p. 2.
[4]MacNeil, p. 4.

ries covered, and emphasizes background and coherence. But television has exacted its price° for MacNeil's rejection of a show business format. By television's standards, the audience is minuscule, the program is confined to public-television stations, and it is a good guess that the combined salary of MacNeil and Lehrer is one-fifth of Dan Rather's or Tom Brokaw's.°

required payment

Rather and Brokaw are anchors of news programs on major commercial television networks.

17   If you were a producer of a television news show for a commercial station, you would not have the option of defying television's requirements. It would be demanded of you that you strive for the largest possible audience, and, as a consequence and in spite of your best intentions, you would arrive at a production very nearly resembling MacNeil's description. Moreover, you would include some things MacNeil does not mention. You would try to make celebrities of your newscasters. You would advertise the show, both in the press and on television itself. You would do "news briefs," to serve as an inducement to viewers. You would have a weatherman as comic relief, and a sportscaster whose language is a touch uncouth (as a way of his relating to the beer-drinking common man). You would, in short, package the whole event as any producer might who is in the entertainment business.

18   The result of all this is that Americans are the best entertained and quite likely the least well-informed people in the Western world. I say this in the face of the popular conceit that television, as a window to the world, has made Americans exceedingly well informed. Much depends here, of course, on what is meant by being informed. I will pass over the now tiresome polls that tell us that, at any given moment, 70 percent of our citizens do not know who is the Secretary of State or the Chief Justice of the Supreme Court. Let us consider, instead, the case of Iran during the drama that was called the "Iranian Hostage Crisis." I don't suppose there has been a story in years that received more continuous attention from television. We may assume, then, that Americans know most of what there is to know about this unhappy event. And now, I put these questions to you: Would it be an exaggeration to say that not one American in a hundred knows what language the Iranians speak? Or what the word "Ayatollah" means or implies? Or knows any details of the tenets of Iranian religious beliefs? Or the main outlines of their political history? Or knows who the Shah was, and where he came from?

19   Nonetheless, everyone had an opinion about this event, for in America everyone is entitled to an opinion,

and it is certainly useful to have a few when a pollster shows up. But these are opinions of a quite different order from eighteenth- or nineteenth-century opinions. It is probably more accurate to call them emotions rather than opinions, which would account for the fact that they change from week to week, as the pollsters tell us. What is happening here is that television is altering the meaning of ''being informed'' by creating a species of information that might properly be called *disinformation*. I am using this word almost in the precise sense in which it is used by spies in the CIA or KGB°. Disinformation does not mean false information. It means misleading information—misplaced, irrelevant, fragmented or superficial information— information that creates the illusion of knowing something but which in fact leads one away from knowing. In saying this, I do not mean to imply that television news deliberately aims to deprive Americans of a coherent, contextual understanding of their world. I mean to say that when news is packaged as entertainment, that is the inevitable result. And in saying that the television news show entertains but does not inform, I am saying something far more serious than that we are being deprived of authentic information. I am saying we are losing our sense of what it means to be well informed. Ignorance is always correctable. But what shall we do if we take ignorance to be knowledge?

The CIA is the Central Intelligence Agency of the United States. It gathers information about the activities of other countries. The KGB performs the same function for the Soviet Union.

20   Here is a startling example of how this process bedevils us. A *New York Times* article is headlined on February 15, 1983:

REAGAN MISSTATEMENTS GETTING LESS ATTENTION[5]

The article begins in the following way:

> President Reagan's aides used to become visibly alarmed at suggestions that he had given mangled and perhaps misleading accounts of his policies or of current events in general. That doesn't seem to happen much anymore.
>
> Indeed, the President continues to make debatable assertions of fact but news accounts do not deal with them as extensively as they once did. In the view of White House officials, the declining news coverage mirrors a *decline in interest by the general public.* [my italics]

21   . . . But there is a subtler point to be made here.

---

[5]Copyright © 1983 by The New York Times Company. Reprinted by permission.

Many of the President's "misstatements" fall in the category of contradictions—mutually exclusive assertions that cannot possibly both, in the context, be true. "In the same context" is the key phrase here, for it is context that defines contradiction. There is no problem in someone's remarking that he prefers oranges to apples, and also remarking that he prefers apples to oranges—not if one statement is made in the context of choosing a wallpaper design and the other in the context of selecting fruit for dessert. In such a case, we have statements that are opposites, but not contradictory. But if the statements are made in a single, continuous, and coherent context, then they are contradictions, and cannot both be true. Contradiction, in short, requires that statements and events be perceived as interrelated aspects of a continuous and coherent context. Disappear the context, or fragment it, and contradiction disappears. This point is nowhere made more clear to me than in conferences with my younger students about their writing. "Look here," I say. "In this paragraph you have said one thing. And in that you have said the opposite. Which is it to be?" They are polite, and wish to please, but they are baffled by the question as I am by the response. "I know," they will say, "but that is *there* and this is *here*." The difference between us is that I assume "there" and "here," "now" and "then," one paragraph and the next to be connected, to be continuous, to be part of the same coherent world of thought. That is the way of typographic discourse, and typography is the universe I'm "coming from," as they say. But they are coming from a different universe of discourse altogether: the "Now . . . this" world of television. The fundamental assumption of that world is not coherence but discontinuity. And in a world of discontinuities, contradiction is useless as a test of truth or merit, because contradiction does not exist.

22   My point is that we are by now so thoroughly adjusted to the "Now . . . this" world of news—a world of fragments, where events stand alone, stripped of any connection to the past, or to the future, or to other events—that all assumptions of coherence have vanished. And so, perforce, has contradiction. In the context of *no context*, so to speak, it simply disappears. And in its absence, what possible interest could there be in a list of what the President says *now* and what he said *then*? It is merely a rehash of old news, and there is nothing interesting or entertaining in that. . . .

23   I do not mean that the trivialization of public information is all accomplished *on* television. I mean that television

is the paradigm for our conception of public information. As the printing press did in an earlier time, television has achieved the power to define the form in which news must come, and it has also defined how we shall respond to it. In presenting news to us packaged as vaudeville, television induces other media to do the same, so that the total information environment begins to mirror television.

24 For example, America's newest and highly successful national newspaper, *USA Today*, is modeled precisely on the format of television. It is sold on the street in receptacles that look like television sets. Its stories are uncommonly short, its design leans heavily on pictures, charts and other graphics, some of them printed in various colors. Its weather maps are a visual delight; its sports section includes enough pointless statistics to distract a computer. As a consequence, *USA Today*, which began publication in September 1982, has become the third largest daily in the United States (as of July 1984, according to the Audit Bureau of Circulations), moving quickly to overtake the *Daily News* and the *Wall Street Journal*. . . .

25 It needs also to be noted here that new and successful magazines such as *People* and *Us* are not only examples of television-oriented print media but have had an extraordinary "ricochet" effect on television itself. Whereas television taught the magazines that news is nothing but entertainment, the magazines have taught television that nothing but entertainment is news. Television programs, such as "Entertainment Tonight," turn information about entertainers and celebrities into "serious" cultural content, so that the circle begins to close: Both the form and content of news become entertainment. . . .

26 And so, we move rapidly into an information environment which may rightly be called trivial pursuit.° As the game of that name uses facts as a source of amusement, so do our sources of news. It has been demonstrated many times that a culture can survive misinformation and false opinion. It has not yet been demonstrated whether a culture can survive if it takes the measure of the world in twenty-two minutes. Or if the value of its news is determined by the number of laughs it provides.

"Trivial Pursuit" is a very popular adult game based on questions about a wide variety of individual facts, or trivia.

Checking Your Comprehension

1. Explain the significance of the title "Now . . . This."
2. Does the author accept the idea that the person who presents the news on television must be credible? Why or why not?

3. What similarities between a television news program and a theatrical entertainment does the author suggest?
4. What does the author mean by saying that television news creates "disinformation"?
5. Why, according to the author, is it becoming harder to notice contradictions in arguments?
6. Give two examples of printed communications that are influenced by television. Explain the nature of the influence.
7. In your own words, state the main points of the author's argument.

For Discussion

1. Do you agree or disagree with the author's argument? If you agree, can you suggest additional examples that illustrate any part of the argument? If you disagree, can you suggest any evidence to support your position?
2. Do you think that television news gives a clear, fully balanced understanding of events? Why or why not?
3. How do film clips of events affect your understanding of the news? Give examples.
4. How do you think your attitudes to news events have been affected by
   a. the personalities of the reporters
   b. the brevity of news items
   c. the occurrence of commercials

Analyzing the Structure

1. The author uses a specific technique to involve the reader in his argument. What is this technique? Is it commonly used in academic writing?
2. The repetition of words and of central ideas helps to remind readers of the main points the author wants to make. Find all the repetitions in the passage of the title phrase "Now . . . this." How does this repetition help the author to present his argument?
3. Identify
   a. the full introduction to the thesis of this passage
   b. the thesis statement
4. Identify the conclusion. How does it perform the function of a conclusion as described in Chapter 4? Refer also to the discussion of writing conclusions later in this chapter.
5. A successful argument requires evidence. What evidence does the author offer to support his argument that
   a. television news reporters are considered to be performers
   b. television news shows are like vaudeville acts rather than serious reports of real and complex events

The Writing Process: Conclusions

The conclusion is like the introduction turned upside-down. It begins with a restatement of the thesis. Then it moves through more and more general topics, relating the essay to the world outside the scope of the essay. The main difference between the content of the introduction and that of the conclusion is that the conclusion is more general than the introduction.

A conclusion can perform one or more of several functions. It can, for example, summarize the main points of the essay instead of restating only the thesis statement. It can also state an opinion, i.e., an argument, based on the information or evidence in the essay. Another possible function of the conclusion is to suggest or speculate about how aspects of the essay topic will appear in the future. The conclusion can also suggest other areas to explore or research that will enlarge the reader's understanding of the subject or of related fields.

The writer of the Amazon essay wrote a conclusion and then rewrote it after getting feedback (see Chapter 1). Let us look at his finished conclusion:

> It is clear, therefore, that the destruction of the Amazon rain forest must stop. The harm that this destruction is causing is far greater than any benefits it might bring. All the nations of the world must become involved in this problem, for the entire planet depends on the Amazon forest and the other great tropical forests. This involvement must not be one-sided. We must not expect Brazil alone to bear the responsibility or pay the cost. Ecology is an issue that has no national boundaries. We shall all have to make sacrifices, including contributions of money, work, and time. Only by making such a commitment to our planet can we guarantee a safe and healthful environment for our children.

Notice how the conclusion begins with a restatement of the thesis. Then it moves smoothly through the very general issues of ecology and the environment, which the writer decided were too general for the introduction. It ends with a call to action, according to which all people should work actively to preserve the rain forests, for without them, the planet's future would be endangered. The call to action is an abbreviated argument, based on the information in the passage. This conclusion, therefore, combines the function of stating an opinion with a suggestion about the importance of this topic in the future.

Exercise

Write a short essay of four or five paragraphs on ''The Qualifications of the Ideal Television News Anchor.'' When you are ready to write a conclusion to your essay, consider the information about conclusions given above. Write the first draft of your essay, including the conclusion. Then exchange your essay with your neighbor, and give and get feedback in order to improve your conclusions.

Writing About Reading

1. In one paragraph, make an argument on one of the points made by the author of "Now . . . This."

2. Write a short essay on the above topic. One way to do this is to write one paragraph for each of the main points in your argument.

3. Choose one of the following:
   a. Write an essay of at least two body paragraphs on the topic "The Effect of Television on Political Campaigns." Since this topic is too general for a short essay, make it more specific. For example, you could focus on two effects, such as: (1) how the appearance of candidates on television affects campaigns; and (2) how television news reports about the candidates' speeches affect campaigns. You may use these suggestions or substitute ideas of your own. You may also refer to "Now . . . This" to help you state and support your opinions on this topic.
   b. Choose any other type of television entertainment that you think influences real life. Write a brief essay presenting your ideas on this topic. Be sure to make your topic specific enough for a short essay. For example, if you decide to write about programs dealing with law or law enforcement, you might want to consider whether to focus on fiction or nonfiction. You will also have to decide what aspect or aspects of real life are affected, how they are affected, and which of these you want to include.

4. Use information from "Now . . . This" and from the reading passages of Units One and Three to discuss the concept of an "information age."

Chapter 11

Teaching as an Amusing Activity[1]

CHAPTER FOCUS

As you study this chapter, you should focus on the following important points:

Arrangement of information: bridging

Vocabulary: understanding new words

Signal words and phrases: *from . . . to, then, worst of all, it would appear*

Sentence grammar: active voice, passive voice, parallelism, future perfect tense, verb tenses

Writing: bridging

Content: the influence of television in changing concepts of education

Arrangement of Information

Organization of the Text: Bridging

The idea of making transitions is not new to you. You have already focused on techniques by which the authors of the reading passages move from one sentence to another within a paragraph. You will recall these as pronoun reference, repetition of key words, and transition words such as *however, moreover,* etc. This chapter will discuss transition techniques that help the reader move from paragraph to paragraph within the essay. To differentiate transi-

---

[1]The title and the reading passage of this chapter are taken from *Amusing Ourselves to Death* (Chap. 10, pp. 142–154) by Neil Postman. Copyright © 1985 by Neil Postman. Reprinted by permission of Viking Penguin, a division of Penguin Books USA, Inc.; London: Methuen. **221**

tions between paragraphs from those between sentences, we will call the former *bridging* techniques.

Like transition, bridging is accomplished by reference to words or ideas in the preceding text, repetitions of words or ideas, the use of certain words that establish relationships (the same words that are used in transitions), or combinations of these techniques. Bridging, however, often requires using these techniques on a larger scale. For example, the first sentence or two of a paragraph can summarize a point or an idea that was discussed in a preceding part of the text. This could mean the previous paragraph, an earlier paragraph or paragraphs, or even the entire text up to that point.

For an illustration of this technique, turn back to paragraph 11 of ''Now . . . This'' in Chapter 10. The first sentence reads as follows:

> This perception of a news show as a stylized dramatic performance whose content has been staged largely to entertain is reinforced by several other features, including the fact that the average length of any story is forty-five seconds.

The subject of this sentence (everything before the verb *is reinforced*) summarizes the preceding paragraph. However, it also refers back to the idea of news as entertainment that is first stated in paragraph 4, carried on in paragraph 5 and continued in most of the text that precedes the summary.

The subject of sentence 1 of paragraph 11, then, is a summary that looks back at the previous text. In doing so, it represents one end of the ''bridge.'' The analogy to a bridge is useful, because a bridge must have at least two supports, one on each side of the river. Thus in the bridge sentence of paragraph 11, the subject looks at what came before, and the predicate (everything following the verb *is reinforced*) looks ahead toward the continuation of the text. We now expect to read about ''several other features,'' of which the first to be mentioned is ''the fact that the average length of any story is forty-five seconds.'' And indeed, these features are explored in paragraphs 11, 12, and 13.

Bridging occurs frequently throughout most essays. We can also think of bridging sentences as a series of links that tie paragraphs and larger chunks of text together so that readers can keep track of ideas throughout an entire reading passage. Indeed, sometimes the main or even the whole function of a paragraph is to be a bridge between sections of the essay.

Because bridging words or sentences often refer to abstractions and—as we have seen—to large and scattered chunks of text, one of the reader's major tasks is to identify the references the bridge sentence makes. It is also important to recognize that bridge sentences often function as topic sentences for their paragraphs.

Exercises

1. Explain the bridging function in each of the following paragraphs from the reading passages, including the role of any specific noun or pronoun reference or transition word:

a. in paragraphs 6 and 9 of ''Now . . . This'' in Chapter 10

b. in paragraph 2 of ''Genetic Ethics'' in Chapter 9

2. Choose any of the reading passages in Chapters 1–8, and identify as many bridge sentences as you can. Explain how they function in their paragraphs.

Vocabulary Preview

Words in Context

The following words appear in this chapter's reading passage. Study them in their contexts and carry out the discussion tasks that follow.

> accommodate (v.)
>
> -ion (n.)   accommodation

The employer asked his employees to work overtime for the next month. He realized that they would have to change their personal schedules to work so many extra hours. Therefore, he promised that if they would *accommodate* him by making these changes, he would pay them double their usual salaries. Most of the employees were happy to make the *accommodation* under these conditions.

The conference organizers arranged *accommodations* at the best hotels. However, these hotel rooms were too expensive for most of the conference participants, so they arranged their own *accommodations* at other places.

If another student asks you for your notes, will you accommodate him or her? Why or why not?

> agenda (n.)

There are three items on the *agenda* of tomorrow's meeting: electing a chairman, choosing new members, and deciding on a program for the year. If you have anything to add to this *agenda*, please tell the committee secretary before five o'clock today.

What is your personal agenda for the next year? Are the items on your list all things that you are willing to tell others about? What does it mean to have a ''hidden agenda''?

> cohere (v.)
>
> -ence (n.)   coherence
>
> -ion (n.)   cohesion
>
> -ive (adj.)   cohesive
>
> -ness (n.)   cohesiveness

The members of the winning soccer team worked well together. They understood each other's strengths and weaknesses, and they tried to help each other at all times. They even enjoyed being together when they weren't practicing soccer. Their *cohesion* as a group was an important factor in their success.

Do you think it is possible for a society made up of many different ethnic groups to be cohesive? What are some of the things that could bring about this cohesiveness?

	consequence (n.)
	consequent (adj.)
-ial (adj.)	consequential
-ly (adv.)	consequentially

He suddenly decided to quit his job without thinking about the long-term results of his action. The *consequences* were that he could not find a better position and had to accept a worse one instead.

What decision have you made that has had good consequences for you? What have been the consequences—either good or bad—of your educational background?

	cultivate (v.)
-ion (n.)	cultivation

In the same way that she *cultivated* her garden by loosening the soil, applying fertilizer, and watering the plants, she aided the development of her mind by reading great literature and attending lectures on many subjects.

What is the best way, in your opinion, to cultivate friendship?

	dynamic (adj.)
-ism (n.)	dynamism
-ics (n.)	dynamics

He is successful as a businessman because of his *dynamic* personality. He seems to have unlimited energy. Another reason for his success is that he understands the *dynamics* of his company, so he encourages its managers and divisions to work together.

Describe the most dynamic person you know. How does this person use his or her dynamism?

	emerge (v.)
-ence (n.)	emergence
-ent (adj.)	emergent

Whales, seals, and dolphins are among the mammals that live in the sea. Because they have lungs instead of gills, they must *emerge* from the water regularly to breathe.

Explain the meanings of the following:

The butterfly emerged from its cocoon.
The bear emerged from its cave in the spring.
After exam week, the students emerged from their complete absorption in notes and textbooks.

	emphasize (v.)
	emphasis (n.)
-ic (adj.)	emphatic
-ally (adv.)	emphatically

When you go for your job interview, try to *emphasize* your years of experience and education. Do not put great *emphasis* on your own opinion of yourself.

If you were asked to recommend someone for a part-time job as a salesperson, what qualities would you emphasize?

	exposition (n.)
-tory (adj.)	expository

He was very good at *exposition*. That is why he was always asked to explain the philosophy of the company to new managers, and to explain new methods and processes to clients.

Even though I understand the subject, I don't do well on essay exams because my *expository* writing is poor.

In what ways is exposition different from narration, description, and argument?

	facile (adj.)
-ity (n.)	facility
-ate (v.)	facilitate
-ion (n.)	facilitation

Having sharp knives *facilitates* food preparation tasks such as slicing meat or chopping vegetables. Having dull knives, on the other hand, makes it easier to cut one's fingers.

What does it mean to have a facility with numbers? If someone gives you a facile excuse, should you believe him? Why would putting oil on a machine facilitate its operation?

	focus (n. or v.)
-al (adj.)	focal
	focal point (noun phrase)

When I looked at the painting of the fisherman, I noticed first his powerful hands. They were the *focal point* of the composition, because the strong contrast between light and shadow drew my eye to that spot.

What happens when you focus a camera? What is meant by the focal point of a discussion?

	hierarchy (n.)
-ical (adj.)	hierarchical

Most businesses have a *hierarchical* structure. This means that there are several levels of responsibility. The chief executive officer is at the top, upper management is on the next level down, middle managers are another step down, and so on. My cousin started working as a teller at a bank. She moved up the *hierarchy* until she became vice president in charge of marketing.

What other examples can you give of organizations that have hierarchical structures? The reading passage in this chapter refers to learning as hierarchical. What do you think this means?

	hypothesis (n.)
-ize (v.)	hypothesize
-ical (adj.)	hypothetical
-ly (adv.)	hypothetically

Before she began her experiment on the effects of television violence on children, she *hypothesized* that the results would show that more violent acts are committed by children who watch violence on TV than by children who do not. Although this *hypothesis* seemed logical, the results of the study were not clear. Apparently, she had made some mistakes when she designed the experiment.

Before you begin to read, do you hypothesize about the content of the material? If so, on what do you base your hypothesis? When weather patterns are unusual—when it is warm in winter or cold in summer, for example—people often have hypotheses about the causes. What hypotheses have you heard as explanations for strange weather conditions?

	orient (v.)
-ation (n.)	orientation
re- (= *again*	reorient (v.)
or *back*)	reorientation (n.)

When I am in a strange city, I have trouble *orienting* myself to the street plan. Whenever I have walked a few blocks, I have to look at a map or ask directions to make sure I am going the right way. Without this frequent *reorientation* I would certainly get lost.

The reading passage in this chapter refers to a "massive reorientation toward learning." What do you think the author means?

paramount (adj.)

For many students, getting high marks is *paramount*. For others, however, high marks are not as important as the experience of learning new things.

What aspect of a university education is paramount for you? Of the main influences on your life, which one has been paramount?

	perplex (v.)
-ity (n.)	perplexity

He was trying to put together the pieces of the new bicycle, but he seemed *perplexed* about what to do next. When I looked at the instructions, I was just as puzzled as he was. Our *perplexity* increased when we saw that this bicycle seemed to have three wheels.

Do you know what your career will be, or are you perplexed about what to choose? Describe a recent situation in which you were perplexed.

	potent (adj.)
-cy (n.)	potency
im- (= *not*)	impotence (n.)
	impotent (adj.)

The *potency* of some illegal drugs is hard to predict. Sometimes they are so powerful that they cause instant death. So far, society has been *impotent* in preventing the spread of drug abuse.

What do you think is the most potent argument for or against the exploration of space?

	prejudice (n.)
-ial (adj.)	prejudicial
-ly (adv.)	prejudicially

If a big company and a small company can have an equal chance to win the contract, then my small company can apply without *prejudice*. However, if you have decided in advance that you prefer to give the contract to a big company, that decision is *prejudicial* to my chances.

Explain the relationship between the above use of *prejudice* and its use in the following sentence:

Prejudice against people who look, speak, or dress differently from others is an attitude children often learn from their parents.

	prestige (n.)
-ous (adj.)	prestigious

There is great competition among students to enter the most *prestigious* universities, because graduates of these well-known and respected schools usually get the best jobs.

Some people like to acquire symbols of prestige to show that they are important. What, in your opinion, are some of these symbols of prestige?

	sequence (n.)
-ial (adj.)	sequential
-ly (adv.)	sequentially

There are five even numbers from 1 to 10. In *sequence* they are 2, 4, 6, 8, 10. If we write them in a different order—for example 6, 2, 10, 4, 8—they are out of *sequence*.

First, Sharon and Alice had an argument; next, Alice moved out of the apartment; then, Sharon decided to go back to her parents' house. That was the *sequence* of events.

What do you think a musical sequence is? a dance sequence? a tragic sequence of events?

	sign (n.)
-ify (v.)	signify
-ation (n.)	signification
-ance (n.)	significance
-ant (adj.)	significant
-ly (adv.)	significantly

The results of the election show that people are looking for a change of leadership. That is the *significance* of the defeat of the leader of the party and the reelection of the other party candidates.

If you make a significant contribution to a charity, are you giving a large or a small amount? Could your contribution to a discussion be both small and significant at the same time? Explain.

	simulate (v.)
-ion (n.)	simulation
-or (n.)	simulator

In the driver safety program, students can test their driving abilities by using a machine that *simulates* road conditions. Practicing their skills using *simulation* is a good way to prepare for real events without actually experiencing them.

Name some ways that simulations can be used. Describe one of these.

	tyrant (n.)
-ical (adj.)	tyrannical
-ly (adv.)	tyrannically
-ize (v.)	tyrannize

Kings and dictators are not always *tyrannical*. Sometimes they are just and rule gently. Moreover, the world's history tells stories of many kinds of *tyranny* in so-called democracies as well as in countries ruled by single individuals.

What is a family tyrant? Imagine what each member of a family could do to become a family tyrant.

> under- (=   undermine (v.)
>   *beneath* or
>   *below*)

At the beginning, the young lawyer was certain that he would succeed at his profession. After losing his first three cases in court, however, he became less sure of his ability. His failures had begun to *undermine* his confidence in himself.

What will happen if you undermine a building? If an employee wanted to undermine the reputation of another employee, what could he or she do?

> under- (=   underscore (v.)
>   *beneath* or
>   *below*)

To mark the most important sentence in the paragraph, *underscore* it three times.

To *underscore* her disapproval of gossip, she refused to talk about anyone, either to disparage or to praise.

Think of an idea that you would like to emphasize by showing how true or important it is. How would you underscore that idea?

Discovering Word Meanings

Use (1) context clues; (2) your knowledge of prefixes, suffixes, and roots; and (3) a dictionary, if necessary, to discover the meanings of the italicized words in the following sentences from this chapter's reading passage.

1. . . . television's principal contribution to educational philosophy is the idea that teaching and entertainment are *inseparable*.

   (Do you recognize the prefix, suffix, and root of the word? Do you know any pair of friends who are so close that they can be called inseparable?)

2. There must not be even a hint that learning is hierarchical, that it is an *edifice* constructed on a foundation.

   (What is constructed on a foundation? What are two clues in the sentence that *edifice* is a noun?)

3. In television teaching, perplexity is a superhighway to low ratings. A perplexed learner is a learner who will turn to another station. This means that there must be nothing that has to be remembered, studied, applied or, worst of all, endured. It is assumed that any information, story or idea can be made immediately *accessible*, since the contentment, not the growth, of the learner is paramount.

(What does it mean for a building to be wheel-chair accessible? Is there any difference between this meaning of *accessible* and its meaning in the above quotation?)

4. The consequences of this reorientation [to learning] are to be observed not only in the decline of the potency of the classroom but, paradoxically, in the *refashioning* of the classroom into a place where both teaching and learning are intended to be vastly amusing activities.

(Is the meaning of this word simply *re* + *fashion*, or is something more added?)

5. The television programs, which teachers are free to record off the air and use at their convenience, are *supplemented* by a series of books and computer exercises that pick up four academic themes . . . .

(What can one do to supplement a diet or an income? In the sentence quoted above, what is it that is supplemented?)

Signal Words and Phrases

Study the following signal words and phrases that appear in this chapter's reading passage.

1. from . . . to

This expression shows a range of characteristics among members of a group. To show that the group is large or that the members' characteristics have a number of variations, a writer can expand the use of this signal, i.e., "from *x* to *y* to *z*," or "from *x* to *y*, and from *p* to *q*," or "from *x* to *y* and *p* to *q* to *r*." A number of other variations are also possible.

Financial difficulties are threatening all kinds of universities, *from* the largest *to* the smallest, *from* the most *to* the least prestigious, and *from* the privately *to* the publicly funded.

2. then

As a signal, *then* may mean "the next thing, event, or action in a sequence." When it has this meaning, *then* is not set off by commas except—occasionally—when it begins a sentence.

To bake a cake successfully, be sure to preheat the oven. *Then* measure and combine the ingredients carefully according to the recipe.

3. worst of all

The writer identifies what follows this phrase as the worst of several possibilities that have been mentioned. Commas separate this phrase from the rest of the sentence. (Note that the judgment that an item is the worst of a group of items represents only the opinion of the writer. Others might disagree with that judgment.) A number of similar phrases express varying degrees of good or bad in the opinion of the writer, e.g., *best of all, better yet, better and better,* and *from bad to worse.*

The book we had to read for class was long, difficult, and, *worst of all,* boring.

4. it would appear

This signal implies that what follows is based on some evidence, but is nevertheless the writer's interpretation. Unless it is used as part of a noun clause (*it would appear that* . . .), commas separate this signal from the rest of the sentence. Other signals with a similar meaning include *it seems* and *apparently.*

People who want to be fashionable must be willing to spend a great deal of money. Thrift, *it would appear,* is no longer in style.

Grammar Preview

The sentences below are from the reading passage in this chapter. With reference to the italicized words or phrases, answer the questions that refer to the sentences.

1. In searching the literature of education, *you will find it said by some* that children will learn best when they are interested in what they are learning. *You will find it said*—Plato and Dewey emphasized this—that reason is best cultivated when it is rooted in robust emotional ground. *You will even find some who say* that learning is best facilitated by a loving and benign teacher.

Compare the author's use of the italicized structures. Do you prefer one form to another? If so, which one and why?

2. And when *one* considers that save for sleeping there is no activity that occupies more of an American youth's time than television-viewing, *we cannot avoid the conclusion* that a massive reorientation toward learning is now taking place. . . . The consequences of this reorientation *are to be observed* not only in the decline of the potency of the classroom but, para-

doxically, in the refashioning of the classroom into a place where both teaching and learning are intended to be vastly amusing activities.

Restate the meaning of *we cannot avoid the conclusion*. What can be substituted for *are to be* in the phrase *are to be observed* without changing the meaning? Change all three italicized parts of this passage by using parallelism and the active voice. Do you think this makes the passage easier to understand?

3. a. Explain the order of the italicized actions.

   Since our students *will have watched* approximately sixteen thousand hours of television by high school's end, questions *should have arisen* . . . about who will teach our students how to look at television. . . .

   b. Draw a diagram that illustrates the time reference of the italicized phrases.

   And, in the end, what *will the students have learned?* They *will*, to be sure, *have learned* something about whales . . . .

Getting Ready to Read

The reading passage in this chapter is taken from *Amusing Ourselves to Death: Public Discourse in the Age of Show Business* by Neil Postman. In "Teaching as an Amusing Activity," the author examines television's influence on the way we think about teaching and learning.

1. Postman refers to two major points he intends to make. By scanning the passage, find the sentences that state these points.

2. In the schools of your native country, did you ever experience an educational method that would fit the category of entertainment? If so, describe it.

3. Since you have been in this country, has any kind of entertainment been part of your education? Explain.

4. In your opinion, what must the student contribute in order to learn something? What should be the contributions of the teacher and/or the learning materials?

5. Do you think that it is a good idea to bring television into the classroom? Why or why not?

Now read the passage to the end. As you read, note the similarities and differences between educational television programs and classroom learning.

Teaching as an Amusing Activity

1 [The chapter begins with a discussion of "Sesame Street," the famous children's program on educational television. "Sesame Street" uses techniques of television entertainment to achieve its goals. These techniques include using the methods of television commercials to teach letters and numbers to preschoolers. Postman suggests that the very success of "Sesame Street" undermines the attitudes that children will bring to classroom learning. He points out that the attitudes we absorb about *how* we learn are more important than *what* we learn, and that the way we learn from television is totally different from the way we learn from books. He considers this "the primary educational issue in America today." Postman calls television a curriculum because it controls the way that today's young people are educated. In describing television's impact on education in America, he observes that as a curriculum it competes successfully with the curriculum of the schools.]

2   Having devoted an earlier book, *Teaching as a Conserving Activity*, to a detailed examination of the antagonistic nature of the two curriculums—television and school—I will not burden the reader or myself with a repetition of that analysis. But I would like to recall two points that I feel I did not express forcefully enough in that book and that happen to be central to this one. I refer, first, to the fact that television's principal contribution to educational philosophy is the idea that teaching and entertainment are inseparable. This entirely original conception is to be found nowhere in educational discourses, from Confucius to Plato to Cicero to Locke to John Dewey.° In searching the literature of education, you will find it said by some that children will learn best when they are interested in what they are learning. You will find it said—Plato and Dewey emphasized this—that reason is best cultivated when it is rooted in robust emotional ground. You will even find some who say that learning is best facilitated by a loving and benign teacher. But no one has ever said or implied that significant learning is effectively, durably and truthfully achieved when education is entertainment. Education philosophers have assumed that becoming acculturated° is difficult because it necessarily involves the imposition of restraints. They have argued that there must be a

great thinkers who have discussed their ideas about education

learning cultural patterns

sequence to learning, that perseverance° and a certain measure of perspiration are indispensable, that individual pleasures must frequently be submerged in the interests of group cohesion, and that learning to be critical and to think conceptually and rigorously do not come easily to the young but are hard-fought victories. Indeed, Cicero remarked that the purpose of education is to free the student from the tyranny of the present, which cannot be pleasurable for those, like the young, who are struggling hard to do the opposite—that is, accommodate themselves to the present.

trying again and again to achieve something

3   Television offers a delicious and, as I have said, original alternative to all of this. We might say there are three commandments that form the philosophy of the education which television offers. The influence of these commandments is observable in every type of television programming—from "Sesame Street" to the documentaries of "Nova" and "The National Geographic" to "Fantasy Island" to MTV.° The commandments are as follows:

American television programs

Thou° shalt have no prerequisites.

you (singular) in biblical or poetic language

4   Every television program must be a complete package in itself. No previous knowledge is to be required. There must not be even a hint that learning is hierarchical, that it is an edifice constructed on a foundation. The learner must be allowed to enter at any point without prejudice. This is why you shall never hear or see a television program begin with the caution° that if the viewer has not seen the previous programs, this one will be meaningless. Television is a nongraded curriculum and excludes no viewer for any reason, at any time. In other words, in doing away with° the idea of sequence and continuity in education, television undermines the idea that sequence and continuity have anything to do with thought itself.

warning

getting rid of or abolishing

In the Bible, the story is told that the Israelites were slaves in Egypt, and that the king of Egypt refused to let them go. The Egyptians then suffered a series of plagues—severe punishments, some of which were sicknesses—until, after the tenth plague, the king agreed to release the Israelites. The language used here, i.e., "Thou shalt . . . ," imitates the language of well-known English translations of the Ten Commandments of the Bible. The purpose is to imply that these "commandments" of television are as important and as basic as these religious commandments of the Bible.

Thou shalt induce no perplexity.

5   In television teaching, perplexity is a superhighway to low ratings. A perplexed learner is a learner who will turn to another station. This means that there must be nothing that has to be remembered, studied, applied or, worst of all, endured. It is assumed that any information, story or idea can be made immediately accessible, since the contentment, not the growth, of the learner is paramount.

Thou shalt avoid exposition like the ten plagues visited upon Egypt.°

6   Of all the enemies of television-teaching, including continuity and perplexity, none is more formidable° than exposition. Arguments, hypotheses, discussions, reasons, refutations or any of the traditional instruments of reasoned discourse turn television into radio or, worse, third-rate printed matter. Thus, television-teaching always takes the form of story-telling, conducted through dynamic images and supported by music. . . . Nothing will be taught on television that cannot be both visualized and placed in a theatrical context.

feared or dreaded

7   The name we may properly give to an education without prerequisites, perplexity and exposition is entertainment. And when one considers that save for° sleeping there is no activity that occupies more of an American youth's time than television-viewing, we cannot avoid the conclusion that a massive reorientation toward learning is now taking place. Which leads to the second point I wish to emphasize: The consequences of this reorientation are to be observed not only in the decline of the potency of the classroom but, paradoxically, in the refashioning of the classroom into a place where both teaching and learning are intended to be vastly amusing activities.

except for

8   I have already referred to the experiment in Philadelphia° in which the classroom is reconstituted as a rock concert. But this is only the silliest example of an attempt to define education as a mode of entertainment. Teachers,

Chapter 6, p. 94, of Amusing Ourselves to Death

FIGURE 11–1   Classroom of the future?

from primary grades through college, are increasing the visual stimulation of their lessons; are reducing the amount of exposition their students must cope with;° are   *manage*
relying less on reading and writing assignments; and are reluctantly concluding that the principal means by which student interest may be engaged is entertainment. . . . I will rest my case° with "The Voyage of the Mimi," which   *present my last argument*
may be taken as a synthesis, if not an apotheosis,° of the   *making into a god*
New Education. "The Voyage of the Mimi" is the name of an expensive science and mathematics project that has brought together some of the most prestigious institutions in the field of education. . . . To describe the project succinctly, I quote from four paragraphs in *The New York Times* of August 7, 1984:

> Organized around a twenty-six-unit television series that depicts the adventures of a floating whale-research laboratory, [the project] combines television viewing with lavishly illustrated books and computer games that simulate the way scientists and navigators work. . . .
>
> "The Voyage of the Mimi" is built around fifteen-minute television programs that depict the adventures of four young people who accompany two scientists and a crusty sea-captain on a voyage to monitor the behavior of humpback whales off the coast of Maine.° The crew of the converted   *state on the northeastern coast of the United States*
> tuna trawler navigates the ship, tracks down the whales and struggles to survive on an uninhabited island after a storm damages the ship's hull. . . .
>
> Each dramatic episode is then followed by a fifteen-minute documentary on related themes.°   *subjects*
> One such documentary involved a visit by one of the teen-age actors to Ted Taylor, a nuclear physicist in Greenport, L.I.,° who has devised a way of   *Long Island, a part of metropolitan New York*
> purifying sea water by freezing it.
>
> The television programs, which teachers are free to record off the air and use at their convenience, are supplemented by a series of books and computer exercises that pick up four academic themes that emerge naturally from the story line: map and navigational skills, whales and their environment, ecological systems and computer literacy. . . .[1]

9   . . . What is of greatest significance about "The Voyage of the Mimi" is that the content selected was obviously chosen because it is eminently *televisable*. Why are these students studying the behavior of humpback whales? How

[1]Copyright © 1984 by The New York Times Company. Reprinted by permission.

critical is it that the "academic themes" of navigational and map-reading skills be learned? Navigational skills have never been considered an "academic theme" and in fact seem singularly° inappropriate for most students in big cities. Why has it been decided that "whales and their environment" is a subject of such compelling interest that an entire year's work should be given to it?

especially

10   I would suggest that "The Voyage of the Mimi" was conceived by someone's asking the question, What is television good for?, not, What is education good for? Television is good for dramatizations, shipwrecks, seafaring adventures, crusty old sea captains, and physicists being interviewed by actor-celebrities. And that, of course, is what we have got in "The Voyage of the Mimi." The fact that this adventure sit-com° is accompanied by lavishly illustrated books and computer games only underscores that the television presentation controls the curriculum. The books whose pictures the students will scan and the computer games the students will play are dictated by the content of the television shows, not the other way around. Books, it would appear, have now become an audio-visual aid; the principal carrier of the content of education is the television show, and its principal claim for a preeminent place in the curriculum is that it is entertaining. Of course, a television production can be used to stimulate interest in lessons, or even as the focal point of a lesson. But what is happening here is that the content of the school curriculum is being determined by the character of television, and even worse, that character is apparently not included as part of what is studied. One would have thought that the school room is the proper place for students to inquire into the ways in which media of all kinds—including television—shape people's attitudes and perceptions. Since our students will have watched approximately sixteen thousand hours of television by high school's end, questions should have arisen, even in the minds of officials at the Department of Education, about who will teach our students how to look at television, and when not to, and with what critical equipment when they do. . . .

situation comedy, a type of television show

11   "The Voyage of the Mimi," in other words, spent $3.65 million for the purpose of using media in exactly the manner that media merchants want them to be used— mindlessly and invisibly, as if media themselves have no epistemological or political agenda. And, in the end, what will the students have learned? They will, to be sure, have learned something about whales, perhaps about navigation and map reading, most of which they could have

learned just as well by other means. Mainly, they will have learned that learning is a form of entertainment or, more precisely, that anything worth learning can take the form of an entertainment, and ought to. And they will not rebel if their English teacher asks them to learn the eight parts of speech through the medium of rock music. Or if their social studies teacher sings to them the facts about the War of 1812. Or if their physics comes to them on cookies and T-shirts. Indeed, they will expect it and thus will be well prepared to receive their politics, their religion, their news and their commerce in the same delightful way.

Checking Your Comprehension

1. The author lists a number of conditions that are important for learning to take place. What are they?
2. According to the author, why can television programs have no prerequisites?
3. Why, according to the author, must television programs avoid perplexity?
4. Explain exposition, and compare or contrast it with *television-teaching*.
5. What topics are taught in connection with ''The Voyage of the Mimi''? What is the author's attitude toward these topics? What is the author's main objection to ''The Voyage of the Mimi''? Explain.

For Discussion

1. What advantages can you suggest that learning from books might have over learning from television?
2. In your own experience, have you learned more from teachers who entertain or from teachers who take a more serious approach to learning? Why?
3. Compare the ''commandments'' for educational television programs to the requirements for television news programs discussed in Chapter 10.

Analyzing the Structure

1. Find the three sentences in the reading passage that together make its thesis statement. What is unusual about the placement of these sentences?
2. The author argues against the idea that ''teaching and entertainment are inseparable.'' Describe how this argument is structured.
3. The author states that television is responsible for changing the classroom into a place where teaching and learning are amusing activities. What

is his main piece of evidence to support this statement? What sentence introduces this evidence? What comparison does this sentence suggest?
4. Find the segment of text that acts as a bridge between the general discussion of education as entertainment and the author's main example.

The Writing Process: Bridging

As we saw earlier in this chapter, *bridging* refers to transitions between paragraphs of a text. Writers must show the relationships and connections among paragraphs as well as between sentences within a paragraph. Just as writers do not all follow the same order in other parts of the writing process, they may also differ as to when they introduce paragraph bridges. Some writers include bridging techniques as part of their first drafts or possibly even in the outline stage. However, even those who use bridging techniques in the early versions of their writing usually find that they must eventually revise or refine their paragraph bridges.

Let us look once again at the rain forest essay (see Chapter 1). Feedback from a reader not only resulted in improvements to the transitions *within* the paragraphs, but also suggested the need for bridges *between* the paragraphs.

The first paragraph bridge –sentence 1 of paragraph 2—echoes the last sentence of the introduction: "Some of these consequences" in paragraph 2 refers to "consequences" in paragraph 1. This bridge was strengthened with the insertion of "these" to improve coherence (see Chapter 7).

The second paragraph bridge occurs in sentence 1 of paragraph 3. Thus as often happens, this sentence is both the topic sentence of its own paragraph and the bridge to the previous paragraph. Notice that adding the signal "as well" (see Chapter 8) provided part of this bridging function, but it was not enough for a smooth transition. Therefore the writer added to the sentence a summary of the previous paragraph. In fact, what was added was really a restatement of the topic sentence of paragraph 2. Thus the paragraph bridge now looks back toward paragraph 2 at the same time as it states the topic of paragraph 3.

The third paragraph bridge opens paragraph 4 (the conclusion). The use of "therefore" in the first sentence of paragraph 4 links the conclusion not only to the previous paragraph but also to the essay as a whole. The word "therefore" refers to the writer's belief that all of the information in the essay supports his conclusion that "the destruction of the Amazon rain forest must stop."

In the following abbreviated version of the essay, the three paragraph bridges are numbered and underlined. Examine them carefully, using the above explanations.

> . . . Many people do not seem to understand that the failure to preserve the Amazon rain forest could have serious consequences for all living things.

①   Some of these consequences are physical or biological. It is estimated, for example, that one million species of animal and plant life depend on the rain forests and on each other to survive. Without this ecosystem, these species, which live nowhere else on earth, would quickly become extinct. Destroying the forests would also speed up the so-called greenhouse effect, which may be causing the earth's temperature to rise at an alarming rate. The rain forests absorb a large amount of carbon dioxide. Scientists believe that this gas is partly responsible for the rising temperatures. A third consequence is the increase in diseases such as malaria. As forests are cleared to make room for hydroelectric dams, large stagnant lakes are formed. These provide breeding grounds for malarial mosquitoes. A final physical consequence of the loss of the Amazon forests might be a significant reduction in the amount of oxygen in the atmosphere. Without the earth's large forests, we might soon run out of air to breathe.

②   In addition to the physical effects caused by the destruction of the rain forests, there are social and economic effects as well. The Amazon forests contain many of the world's rubber trees, which are a major source of income for people living in the area. These people would have to find other ways to make a living if the forest disappeared. An even more serious consequence is the introduction of previously unknown diseases, such as malaria, into the region. Poor people, who cannot easily get medicines, often have no protection against these diseases. In addition, native peoples whose tribes have lived for centuries in the area are now being forced to move to escape disease and to find new sources of food as the forests disappear. However, many of the native peoples are hunters and gatherers who are unable to change their way of life. They cannot find food in the areas where they must live. The result is that these people are dying from disease and starvation, and their cultures are vanishing.

③   It is clear, therefore, that the destruction of the Amazon rain forest must stop. . . .

Exercise

Write an essay of about five paragraphs on the role of television in your own learning experiences. When you are ready for comments on the bridging between the paragraphs of your essay, exchange essays with your neighbor, and give and receive suggestions for improvement.

Writing About Reading

1. In one paragraph, write an argument in favor of learning English from television.

2. Write a short essay on the above topic. One way to do this is to divide the main points in your argument into two or more paragraphs.

3. Discuss the ways in which an educational television program could overcome at least some of the faults mentioned in the reading passage.

4. Discuss how television news and educational television programming illustrate the intrusion of entertainment into various areas of public life.

Chapter 12

Reading, Writing, and Broadcast News[1]

CHAPTER FOCUS

As you study this chapter, you should focus on the following important points:

Arrangement of information: comparison and contrast

Vocabulary: understanding new words

Signal words and phrases: *both, also*

Sentence grammar: reference, parallel forms, complex structures

Writing: editing

Content: using television news programs in high school classes

Arrangement of Information

Organization of the Content: Comparison and Contrast

One of the most important ways that information is arranged in texts is by showing or stating that two things or ideas or actions are like each other, or that they are different from each other. When we say that they are alike, we are using comparison; when we say that they are different, we are using contrast. Although you will find in texts examples of comparison alone or

[1]The title and the reading passage of this chapter are taken from Susan Chira (1990, March 6). Reading, Writing, and Broadcast News. *New York Times,* p. B1. Copyright © 1990 by the New York Times Company. Reprinted by permission.

contrast alone, these methods are most often used together, for when there are similarities between things, there are usually differences as well.

It is essential for the reader of a text to be able to recognize when and on what basis comparisons and contrasts are being made. The use of comparison and contrast can be simple enough to be stated in one sentence, or it can be so complex that many similarities and differences can be woven together. It can be a small part of a text, or it can be the basis for the text as a whole. For example, an entire essay could consist of a comparison and contrast of two characters in a play or of two economic systems.

Any comparison or contrast must be made according to some principle, i.e., there must be a basis for the comparison or contrast. This is true even in single sentences such as the following:

Her essay is as long as yours.
His essay is longer than hers.
The essay she wrote yesterday is more ambitious than the one she wrote
  last week in that it is twice as long.
Both his essay and hers are very long.

The basis of comparison or contrast in all of these sentences is the quality of length. In order to understand the comparison or contrast, it is necessary to identify this basis. In longer and more complex texts, the basis of comparison or contrast is not always so easy to identify.

While there must always be a basis for a valid comparison or contrast, several methods are used in texts to express these relationships. One of these is the point-by-point method, in which one point at a time is discussed and compared or contrasted. Another method describes a subject by giving a set of characteristics, and then describes another subject by giving a similar set of characteristics (comparison) or a dissimilar set of characteristics (contrast). While both of these methods can be used equally well for comparison or contrast, the third method is used primarily for comparisons. This is the use of a figure of speech, such as a simile or a metaphor. These are literary techniques that suggest similarities in things that are otherwise dissimilar. They are often used to illuminate or explain processes or ideas that might be difficult to understand or imagine. For example, to suggest that "angry looks are tiny daggers that pierce the heart" is to use a metaphor to make a reader understand an abstract idea in a physical context. Sometimes such metaphors are extended, i.e., carried on through larger segments of text.

Let us look at an example of each of these three methods, keeping in mind that any of them can be used in combination as well as separately.

The first example uses the point-by-point method. It contrasts the characteristics of the educational television program "Sesame Street" with the characteristics of traditional classroom education.

> We now know that "Sesame Street" encourages children to love school only if school is like "Sesame Street." Which is to say, we now know that "Sesame Street" undermines what the traditional idea of schooling

represents. Whereas a classroom is a place of social interaction, the space in front of a television set is a private preserve. Whereas in a classroom, one may ask a teacher questions, one can ask nothing of a television screen. Whereas school is centered on the development of language, television demands attention to images. Whereas attending school is a legal requirement, watching television is an act of choice. Whereas in school, one fails to attend to the teacher at the risk of punishment, no penalties exist for failing to attend to the television screen. Whereas to behave oneself in school means to observe rules of public decorum, television watching requires no such observances, has no concept of public decorum. Whereas in a classroom, fun is never more than a means to an end, on television it is the end in itself.[2]

Notice that the basis of contrast is stated in the second sentence. Notice also that the author uses the same grammatical structure for each point of the contrast. This strengthens the impact of the contrast, like a hammer hitting a nail again and again until the task is completed. However, various grammatical structures can be—and usually are—used in the point-by-point method.

The second example presents one set of characteristics at a time. It compares adherence to an organized religion with membership in certain types of secular groups. The basis of comparison is the fulfillment of needs. In this comparison there are four needs: (1) to feel a sense of moral purpose; (2) to proselytize; (3) to develop discipline; and (4) to have a focal point for a variety of activities. This comparison first discusses how adherence to an organized religion satisfies these four needs. It then considers how joining certain secular groups fills these same needs.

Adherence to an organized religion fulfills needs for some people that adherence to a particular set of secular rules fulfills for others. First, being a member of a religious faith implies a moral purpose. A religious person generally believes that some values are higher or more important than any individual's ideas or wishes. Religion is a guide to this person, helping him or her decide what is right and what is wrong. It also teaches him or her that there *is* right and wrong in the first place. Frequently, strong believers try to persuade others to become a part of this group, which understands the "correct" way to live. Belonging to a religion also develops a certain amount of discipline, for members are often expected to do some things and forbidden to do others. For example, Hindus may not eat beef, Jews and Moslems may not eat pork, and at least one Christian denomination forbids the drinking of any "strong" beverages, including coffee and tea. Finally, being a member of an organized religious group can also provide a focal point for a variety of social relations, recreational activities, and business contacts.

A sense of moral purpose, the desire to proselytize—or convert others, the development of discipline, and the possession of a focal point for a variety of activities are needs that can also be fulfilled by joining groups that are completely secular, that is, groups that have no connection with religion. Examples include vegetarians, environmentalists, and health and fitness enthusiasts. Indeed, members of such groups sometimes have much in common with members of religious groups. The belief of many vegetarians that animals should not be killed to provide people with food gives them a sense of moral purpose. Similarly, the moral purpose of environmentalists is a commitment to preserving the earth for future generations. And fitness buffs are convinced that physical exercise influences and enhances every aspect of their lives. Like members of religious groups, some of these believers may try to persuade others that theirs is the best way of life. Members of these groups also need to develop discipline. For example, vegetarians do not allow themselves to eat many foods that are available to others; environmentalists do not permit themselves to use many of the convenience products that add to waste and pollution; and fitness enthusiasts maintain a regular schedule of exercise. Finally, at restaurants, meetings, conferences or health clubs members of all these groups can meet others who share their interests and beliefs.

Notice that in paragraph 2 there are also two point-by-point comparisons within the larger comparison: the three secular groups are compared with regard to the way each of them requires a sense of moral purpose and the way each develops discipline. Notice also that this passage has very little language that is specific to comparison. In fact, there is only one such phrase that is specific to the main comparison, i.e., "have much in common" in sentence 3 of paragraph 2. The other expression specific to comparison is "similarly" in sentence 5 of paragraph 2, which relates to the secondary point-by-point comparison. How, then, is this comparison accomplished? In each paragraph, the set of characteristics is presented in the same order, making the comparison easier to see. Furthermore, the needs that are described in paragraph 1 are summarized in the first sentence of paragraph 2. The fulfillment of these needs is then detailed in the rest of that paragraph. In this way the basis of comparison is repeated and highlighted.

The third example is an extended metaphor that compares the grip of communism in eastern Europe to the grip of ice on a river.

> For 40 years, eastern Europe looked like a frozen river. Nothing seemed to happen there. All was still and immutable in a series of societies at the margin of the world's consciousness. Beneath the ice, however, small currents of dissent whirled. But whenever they cracked through the ice, they were quickly sealed over by yet another political frost.
>
> Beginning in the fall of 1988 and continuing through 1989, those currents whirled faster and faster, at first cracking the ice of Communist rule, then sweeping the ice completely away.[3]

Notice that this passage begins with an explicit comparison: ". . . Europe looked like a frozen river." It continues, however, as a metaphor that explains what the explicit comparison means.

[3]*Source:* Jeffrey Simpson (1990, June 9). How the Ice Cracked, a book review of *The Collapse of Communism*, edited by Bernard Gwertzman and Michael Kaufman [Random House, 1990]. The review appeared in the *Globe and Mail* (Toronto), p. C17.

Although comparisons and contrasts can be accomplished without the use of specific comparison/contrast language, as we have seen in our examples, they are often signaled in a text by a variety of words and phrases. Many of these expressions have been discussed in the "Signal Words and Phrases" sections of this text. To help you spot such signals in your reading, we list some of the most important ones below:

Contrast: *but, however, instead, unlike, in contrast, on the other hand, some . . . others, unlike, while, whereas, dissimilar, more/ less, more (-er) . . . than*

Comparison: *like, as . . . as; neither . . . nor; similar(ly); just as x, so y; both x and y.*

In addition, the basis of the comparison is often indicated by expressions such as *in that* and *on the basis of:*

This car is better than that one *in that* it is more sturdily built.

This car is better than that one *on the basis of* its construction.

Combining Ways of Arranging Information

In the preceding chapters of this book, you learned about several ways that information is arranged in texts. You also learned that these methods are normally combined in most texts. A good example of such combination is the second passage above that was used to illustrate comparison. Included in those two paragraphs are several examples of enumeration and one example of informal definition. Classification is also represented by the naming of four kinds of needs that religions and secular groups fulfill. The passage also illustrates methods of developing paragraphs and of achieving unity and coherence. Note in particular the important role of the bridge sentence that begins paragraph 2.

Exercises

1. Analyze the short passage below in terms of the following:
   a. What method of comparison/contrast does the passage use?
   b. Name the bases of comparison and contrast.
   c. Indicate which bases are being compared and which are being contrasted.

   José and Arigo are very good friends. Although they come from very different family backgrounds, they have many things in common. Both of them are excellent students, and they are both interested in the sciences. Their personalities are also similar in that they are both cheerful, friendly, and sensitive people. In addition, each of them participates in a sport, although Jose plays baseball, while Arigo is a basketball player.

2. Reorganize the above passage on religious versus secular groups into a point-by-point comparison.

Vocabulary Preview

Words in Context

The following words appear in this chapter's reading passage. Study them in their contexts and write the correct forms of the words in the blanks in the exercises that follow. In some cases you may have to include another word, such as a preposition.

	adapt (v.)
-ation (n.)	adaptation
-able (adj.)	adaptable
-ity (n.)	adaptability

It took us a few months to _____ to our new school. Our parents tell us that we were more _____ when we were small children. Each time our parents were transferred to a new city, we had to adjust ourselves to a new house, new friends, and a new neighborhood. Now that we are teenagers, our _____ is decreasing with every move to new surroundings. We are tired of starting over again and again.

	apathy (n.)
-tic (adj.)	apathetic
-ally (adv.)	apathetically

The child has a high fever. She is just lying in bed instead of running energetically around the house as she usually does. Her _____ is frightening because it makes her seem very sick. Being _____ can be a sign of serious illness.

	ban (n. or v.)

Many people favor a _____ on advertising liquor and cigarettes. They say that not permitting publicity for these products will prevent the addiction of many young people. So far, however, they have not been successful in totally _____ mass media advertising.

concern (n. or v.)

Nuclear power causes many people to worry about safety. They

are _____ about radiation leaks and about nuclear acci-

dents. Their _____ include finding safe ways to store radio-

active wastes. On the other hand, people know that there are also

problems _____ oil, gas, and coal.

constrain (v.)
constraint (n.)

He would like to quit his job, but there are several _____ fac-

tors. One _____ is his lack of money in the bank. Another

is the scarcity of other jobs in his field. In addition to these

_____, he would lose the medical insurance benefits

that are paid by his employer.

	corpus (n.)
-ate (adj.)	corporate
in- (= in; v.)	incorporate
-ion (n.)	corporation
in- (= in)	incorporation

I don't like that composer's music. In the entire _____ of his

work there is not one composition I enjoy hearing. One technique

of his that I particularly dislike is the way he _____ the

sounds of everyday life into his music. However, many people must

disagree with me, for the _____ that sells his recordings has

made a large profit.

counter (v.)
counter to (prep.)

All the people on the street were suspicious of Harry, their new

neighbor. To _____ their distrust, Harry invited them all

to a big party at his house. They all enjoyed it very

much, _____ _____ their expectations, and they

decided that Harry was wonderful, even though he did have a motor-

cycle.

debut (n.)

She has appeared in several plays, but tonight she is making

her _____ as a singer in a musical performance. She is al-

ways especially nervous when she makes her first appearance in a

role.

	evidence (n.)
	evident (adj.)
-ly (adv.)	evidently

The detective thought he knew who had stolen the money, but he

needed _____ to prove it. It was _____ that the

guilty person must have known where the money was

kept. _____, there were only three people who had had

both the knowledge and the opportunity.

fall behind (v.)

He liked going to parties more than studying, so

he _____ _____ in his work. Consequently, he

had so much work to do at the end of the course that he couldn't

finish it on time.

	furor (n.)
	fury (n.)
-ous (adj.)	furious
-ly (adv.)	furiously
in- (= *in*)	infuriate
+ -ate (v.)	

The city government's decision to spend a million dollars on a modern

sculpture to put in the park caused a _____. Some people

demonstrated _____ against the decision. Others showed

their _____ by writing letters to the newspapers. Still oth-

ers were _____ by the use of public funds for a luxury in-

stead of for social services.

	fragment (n. or v.)
-ation (n.)	fragmentation

After the accident, the road was covered with tiny _____ of

glass.

Politicians sometimes use opinion polls to try to find out what the public wants. However, these polls often result in the _____ of public opinion. It is difficult for the politician to decide what to do to unify his supporters rather than to _____ them.

pace (n. or v.)

Your house is only twenty _____ from mine, but those twenty steps measure only the physical difference between the two buildings. Your house has kept _____ with all the modern technology that is available today, while my house is very old-fashioned. Similarly, you live a very fast-_____ life, while my life is very quiet and uninteresting.

phase (n.)
phase in (v.)
phase out (v.)

Parents often say their children are "going through a _____." This usually refers to a period of time when the children are difficult to control.

The office manager told his employees that he was planning to _____ _____ new computer equipment. He thought that bringing it in little by little would make it easier for employees to accept it.

	simple (adj.)
-ity (n.)	simplicity
-tic (adj.)	simplistic
-ally (adv.)	simplistically

She likes to wear very _____ clothes because she knows that _____ is the basis of elegance. However, it would be _____ to think that elegance is easy to achieve. On the contrary, it is very difficult.

	sophisticate (n. or v.)
-ion (n.)	sophistication

He has very _____ tastes. For example, he drinks very fine
wines and eats gourmet food. Traveling around the world has also
helped to _____ him. Because he is such a _____,
he would not enjoy my way of life, which is simple and
without _____.

	superficial (adj.)
-ly (adv.)	superficially
-ity (n.)	superficiality

Her knowledge of the subject was very _____. She knew the
right words to use, but she understood only the surface of the topic.
The _____ became obvious when she was unable to explain
any of her statements in greater depth. She herself had probably
been _____ taught.

Discovering Word Meanings

Use (1) context clues; (2) your knowledge of prefixes, suffixes, and roots, and
(3) a dictionary, if necessary, to discover the meanings of the italicized words
in the following sentences from this chapter's reading passage.

1. Television news has arrived in the classroom, and today's *debut* of Chan-
    nel One in 400 schools across the country brings one of the fiercest educa-
    tional battles in years to a new phase.

    (Compare the above use of the word to its use in the following sentence:
    "A film actor made his *debut* last night as a stage performer." What is the
    origin of the word?)

2. Banned in New York, California and Rhode Island, Channel One has
    been branded a pernicious, cynical attempt to make profits from school
    children under the *guise* of educational television.

    (Does this sentence express approval or disapproval of making profits
    under the guise of educational television? What other preposition in addi-
    tion to *under* is used with *the guise of*?)

3. Both programs, Channel One and CNN Newsroom, aim to teach teen-
    agers about world events and to *counter* political apathy.

    (*Counter* has many meanings. Which part of speech should you look for
    in your dictionary?)

4. But Herbert Kohl, a former teacher and author of several books on education, worries that the brevity of the program will leave students with *superficial* knowledge of world affairs.

(What does *brevity* suggest about the meaning of this word?)

5. "What I don't like is the Japanese can get a scholarship before another guy," said Don Matera. His teacher pointed out that a student interviewed on the program had expressed the same fear, but that it had been shown to be not necessarily true. Many students expressed *resentment* that Japanese lived in the United States, but did not choose American high schools.

(Does *resentment* express a positive or a negative attitude? What clue does the context give you? What part of speech is indicated by the suffix?)

Signal Words and Phrases

Study the following signal words and phrases that appear in this chapter's reading passage.

1. both

This word can be used as a pronoun, an adjective, or a conjunction (when it is used with *and*.) It suggests that a comparison is being made.

> *Both* programs . . . aim to teach teen-agers about world events and to counter political apathy.

> *Both* Channel One *and* CNN Newsroom are similar in their program design.

2. also

This word is used as an adverb or as part of the correlative conjunction *not only . . . but also*. It means *as well, besides, too,* or *in addition*.

> The 15-minute CNN Newsroom *also* includes daily longer features. . . .

> We had car trouble during our trip. *Also,* one of the children got sick.

Grammar Preview

The exercises below are based on sentences from the reading passage in this chapter. The purpose of these exercises is to help you to break down complex grammatical structures in order to understand their meanings more easily.

1. **Reference.** In the following sentences there are several italicized words. Identify the word(s) or group(s) of words to which the italicized words refer or are otherwise related, and specify the relationship.

   a. Television news has arrived in the classroom, and today's *debut of Channel One in 400 schools across the country* brings one of the fiercest educational battles in years to a new phase.

   b. *Banned in New York, California and Rhode Island,* Channel One has been branded a pernicious, cynical attempt to make profits from school children under the guise of educational television. *Others* call *it* visionary, applauding the idea of tailoring a *news program* for teen-agers and arguing that the much-needed video equipment that schools receive free for subscribing to *the program* outweighs two minutes of commercials a day.

   c. Mr. Griest has shown CNN Newsroom to *his* government and economics students every school . . . day since September, and *he* believes *he* can already detect improvement in *their* ability to find countries on maps, *their* knowledge of world affairs and *their* understanding of economics and government. *He* said the program particularly appeals to students who are uninterested in traditional textbooks.

2. **Parallel Forms.** Identify the use of parallelism in each of the following, according to the example.

   > Mr. Griest has shown CNN Newsroom to his government and economics students every school . . . day since September, and he believes he can already detect improvement in *their ability* to find countries on maps, *[in] their knowledge* of world affairs and *[in] their understanding* of economics and government.

   a. Channel One and CNN Newsroom have similar formats, opening with fairly fast paced, brief news reports, slowing to focus on a few events in more detail, cutting to graphics like pop quizzes or quotations of the day and slowing again for one or two longer features.

   b. In Rita Duane's journalism class and Tom Quinn's social studies class, students watched as Channel One moved quickly through some top reports: the death of a college basketball star, the Cuban defector who windsurfed to the United States, President Bush's meeting with Prime Minister Toshiki Kaifu of Japan, the landing of the space shuttle Atlantis.

   c. The 12-minute Channel One program broadcasts a five-part series every week on one topic, like Eastern Europe, drugs or summer jobs. The 15-minute CNN Newsroom also includes daily longer features, like reports on American Indians' anger over celebrations of Columbus's discovery of America or a debate on whether to end Baylor University's 145-year-old ban on dancing.

3. **Complex structures.** Simplify the following sentences according to the instructions given for each item. Study the example below.

Rewrite the following sentence as five shorter sentences:

Channel One and CNN Newsroom have similar formats, opening with fairly fast paced, brief news reports, slowing to focus on a few events in more detail, cutting to graphics like pop quizzes or quotations of the day and slowing again for one or two longer features.

Channel One and CNN Newsroom have similar formats. They open with fairly fast paced, brief news reports. They slow to focus on a few events in more detail. They cut to graphics like pop quizzes or quotations of the day. They slow again for one or two longer features.

a. Rewrite the following sentence so that it begins with the subject. Underline the complete subject.

Even more important than the format, said Terry Baker, dean of the research division at Bank Street College in New York City, is how teachers incorporate the programs into their curriculum.

b. Rewrite the following sentence as four simpler sentences.

Others call it visionary, applauding the idea of tailoring a news program for teen-agers and arguing that the much-needed video equipment that schools receive free for subscribing to the program outweighs two minutes of commercials a day.

c. Explain in three or four simpler sentences why the Japanese high school was founded in the United States. Omit the first six words of the given sentence.

The report did not explain that the Japanese high school was founded because Japanese students educated overseas often fall behind their classmates at home and then fail the competitive examinations necessary for college, and future success, in their country.

d. Rewrite the following sentence in four simpler sentences.

Explaining the need for the programs to slow their pace, Carla Seal-Wanner of Columbia University's Teacher's College said her research shows that teen-agers learn more from a magazine-style format, including [historical] background and a focus on how the news affects people their age.

Getting Ready to Read

The reading passage in this chapter, "Reading, Writing, and Broadcast News," is taken from an article that appeared in the *New York Times* on March

6, 1990. It discusses the introduction of two television news programs to high school classrooms. These programs have been specially created for schools, and their use raises several educational questions.

1. Keeping in mind the readings in Chapters 10 and 11, what do you think of the idea of showing television news in classrooms?

2. Do you think commercials should be used to help pay for the use of television in the classroom? Why or why not?

3. Reading and writing are not discussed in the article. Why do you think the writer used those words in the title instead of a more general word like *education?*

4. Skim quickly through the first two paragraphs. What information do you get from them? How do they set the scene for the article?

5. Quickly read the first sentences of the rest of the paragraphs in the article. What do you think are the writer's main points? What basic method has she used to organize the content, i.e., definition, classification, argument, comparison/contrast, etc.?

6. Scan the article to find two quoted opinions of high school students about television news in their classrooms.

7. Scan the article to find the names of five experts whose opinions are presented.

8. Remember that the article describes television news programs for classes of English-speaking students. What differences would there be in using such programs for students of English as a second language?

Now read through this chapter's reading passage. Note the questions raised by the introduction of television news to the classroom, and the similarities and differences between the two programs described in the article.

READING PASSAGE

Reading, Writing, and Broadcast News

1   The camera pans° the Berlin wall as the narrator discusses the divided city and the outbreak of the cold war.

2   Cut° to a cartoon cheetah. Students at Union High School laugh as the animal is <u>flattened</u> by <u>trucks</u> and falls into <u>manholes</u> in his pursuit of Cheetos, the cheese snack.

> pans, cut, fade out, *and* zoom *have special meanings here. What do they have in common in this context?*

Fade out° for the first day of Channel One, a news show for teen-age students complete with commercials.

3   Zoom° across the state line to Peekskill, N.Y., where Michael E. Griest's students watch news too, but without commercials. Mr. Griest uses the program CNN Newsroom to test his government and economics students' understanding of current topics, from world events to geography to marketing principles.

4   Television news has arrived in the classroom, and today's debut of Channel One in 400 schools across the country brings one of the fiercest educational battles in years to a new phase.

5   Banned in New York, California and Rhode Island,° Channel One has been branded° a pernicious, cynical attempt to make profits from school children under the guise of educational television. Others call it visionary, applauding the idea of tailoring° a news program for teen-agers and arguing that the much-needed video equipment that schools receive free for subscribing to the program outweighs° two minutes of commercials a day.

three states in the United States

To brand *is to mark permanently with an identifying symbol. Here* branded *means* _____.

Tailors *make clothes to fit individuals. Here* tailoring *means* _____.

What is being weighed here?

Education questions raised

6   The furor surrounding Channel One raises other, broader educational concerns. Is television the way to reach the majority of teen-agers who say the tumult in Eastern Europe leaves them cold.° Can a brief daily news program interest and inform them or does it present too simplistic and fragmented a picture? Is this a genuine educational innovation or a quick-fix for historical and geographical ignorance that will not genuinely deepen teen-agers' knowledge?

A hot topic is one that many people are interested in. Therefore, something that leaves them cold is _____.

7   Both programs, Channel One and CNN Newsroom, aim to teach teen-agers about world events and to counter political apathy. But whether either program will achieve its goal depends on their formats° and how well teachers use them, say experts on technology in the classroom.

the ways they are arranged and presented

8   "Learning about contemporary events from television, it's a natural," said Sam Gibbon, director of the award-winning science television show, "Voyage of the Mimi," from Bank Street College of Education. "As far as the power of television to transport students to other worlds, to teach, to introduce a variety of subjects to the classroom, I think its power is very well established."

9   But Herbert Kohl, a former teacher and author of several books on education, worries that the brevity of the program will leave students with superficial knowledge of

FIGURE 12–1 Here a toddler examines the news of the day. Will television in the classroom help schoolage children achieve a better understanding of current events? (Source: Laimute E. Druskis)

world affairs. "The claims being made for this have no relation to what will actually be taught," he said. "You can put this on, let it play, and have no responsibility for going deeper. It won't provide extra learning that teachers don't provide, but administrators find this a cheap and easy way to look good." . . .

10 Channel One and CNN Newsroom have similar formats, opening with fairly fast paced, brief news reports, slowing to focus on a few events in more detail, cutting to graphics like pop quizzes or quotations of the day and slowing again for one or two longer features.

11 The 12-minute Channel One program broadcasts a five-part series every week on one topic, like Eastern Europe, drugs or summer jobs. The 15-minute CNN Newsroom also includes daily longer features, like reports on American Indians' anger over celebrations of Columbus's discovery of America or a debate on whether to end Baylor University's 145-year-old ban on dancing.

12 Channel One has flashier graphics and more music; CNN Newsroom looks more like a standard news program.

13 Educators who have seen both programs say their producers need to slow down the pace and create more

material especially for teen-agers. Even more important than the format, said Terry Baker, dean of the research division at Bank Street College in New York City, is how teachers incorporate the programs into their curriculum.

14   "If this is used by itself, it's not going to be used effectively," he said. "It depends on whether teachers prepare to do something with it." . . .

15   Mr. Griest has shown CNN Newsroom to his government and economics students every school . . . day since September, and he believes he can already detect improvement in their ability to find countries on maps, their knowledge of world affairs and their understanding of economics and government. He said the program particularly appeals to students who are uninterested in traditional textbooks.

16   His students, for the most part, agree. "It's good because some people don't watch the news at home," said Aaron Paige. "It gives us more knowledge about the world and what's going on. A lot of people don't know about East Germany, or why the wall is coming down.° This makes you a worldly person. You can talk about anything."

the wall built by the East Germans to separate the communist and noncommunist sections of Berlin.

17   At Union High School, students generally liked their first look at Channel One, too. In Rita Duane's journalism class and Tom Quinn's social studies class, students watched as Channel One moved quickly through some top reports: the death of a college basketball star, the Cuban defector who windsurfed to the United States, President Bush's meeting with Prime Minister Toshiki Kaifu of Japan, the landing of the space shuttle Atlantis.

18   The program offered a Japanese high school in Tennessee, the history of the Berlin wall and the stricter educational requirements of the United States Army. Some students watched the screen; some quietly painted their nails or applied lipstick and hairspray.

High school piques interest

19   The feature on the Japanese high school clearly sparked° the most interest.

20   "What I don't like is the Japanese can get a scholarship before another guy," said Don Matera. His teacher pointed out that a student interviewed on the program had expressed the same fear, but that it had been shown to be not necessarily true. Many students expressed resentment that Japanese lived in the United States, but did not choose American high schools.

A spark from a fire can cause another fire to start. What does it mean to spark a person's interest?

21   The report did not explain that the Japanese high school was founded because Japanese students educated overseas often fall behind their classmates at home and then fail the competitive examinations necessary for college, and future success, in their country.

22   Problems with sophistication and nuance were evident with both programs. For instance, even though the students had been watching discussions of Eastern Europe on CNN Newsroom for months, few moved beyond comments like, "Communism is really falling apart." In both schools, discussion of issues raised by the programs was fairly brief, given° the constraints of a 45- to 50-minute class period and other material teachers had to cover. . . .

Here the constraints of time and of other subjects are givens, i.e., accepted facts.

23   Explaining the need for the programs to slow their pace, Carla Seal-Wanner of Columbia University's Teacher's College said her research shows that teen-agers learn more from a magazine-style format, including [historical] background and a focus on how the news affects people their age.

24   Ms. Seal-Wanner, director of the graduate program in instructional technology, praised Channel One's long features with their emphasis on teen-ager[s], but she found the program too fast-paced and simplistic.

25   CNN Newsroom did a better job presenting the news, she said, but failed to adapt the news to its audience by interviewing teen-agers.

26   "CNN has skewed° it a little too much to making a news program and repackaging it for kids," she said. "Whittle° tried to make it too entertaining, assuming that kids aren't going to be interested."

distorted or twisted out of shape

Whittle Communications, a unit of Time Warner, Inc.

Checking Your Comprehension

1. In the opening paragraphs of the article, the writer has used the words *pans, cut, fade out* and *zoom.* Why has she done so?
2. Which was the first news program to be used in classrooms?
3. Why is Channel One not permitted in classrooms in some parts of the United States?
4. What argument is given for using commercials in the classroom, and what argument is given against it?
5. Describe the similarities and differences between the two news programs.

6. According to the article, what is the purpose of using specially prepared television news programs in high school classes? What will determine whether this purpose is accomplished?

7. What educational concerns are mentioned in the article? What examples of these concerns are discussed?

8. Reread the last six paragraphs of the article. What observations are made that support the views expressed in Chapters 10 and 11?

For Discussion

1. Paragraphs 17 and 18 of the reading passage list the topics covered on a Channel One program. Do you think these are good choices ? Will they accomplish the aims mentioned in paragraph 7? Suggest some reasons why these topics might have been chosen.

2. The article mentions that some people oppose Channel One's "attempt to make profits from school children under the guise of educational television." It also says that since schools receive video equipment free when they subscribe to the program, having commercials is not such a high price to pay. What is your opinion?

Analyzing the Structure

1. Which paragraphs constitute the introductory section of the article? (Note that paragraph structure in newspaper articles is different from paragraph structure in essays. In newspapers, paragraphs can sometimes consist of one sentence.)

2. Identify the thesis statement of the article.

3. What is the purpose of the subheadings in the article?

4. What is the bridge between paragraphs 5 and 6? 16 and 17?

5. There are many quotes in the article. Why are they used?

6. Find the statements in the article that present an opinion of the writer.

7. To what extent is the article an argument? What kinds of evidence does the writer use to support the points in the argument?

8. Find all the parts of the article that use comparison and contrast.

9. Does the article have a conclusion? If so, identify it.

The Writing Process: Editing

After you have made the changes that the readers of your draft suggested, you are ready to make your final revisions. Most of these will involve what is known as mechanics. Mechanics includes spelling, punctuation, forms for quotations and other references, paragraph indentation, and margins for the sides, top, and bottom of your final copy.

In addition, there might be a few remaining errors in grammar or some passages where meaning is still not clear. The best way to discover these errors is by asking a native speaker of English to read and comment on the essay. However, to get the specific kind of response that you need from this reader, it is a good idea to tell him or her exactly what to look for. It is especially helpful, to both you and the reader, to keep a checklist of the sorts of errors that you are most likely to make. For example, you may have trouble with run-on sentences or with subject-verb agreement; or punctuation might be your particular weakness. Knowing this, the reader can be especially alert for errors of these kinds.

After correcting all the errors that he and his readers could find, the writer of the Amazon essay prepared his final draft, as follows:

Consequences of Damaging the Amazon Rain Forest

Living things often depend on each other to survive. In some places, such as the oceans and the tropical forests, thousands of species may be living together in this way. These living creatures also interact with the nonliving, or inorganic, things around them. Such areas of close interdependence in nature are known as ecosystems. These ecosystems, however, do more than support the plants and animals that live in them. They also influence the environment of the entire planet. The ecosystems of tropical rain forests, for example, protect the entire planet by returning water to the air as vapor and by providing much of the oxygen that we breathe. One of the largest of these is the rain forest of the Amazon River Basin in Brazil. This forest is almost as large as the United States. It protects many unique species, and it plays a major role in controlling the earth's atmosphere and weather. However, it is being destroyed to provide farm land. Little is being done to prevent this destruction. Many people do not seem to understand that the failure to preserve the Amazon rain forest could have serious consequences for all living things.

Some of these consequences are physical or biological. It is estimated, for example, that one million species of animal and plant life depend on the rain forests and on each other to survive. Without this ecosystem, these species, which live nowhere else on earth, would quickly become extinct. Destroying the forests would also speed up the so-called greenhouse effect, which may be causing the earth's temperature to rise at an alarming rate. The rain forests absorb a large amount of carbon dioxide. Scientists believe that this gas is partly responsible for the rising temperatures. A third consequence is the increase in diseases such as malaria. As forests are cleared to make room for hydroelectric dams, large stagnant lakes are formed. These provide breeding grounds for malarial mosquitoes. A final physical consequence of the loss of the Amazon forests might be a significant reduction in the amount of oxygen in the atmosphere. Without the earth's large forests, we might soon run out of air to breathe.

In addition to the physical effects caused by the destruction of the rain forests, there are social and economic effects as well. The Amazon forests contain many of the world's rubber trees, which are a major source of income for people living in the area. These people would have to find other ways to make a living if the forest disappeared. An even more serious consequence is the introduction of previously unknown diseases, such as malaria, into the region. Poor people, who cannot easily get medicines, often have no protection against these diseases. In addition, native peoples whose tribes have lived for centuries in the area are now being forced to move to escape disease and to find new sources of food as the forests disappear. However, many of the native peoples are hunters and gatherers who are unable to change their way of life. They cannot find food in the areas where they must live. The result is that these people are dying from disease and starvation, and their cultures are vanishing.

It is clear, therefore, that the destruction of the Amazon rain forest must stop. The harm that this destruction is causing is far greater than any benefits it might bring. All the nations of the world must become involved in this problem, for the entire planet depends on the Amazon forest and the other great tropical forests. This involvement must not be one-sided. We must not expect Brazil alone to bear the responsibility or pay the cost. Ecology is an issue that has no national boundaries. We shall all have to make sacrifices, including contributions of money, work, and time. Only by making such a commitment to our planet can we guarantee a safe and healthful environment for our children.

Exercise

Choose any essay you have already written and revised. Edit it, make a list of your errors, and categorize them. Exchange papers with a partner for final feedback and correction.

Writing About Reading

1. In a single paragraph, compare and/or contrast either two courses you have taken, or two books or films having similar themes.

2. Write a short essay on the above topic.

3. Write an essay that compares and/or contrasts the approaches to television news in the classroom. Be sure to make clear the basis on which you do so.

4. Write an essay that compares and/or contrasts the effects of television's mode of discourse on news broadcasting and on classroom learning. Refer to the reading passages in Chapters 10–12.

Appendix A

Researching and Referencing

Researching

Once you have chosen a topic for a research paper, you are ready to begin researching it in the university library. Bring along a package of file cards. Make a card for each source you use (book, article, etc.). These source cards should look like this:

```
┌─────────────────────────────────────────────┐
│  author's name                  call number  │
│  (last name first)                            │
│                                               │
│           title                               │
│           place of publication                │
│           publisher                           │
│           date of publication                 │
└─────────────────────────────────────────────┘
```

File these cards alphabetically by the author's last name. Each time you use another source, make a card for it and file it alphabetically. This will save a lot of work when you make the reference page at the end of your finished paper.

Use another set of cards to keep notes on the information you read. These cards should be made out like this:

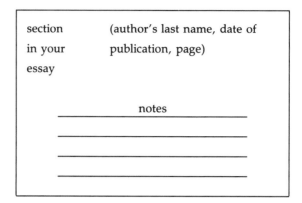

Now go to the reference area of the library to find the information that you need to get started with your research. The reference sources include catalogues of books and other materials located thoughout the library. The following are descriptions of the most important research materials. When you locate an item, be sure to record all bibliographic information on one of your file cards.

Monographs

Monographs are books on one topic, and they are usually located in an area of the library called the stacks. Use the subject catalogues (located in the reference area) to find the bibliographic information (author's name, monograph title, date, call number) of books on the topic of your research paper. The call number is the number on the spine of the book. Books are arranged on the shelves according to their call numbers. When you locate a book in the stacks, look nearby for other books on the same topic.

Periodicals

Periodicals include journals, popular magazines, newspapers, and other sources that are published in frequent, periodic issues (once a day, once a week, four times a year, etc.). A periodical may contain an important article on your topic. Recent periodical articles are likely to be more up-to-date than monographs.

Bibliographic information on articles in periodicals (author's name, title of article, title of serial, date, page numbers) is listed in reference journals called indexes. These are located in the reference section of the library. Many of these indexes are specialized according to subject area (see below). A general index to popular periodicals is the *Reader's Guide to Periodical Literature*. Ask the reference librarian to show you the *Reader's Guide* and to explain how it works. When you find a reference to an article on your topic, use the library's catalogue to find the call number of the periodical.

Specialized Indexes

The *Reader's Guide* is an *index* of periodical literature, but it is very general. Often it is possible to find an indexing journal that specializes in your topic area. Some of these are listed below. Ask the research librarian for other indexing journals in your topic area.

> *Accountant's Index*
> *Anthropological Index*
> *Applied Science and Technology Index*
> *Art Index*
> *Bibliography and Index of Geology*
> *Biography Index*
> *Biological and Agricultural Index*
> *Business Periodicals Index*
> *Canadian Business and Technical Index*
> *Canadian Periodical Index*
> *Current Index to Journals in Education*
> *Dramatic Index*
> *Education Index*
> *Energy Index*
> *Engineering Index*
> *Environment Index*
> *Essay and General Literature Index*
> *Financial Index*
> *Foreign Language Index*
> *Funk and Scott Index (Business)*
> *Humanities Index*
> *Index Medicus*
> *Index of Economic Articles*
> *Index of Mining Engineering Literature*
> *Index to U.S. Government Periodicals*
> *Music Index*
> *PAIS Foreign Language Index*
> *Population Index*
> *Psychological Index*
> *Public Affairs Information Service (PAIS)*
> *Selected Water Resources Index*
> *Social Sciences and Humanities Index*
> *Social Sciences Citation Index*
> *Social Sciences Index*
> *Sport and Recreation Index*
> *United Nations Index*
> *Zoological Record*

Abstracting Journals

Abstracting journals contain abstracts, or summaries, of many current articles in a particular field. You may read the abstract and decide whether the article is useful for your research. As in an indexing journal, in an abstracting journal articles are listed according to subject and year of publication. Often it is possible to find an abstracting journal that specializes in your topic. The list below includes some of the more popular specialized abstracting journals. Ask the research librarian for other abstracting journals in your subject area.

Abstracts in Anthropology
Abstracts of New World Archaeology
Abstracts of Tropical Agriculture
Abstracts on Criminology and Penology
Accounting & Data Processing Abstracts
African Abstracts
America; History and Life
Animal Breeding Abstracts
Biological Abstracts
Child Development Abstracts and Bibliography
Communication Abstracts
Computer Abstracts
Economic Abstracts
Education Abstracts
Education Digest
Electrical Engineering Abstracts
Employment Relations Abstracts
Energy Information Abstracts
Environmental Abstracts
Food Science and Technology Abstracts
Forestry Abstracts
Geophysical Abstracts
Geoscience Abstracts
Historical Abstracts
Human Resources Abstracts
International Political Science Abstracts
Language and Language Behavior Abstracts
Language Teaching and Linguistics Abstracts
Management Abstracts
Meteorological and Geoastrophysical Abstracts
Middle East Abstracts and Indexes
Nutrition Abstracts and Reviews
Physics Abstracts
Plant Breeding Abstracts
Political Science Abstracts
Pollution Abstracts
Psychological Abstracts
Religious and Theological Abstracts
Science Abstracts
Social Science Abstracts

Sociological Abstracts
Statistical Theory and Methods Abstracts
Technical Education Abstracts
Transportation Research Abstracts
Women Studies Abstracts
Work Related Abstracts
World Agricultural Economics and Rural Sociological Abstracts

Encyclopedias

Some of the major encyclopedias are the *World Book Encyclopedia*, the *New Encyclopaedia Britannica, Encyclopedia Americana*, and the *Canadian Encyclopedia*. The easiest of these to understand is the *World Book*. The most difficult and detailed of these is the *Britannica*. Ask the research librarian for specialized encyclopedias in your subject area, such as *The International Encyclopedia of the Social Sciences* and *The Encyclopedia of Education*.

Microforms

Microforms include microfilm (strips of film containing reduced photographs of the pages of books and articles) and microfiche (transparent plastic cards containing greatly reduced photographs of book and periodical pages). Both microfilm and microfiche must be read with special machines. Ask the librarian to help you find a microfiche or microfilm that contains an article on your topic.

Referencing

Using Information from Your Reading

Much written material in academic work contains ideas and statements that have been taken from other sources because the writer wants the reader to know about them or because they support the writer's own discussion of a topic. When a writer uses such ideas and statements, he or she must inform the reader where they originate; otherwise, the writer will be guilty of stealing, or *plagiarizing*. Plagiarism is severely punished in university. A student who plagiarizes may fail the assignment, be removed from the course, or even be expelled from the university.

In academic work researchers and students constantly read material on their subjects before writing papers and essays, and they must give credit to the writers whose work they are using. This is called giving references, or referring. It is possible to refer to someone's work either by quoting, i.e., by using the writer's exact words, or by paraphrasing, i.e., by restating the writer's ideas in your own words. In addition, writers occasionally need to refer by name to a theory, idea, formula, etc., that orginated in another text.

A general rule to follow is to reference all information that is not considered to be commonly known or understood.

Quoting

When we use someone's words, we are quoting the person, and we must show the reader we are doing so. Quotations must always be *exact*. We cannot change any words, even if they are ungrammatical or misspelled. Also, we may not omit some of a person's words in the middle of a quotation unless we indicate that we are doing so. The purpose of this is to show the reader that words or sentences that might change the meaning of the statement have been left out. Usually, a writer who uses a quotation does not—and should not—intend to change its original meaning. Sometimes, however, a quotation is *taken out of context*, i.e., it is removed from the surrounding words of the text so that the original meaning is changed.

To illustrate what could result from quoting out of context, imagine a newspaper advertisement for a film. The ad quotes the words of a film critic who has written ''. . . the best film I have seen this year. . . .'' The dots show that some words have been left out at those places where the dots occur. If we looked at the original review, we might find that the reviewer actually said, ''Although this is certainly not *the best film I have seen this year*, it is mildly entertaining.'' Obviously, the quotation was taken out of context to create an impression certainly not intended by the reviewer.

Thus, the dots, which show *ellipsis* (incompleteness), are a warning signal to the reader that part of the original quotation is missing. Ellipsis may also be used to show that one or more sentences have been omitted from a larger quotation. Ellipsis is a useful and important tool, but it must be used fairly and carefully.

Inserting Quotations into a Text

Quotations should be used so that they become part of a context. The following techniques can be used accomplish this.

1. If a quotation is shorter than forty words, enclose it in quotation marks.

2. If a quotation is forty words or longer, increase the left margin by ten spaces and do not use quotation marks. Leave a blank line before and after the quotation. Such quotations are often single-spaced to differentiate them from the rest of a double-spaced essay.

3. When a quotation begins with a complete sentence, introduce it with a phrase that tells the reader the source of the quotation. This phrase includes the name of the person who is being quoted, or sometimes the name of a newspaper or other document where the information was found. Study the following chart for examples of how to introduce this kind of quotation.

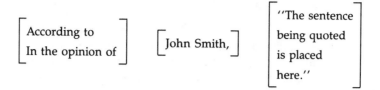

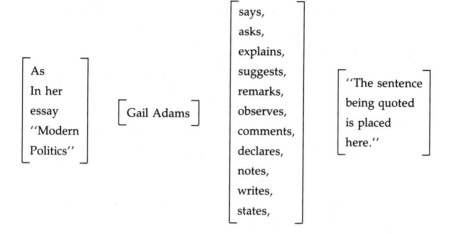

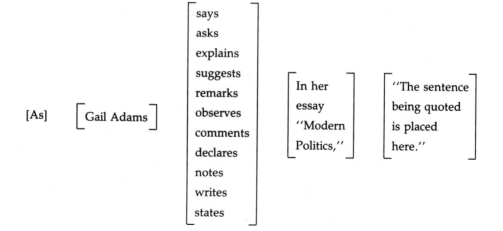

Example

As Gail Adams observes, "Recent events in the Communist world may prove to be a turning point in history as important as the French Revolution" (1990, p. 36).

4. When a quotation is not a complete sentence, it must be logically and grammatically placed in the text:

> The recent upheaval in eastern Europe ''may prove to be a turning point in history as important as the French Revolution'' (Adams, 1990, p. 36). Like the French Revolution. . . .

Notice the punctuation of quotations in the two examples above. A comma follows the introductory phrase in the first example. The partial sentence in the second example fits naturally into the sentence. The end-of-sentence period follows the reference in both examples.

Providing a Reference

It is not enough to identify words or sentences as quotations; it is also essential to provide a reference that gives the source of a quotation. Notice the following in the two examples above.

1. The reference in the first example contains the year of publication of the quoted material. Since the page number is known, it is also given. The author's name is included in the sentence and does not, therefore, need to be repeated in the reference.

2. In the second example, the author's name is not included in the sentence and, thus, must be included in the reference.

Exercise

Read the passage below, and do the quoting and referencing exercises that follow.

Author: R. Weinstock
Date of Publication: 1990

Vacation Stress

One of the greatest benefits of a vacation should be release from the pressures and stresses of daily life. Unfortunately, many people unwittingly forego this benefit by taking their holidays under circumstances that continue these pressures instead of relieving them. Because we are often unaware of the forms that stress can take, we don't know how to avoid it. Most people recognize the stressful nature of their jobs and of family or community responsibilities. But how many of us realize that our social relationships with friends and acquaintances—even though we normally enjoy the company of others—impose on us certain codes of behavior and responsibilities?

Another source of stress is time. In our daily lives we are subject to schedules, whether formal or informal. We are also bombarded by the sounds of traffic, machinery, conversation, and music. Yet many of us perpetuate these stresses when we go on vacation. We travel to resorts where we must obey social rules and where we must arrange our activities around a schedule imposed by others. We visit faraway cities where we are assaulted by the same kinds of noise that cause us stress at home. When we return, we are often secretly puzzled that we are not as rested as we hoped to be. Analyzing the pressures of one's life before planning a vacation could result in a reduction of stress, and therefore in a more relaxing holiday.

1. Quote the author's opinion on why people often do not avoid stress on a vacation. Quote only part of a sentence. Give a reference.

_____

_____

2. Quote what the author says about stress in social situations and how people perpetuate this stress during vacations. Give a reference.

_____

_____

3. Quote the author's observation on one other type of stress. Quote a complete sentence and give a reference.

_____

_____

Paraphrasing

Another way to give information from a source is to paraphrase, i.e., to state the information carefully and accurately, using your own words. Paraphrases, like quotations, require references in the text. You may paraphrase whenever it is not necessary to give the exact words of the author. Observe the following text and the two possible paraphrases.

Text

"The wine barometer built by Pascal is a variation on the more common mercury barometer, except that water or wine is used instead of the much denser mercury, and, as a consequence, the tube must be more than ten meters long" (Jones, 1976, p. 16).

Paraphrase 1

Pascal's wine barometer, which uses fluid much lighter than mercury, requires, therefore, a tube longer than ten meters (Jones, 1976, p. 16).

Paraphase 2

The wine barometer of Pascal operates according to the principle of the mercury barometer. But it requires a very long tube to accommodate fluids such as water or wine, which are much less dense than mercury (Jones, 1976, p. 16).

Exercise

Reread the passage on "Vacation Stress" above, and complete the following tasks.

1. Paraphrase the author's opinion on why people often do not avoid stress on a vacation. Give a reference.

   _____

   _____

2. Paraphrase what the author says about stress in social situations and how people perpetuate this stress during vacations. Give a reference.

   _____

   _____

3. Paraphrase the author's observation on one other type of stress. Give a reference.

   _____

   _____

Note that several methods can be used for referencing. When writing a paper for a particular course, check with the instructor to find out what referencing rules are commonly used in that subject.

The Reference Page

References are given on a separate page or pages at the end of the research paper. For each reference in the text, a corresponding reference on the reference page is shown. The title of the reference page should be "References" or "List of References." Do not make separate sections for books and periodicals. All references should be in alphabetical order. The following models represent one type of referencing. Underline the names of books, but not articles or chapters. Give page numbers wherever possible.

For further information and examples, consult *Publication Manual of the American Psychological Association* (3rd ed.), Washington, D.C., 1984.

1. Book

   In the text: (Ferguson, 1976, p. 54)

On the
reference
page: Ferguson, G. W. (1976). *Statistical Analysis in Psychology and Education* (4th ed.). New York: McGraw-Hill.

2. Article from an edited anthology

In the text: (Crystal & Davy, 1978, pp. 82–84)
On the
reference
page: Crystal, D., & Davy, D. (1978). Stylistic Analysis. In J. P. B. Allen & S. Pit Corder (Eds.), *The Edinburgh Course in Applied Linguistics:* Vol. 1. *Readings for Applied Linguistics* (pp. 69–90). London: Oxford University Press.

3. Periodicals (paginated by issue)

In the text: (Hancock, 1984, p. 14)
On the
reference
page: Hancock, C. R. (1984). Baltimore City Schools Use Computers to Teach Writing. *Calico Journal, 2*(3), 13–16.

The numbers refer to volume 2, number 3, pages 13 to 16.

4. Periodicals (paginated by volume)

In the text: (Kuder & Richardson, 1937, p. 158)
On the
reference
page: Kuder, G. F. & Richardson, M. W. (1937). The Theory and Estimation of Test Reliability. *Psychometrika, 2,* 151–160.

The numbers refer to volume 2, pages 151 to 160.

5. Encyclopedias and almanacs

In the text: (Life-Support Systems, 1981)
On the
reference
page: Life-Support Systems (1981). *Encyclopaedia Britannica* (15th ed.). Vol. 10, pp. 926–27.

6. Bulletins and pamphlets

In the text: (Jackson & Ferguson, 1941)
On the
reference
page: Jackson, R.W.B., & Ferguson, G. A. (1941). *Studies on the Reliability of Tests* (Bulletin 12). Toronto: University of Toronto, Depaitment of Educational Research.

7. Indirect sources

If possible, avoid using secondhand sources. Quote or paraphrase information from the original source instead. If the original source is not available, you may refer to a secondhand source. In the following example, a quotation that originally appeared in a journal article is quoted from a more recent book.

In the text:	(Revenstein, 1885)
On the reference page:	Revenstein, E. G. (1885). The Laws of Migration. *Journal of the Royal Statistical Society, 48,* 167–235. Quoted in Hornby, W. F. & Jones, M. (1985). *An Introduction to Population Geography* (p. 90). Cambridge: Cambridge University Press.

Even though one of the sources was not actually available to the author, it is necessary to give both sources on the reference page. Otherwise it might appear that both sources date from the same year, which in this case is not true.

Appendix B

Lists

Word List

This list contains the words that appear in the "Words in Context" section of each chapter.

Word	Chapter
abrupt (adj.)	6
abruptly (adv.)	6
abruptness (n.)	6
accelerate (v.)	1
acceleration (n.)	1
accelerator (n.)	1
accommodate (v.)	11
accommodation (n.)	11
acquire (v.)	3
acquisition (n.)	3
acquisitive (adj.)	3
adapt (v.)	12
adaptability (n.)	12
adaptable (adj.)	12
adaptation (n.)	12
ad hominem argument (n. phrase)	10
agenda (n.)	11
agricultural (adj.)	2
agriculture (n.)	2
anachronism (n.)	10
anachronistic (adj.)	10

Word	Chapter
anachronistically (adv.)	10
analogize (v.)	4
analogous (adj.)	4
analogy (n.)	4
ancestor (n.)	6
ancestral (adj.)	6
ancestry (n.)	6
animate (v.)	7
animation (n.)	7
antitoxin (n.)	4
apathetic (adj.)	12
apathetically (adv.)	12
apathy (n.)	12
applicable (adj.)	9
application (n.)	9
apply (v.)	9
art (n.)	6
artist (n.)	6
artistic (adj.)	6
artistically (adv.)	6
artistry (n.)	6
assess (v.)	1
assessment (n.)	1
automate (v.)	1
automatic (adj.)	1
automatically (adv.)	1
automation (n.)	1
avoid (v.)	6
avoidable (adj.)	6
avoidance (n.)	6
ban (n. or v.)	12
bed (n. or v.)	10
biological (adj.)	2
biologically (adv.)	2
biologist (n.)	2
biology (n.)	2
block (n. or v.)	6
blockage (n.)	6
brevity (n.)	10
bridge (n. or v.)	3
bridgeable (adj.)	3
brief (adj.)	10
cattle (n.)	8
clone (n. or v.)	8
cohere (v.)	11

Word	Chapter
coherence (n.)	11
cohesion (n.)	11
cohesive (adj.)	11
cohesiveness (n.)	11
combination (n.)	7
combine (v.)	7
complex (adj. or n.)	7
complexity (n.)	7
compose (v.)	6
composite (n.)	6
composition (n.)	6
conceit (n.)	7
conceivable (adj.)	7
conceivably (adv.)	7
conceive (v.)	7
concept (n.)	1
conception (n.)	1
conceptual (adj.)	1
conceptualization (n.)	1
conceptualize (v.)	1
conceptually (adv.)	1
concern (n. or v.)	12
conduce (v.)	4
conducive (adj.)	4
conduciveness (n.)	4
congest (v.)	2
congestion (n.)	2
congestive (adj.)	2
consequence (n.)	11
consequent (adj.)	11
consequential (adj.)	11
consequentially (adv.)	11
constrain (v.)	12
constraint (n.)	12
contemporaneous (adj.)	2
contemporary (adj. or n.)	2
content (adj.)	3
contented (adj.)	3
contentedly (adv.)	3
contentment (n.)	3
context (n.)	10
contextual (adj.)	10
corporate (adj.)	12
corporation (n.)	12
corpus (n.)	12

Word	Chapter
correct (v. or adj.)	8
correction (n.)	8
corrective (adj.)	8
correctly (adv.)	8
counter (v.)	12
counter to (prep.)	12
create (v.)	7
creation (n.)	7
creative (adj.)	7
creatively (adv.)	7
creativity (n.)	7
creator (n.)	7
cripple (v.)	6
critic (n.)	9
critical (adj.)	9
critically (adv.)	9
criticism (n.)	9
criticize (v.)	9
crucial (adj.)	4
crucially (adv.)	4
crux (n.)	4
cultivate (v.)	11
cultivation (n.)	11
curable (adj.)	9
cure (n. or v.)	9
debatable (adj.)	3
debatably (adv.)	3
debate (n. or v.)	3
debater (n.)	3
debut (n.)	12
decipher (v.)	7
decipherable (adj.)	7
decompose (v.)	6
define (v.)	2
definite (adj.)	2
definitely (adv.)	2
definition (n.)	2
definitive (adj.)	2
definitively (adv.)	2
defuse (v.)	10
degenerative (adj.)	6
dense (adj.)	5
densely (adv.)	5
denseness (n.)	5
density (n.)	5

Word	Chapter
descend (v.)	6
descendant (n.)	6
descent (n.)	6
desirable (adj.)	8
desire (n. or v.)	8
devastate (v.)	6
devastation (n.)	6
device (n.)	8
devise (v.)	8
digest (n. or v.)	6
digestible (adj.)	6
digestion (n.)	6
digestive (adj.)	6
discontent (n.)	3
discontented (adj.)	3
discrete (adj.)	10
discretion (n.)	10
disorder (n. or v.)	8
disorderly (adj.)	8
disputable (adj.)	3
disputably (adv.)	3
disputant (n.)	3
disputation (n.)	3
dispute (n. or v.)	3
disrupt (v.)	3
disruption (n.)	3
disruptive (adj.)	3
disruptively (adv.)	3
dissolution (n.)	10
dissolve (v.)	10
diverse (adj.)	8
diversification (n.)	8
diversify (v.)	8
diversity (n.)	8
divide (v.)	8
divisible (adj.)	8
division (n.)	8
divisive (adj.)	8
divisively (adv.)	8
domestic (adj.)	1
domestically (adv.)	1
domesticate (v.)	1
domestication (n.)	1
domesticity (n.)	1
dominance (n.)	9

Word	Chapter
dominant (adj.)	9
dominate (v.)	9
domination (n.)	9
donate (v.)	8
donation (n.)	8
donor (n.)	8
drawback (n.)	5
drift (n. or v.)	5
drifter (n.)	5
dynamic (adj.)	11
dynamics (n.)	11
dynamism (n.)	11
ecological (adj.)	4
ecologically (adv.)	4
ecologist (n.)	4
ecology (n.)	4
economic (adj.)	2
economical (adj.)	2
economically (adv.)	2
economics (n.)	2
economist (n.)	2
economize (v.)	2
economy (n.)	2
embed (v.)	10
emerge (v.)	11
emergence (n.)	11
emergent (adj.)	11
eminence (n.)	7
eminent (adj.)	7
eminently (adv.)	7
emphasis (n.)	11
emphasize (v.)	11
emphatic (adj.)	11
emphatically (adv.)	11
encounter (n. or v.)	5
enforce (v.)	10
enforceable (adj.)	10
enforceably (adv.)	10
enforcement (n.)	10
enterprise (n.)	1
environment (n.)	4
environmental (adj.)	4
environmentally (adv.)	4
environs (n.; pl. only)	4
ethical (adj.)	8

Word	Chapter
ethically (adv.)	8
ethics (n.)	8
evidence (n.)	12
evident (adj.)	12
evidently (adv.)	12
exert (v.)	5
exertion (n.)	5
expect (v.)	9
expectant (adj.)	9
expectation (n.)	9
expend (v.)	4
expenditure (n.)	4
expense (n.)	4
exploit (n. or v.)	7
exploitation (n.)	7
exposition (n.)	11
expository (adj.)	11
extend (v.)	1
extension (n.)	1
extensive (adj.)	1
extensively (adv.)	1
extent (n.)	1
extinct (adj.)	6
extinction (n.)	6
extinguish (v.)	6
extinguishable (adj.)	6
facile (adj.)	11
facilitate (v.)	11
facilitation (n.)	11
facility (n.)	11
fallacious (adj.)	10
fallaciously (adv.)	10
fallacy (n.)	10
fall behind (v.)	12
feasibility (n.)	4
feasible (adj.)	4
feasibly (adv.)	4
feat (n.)	7
ferment (n. or v.)	7
fermentation (n.)	7
fertile (adj.)	7
fertility (n.)	7
fertilization (n.)	7
fertilize (v.)	7
fertilizer (n.)	7

Word	Chapter
focal (adj.)	11
focal point (n. phrase)	11
focus (n. or v.)	11
foresee (v.)	9
foreseeable (adj.)	9
foreseeably (adv.)	9
foresight (n.)	9
fragment (n. or v.)	12
fragmentation (n.)	12
fundamental (adj.)	1
fundamentally (adv.)	1
furious (adj.)	12
furiously (adv.)	12
furor (n.)	12
fury (n.)	12
generate (v.)	6
generation (n.)	6
generative (adj.)	6
hardihood (n.)	4
hardiness (n.)	4
hardy (adj.)	4
hereditary (adj.)	7
heredity (n.)	7
hierarchical (adj.)	11
hierarchy (n.)	11
hurl (v.)	7
hypothesis (n.)	11
hypothesize (v.)	11
hypothetical (adj.)	11
hypothetically (adv.)	11
illegal (adj.)	9
illusion (n.)	2
illusive (adj.)	2
illusory (adj.)	2
immune (adj.)	7
immunity (n.)	7
immunization (n.)	7
immunize (v.)	7
impede (v.)	10
impediment (n.)	10
impending (adj.)	4
implicate (v.)	10
implication (n.)	10
imply (v.)	10
impotence (n.)	11

Word	Chapter
impotent (adj.)	11
imprison (v.)	9
imprisonment (n.)	9
inanimate (adj.)	7
inconceivable (adj.)	7
incorporate (v.)	12
incorporation (n.)	12
incurable (adj.)	9
incurably (adv.)	9
indigestible (adj.)	6
indivisible (adj.)	8
inextinguishable (adj.)	6
infuriate (v.)	12
inherent (adj.)	7
inherently (adv.)	7
inherit (v.)	7
inheritance (n.)	7
innovate (v.)	1
innovation (n.)	1
innovative (adj.)	1
innovatively (adv.)	1
inspiration (n.)	5
inspirational (adj.)	5
inspirationally (adv.)	5
inspire (v.)	5
institute (n. or v.)	9
institution (n.)	9
intolerance (n.)	6
intolerant (adj.)	6
introspection (n.)	10
introspective (adj.)	10
invent (v.)	2
invention (n.)	2
inventive (adj.)	2
inventively (adv.)	2
inventiveness (n.)	2
inventor (n.)	2
irrevocable (adj.)	9
juxtaposition (n.)	10
law (n.)	9
legal (adj.)	9
legalization (n.)	9
legalize (v.)	9
legally (adv.)	9
line of demarcation (n. phrase)	10

Word	Chapter
look to (v.)	5
magnification (n.)	6
magnify (v.)	6
maintain (v.)	1
maintenance (n.)	1
mammal (n.)	8
mammalian (adj.)	8
man (n. or v.)	5
means (n., sing. or pl.)	10
mechanic (n.)	7
mechanical (adj.)	7
mechanically (adv.)	7
mechanics (n., sing.)	7
mechanism (n.)	7
mechanistic (adj.)	7
mechanistically (adv.)	7
mechanize (v.)	7
metaphor (n.)	10
metaphorical (adj.)	10
metaphorically (adv.)	10
misapplication (n.)	9
miscellaneous (adj.)	4
miscellaneously (adv.)	4
miscellany (n.)	4
model (n. or v.)	1
monitor (n. or v.)	5
mutant (adj.)	9
mutate (v.)	9
mutation (n.)	9
norm (n.)	1
normal (adj.)	1
normalize (v.)	1
normally (adv.)	1
nourish (v.)	5
nourishment (n.)	5
nuance (n.)	10
nurture (v.)	10
nutrient (adj. or n.)	4
nutritious (adj.)	4
nutritiously (adv.)	4
nutritiousness (n.)	4
onset (n.)	3
order (n. or v.)	8
ordered (adj.)	8
orderly (adj.)	8

Word	Chapter
orient (v.)	11
orientation (n.)	11
outlaw (n. or v.)	9
overhead (n. or adj.)	4
pace (n. or v.)	12
paradigm (n.)	10
paradigmatic (adj.)	10
paradigmatically (adv.)	10
paramount (adj.)	11
parasite (n.)	8
parasitic (adj.)	8
parasitical (adj.)	8
parasitically (adv.)	8
per capita (adv. or adj.)	1
perceive (v.)	10
perceptible (adj.)	10
perceptibly (adv.)	10
perception (n.)	10
perceptive (adj.)	10
perceptively (adv.)	10
perfect (v. or adj.)	9
perfection (n.)	9
perfectly (adv.)	9
perplex (v.)	11
perplexity (n.)	11
pessimism (n.)	3
pessimist (n.)	3
pessimistic (adj.)	3
pessimistically (adv.)	3
phase (n.)	12
phase in (v.)	12
phase out (v.)	12
phenomenal (adj.)	7
phenomenally (adv.)	7
phenomenon (n., pl., phenomena)	7
plant (n. or v.)	8
poise (n. or v.)	7
polar (adj.)	3
polarity (n.)	3
polarization (n.)	3
polarize (v.)	3
pole (n.)	3
poll (n. or v.)	10
pollster (n.)	10
pollutant (n.)	2

Word	Chapter
pollute (v.)	2
pollution (n.)	2
pose (n. or v.)	9
potency (n.)	11
potent (adj.)	11
precede (v.)	10
precedence (n.)	10
precedent (n.)	10
preeminence (n.)	7
prejudice (n.)	11
prejudicial (adj.)	11
prejudicially (adv.)	11
prestige (n.)	11
prestigious (adj.)	11
prison (n.)	9
prisoner (n.)	9
produce (n. or v.)	7
product (n.)	7
production (n.)	7
prominence (n.)	10
prominent (adj.)	10
prominently (adv.)	10
prototype (n.)	5
prototypical (adj.)	5
prototypically (adv.)	5
race (n.)	9
racial (adj.)	9
racially (adv.)	9
racism (n.)	9
racist (n.)	9
range of factors (n. phrase)	1
rapid (adj.)	9
rapidity (n.)	9
rapidly (adv.)	9
real (adj.)	10
realist (n.)	10
realistic (adj.)	10
realistically (adv.)	10
really (adv.)	10
receipt (n.)	8
receive (v.)	8
recipient (n.)	8
recombine (v.)	7
redefine (v.)	2
reflect (v.)	1

Word	Chapter
reflection (n.)	1
reflective (adj.)	1
reflectively (adv.)	1
reflector (n.)	1
reinforce (v.)	10
relevance (n.)	1
relevant (adj.)	1
remodel (v.)	1
reorient (v.)	11
reorientation (n.)	11
replica (n.)	7
replicate (v.)	7
replication (n.)	7
reproduction (n.)	7
revocable (adj.)	9
revocation (n.)	9
revoke (v.)	9
revolt (n. or v.)	3
revolution (n.)	3
revolutionary (n. or adj.)	3
revolutionize (v.)	3
root (n. or v.)	3
rural (adj.)	1
semiskilled (adj.)	2
sequence (n. or v.)	11
sequential (adj.)	11
sequentially (adv.)	11
sex (n.)	7
sexual (adj.)	7
sexuality (n.)	7
sexually (adv.)	7
shift (n. or v.)	1
shifty (adj.)	1
sign (n.)	11
significance (n.)	11
significant (adj.)	11
significantly (adv.)	11
signification (n.)	11
signify (v.)	11
simple (adj.)	12
simplicity (n.)	12
simplistic (adj.)	12
simplistically (adv.)	12
simulate (v.)	11
simulation (n.)	11

Word	Chapter
simulator (n.)	11
site (n. or v.)	4
situate (v.)	4
situation (n.)	4
skill (n.)	2
skilled (adj.)	2
skillful (adj.)	2
skillfully (adv.)	2
sophisticate (n. or v.)	12
sophistication (n.)	12
spawn (n. or v.)	4
spend (v.)	4
spontaneity (n.)	9
spontaneous (adj.)	9
spontaneously (adv.)	9
spontaneousness (n.)	9
stimulant (n.)	1
stimulate (v.)	1
stimulation (n.)	1
stimulus (n., pl. stimuli)	10
stress (n. or v.)	5
stressful (adj.)	5
subdivide (v.)	8
suburban (adj.)	1
succession (n.)	8
successive (adj.)	8
successor (n.)	8
superficial (adj.)	12
superficiality (n.)	12
superficially (adv.)	12
surreal (adj.)	10
surround (v.)	7
surroundings (n., pl. only)	7
synthesis (n., pl. syntheses)	7
synthesize (v.)	7
synthetic (adj.)	7
synthetically (adv.)	7
talent (n.)	2
talented (adj.)	2
tap (n. or v.)	5
tenet (n.)	10
terms (n., pl.)	1
theoretical (adj.)	2
theoretically (adv.)	2

Word	Chapter
theorize (v.)	2
theory (n.)	2
tolerance (n.)	6
tolerant (adj.)	6
tolerate (v.)	6
tow (n. or v.)	5
toxic (adj.)	4
toxicity (n.)	4
toxin (n.)	4
trait (n.)	9
transplant (n. or v.)	8
trend (n. or v.)	1
trendiness (n.)	1
trendy (adj.)	1
trigger (n. or v.)	1
tyrannical (adj.)	11
tyrannically (adv.)	11
tyrannize (v.)	11
tyrant (n.)	11
unavoidable (adj.)	6
unbridgeable (adj.)	3
undergo (v.)	9
undermine (v.)	11
underscore (v.)	11
undesirable (adj.)	8
unforeseen (adj.)	9
unprecedented (adj.)	9
uproot (v.)	3
urban (adj.)	1
urbanization (n.)	1
urbanize (v.)	1
variability (n.)	1
variable (adj. or n.)	1
variation (n.)	1
varied (adj.)	1
variety (n.)	1
various (adj.)	1
vary (v.)	1
visual (adj.)	7
visualization (n.)	7
visualize (v.)	7
visually (adv.)	7
worthwhile (adj.)	3
zone (n. or v.)	5

List of Signal Words and Phrases

This list contains only those words that appear in the "Signal Words and Phrases" section of each chapter. Other lists of signal words relevant to the logical arrangement of information appear in the "Arrangement of Information" sections of several chapters.

Signal Word or Phrase	Chapter
above all	9
accordingly	5
according to	2
according to which	8
additionally	2
a final	1
a further	1, 3
also	12
among others	7
another	1, 3
anyhow	10
anyway	10
apparently	11
as a consequence	3
as a matter of fact	8
as an example	4
as a result	1, 3, 5
as such	10
as we have seen	6
as well	12
at least	10
at the very least	10
besides	12
best of all	11
better and better	11
better yet	11
both	12
but	1
but . . . anyway	5, 6
by means of which	8
clearly	9
consequently	3, 5
despite	5
first	2
for example	2, 4
for instance	2, 4
for these reasons	5
for this reason	5

Signal Word or Phrase	Chapter
from bad to worse	11
from . . . to	11
furthermore	2, 6
hence	1
however	1, 5, 6
I admit that	1
in addition	2, 6
in any case	10
in any event	10
indeed	1, 8
in fact	1, 8
in other words	9
in short	10
in spite of	5
in spite of that	5, 6
instead	7
in that case	10
in the meantime	9
in this way	6
in turn	3
it is true that	1
it seems	11
it would appear	11
like	7
meanwhile	9
moreover	2, 6
most importantly	9
naturally	9
nevertheless	5, 6
next	4
nonetheless	5, 6
not only . . . but also	12
obviously	9
of course	9
on the contrary	1
on the other hand	3
rather	1
second	2
similar to	7
so	5
some . . . others	6
still	5, 6
still another	1, 6
that is	9
that is to say	9

Signal Word or Phrase	Chapter
the final	1
then	10, 11
therefore	1, 5, 10
third	2
thus	1
too	12
unlike	7
whereby	8
worst of all	11
yet another	1, 6

List of Grammar Items

This list contains the grammar items that appear in the "Grammar Preview" section of each chapter.

Grammar Item	Chapter
active voice	11
adjective clauses	1, 2, 6, 8
adjective clauses, reduction of	3, 6
adverb clauses	4, 6
articles	8
complex structures	12
coordination	1
future perfect tense	11
future tense	2–4
gerunds	3, 4
hypothetical *would*	3, 5
modal verbs	2
noun clauses, interpretation of	7
noun forms	11
noun + verb combination	4
parallelism	2, 8, 10, 11, 12
participles	9
passive voice	4, 10, 11
past perfect tense	7
past tense	1, 6
present perfect tense	1
reference	12
sentence structure	8
transitions	9
verb forms	9, 11
verb + verb combinations	4
verb tenses	8, 11